JOBS
IN
ARTS
AND
MEDIA
MANAGEMENT

J O B S
IN
A R T S
AND
M E D I A
M A N A G E M E N T

STEPHEN LANGLEY
JAMES ABRUZZO

αcα BOOKS
American Council for the Arts
New York, New York
Copublished with Allworth Press

Jacket design by Celine Brandes, *Photo Plus Art*

Director of Publishing: Robert Porter
Associate Director of Publishing: Doug Rose
Publishing Assistant: Tiffany Chez Robinson

95 94 93 92   10 9 8 7 6 5 4 3 2 1

Library of Congress Cataloging-in-Publication Data

Langley, Stephen.

Jobs in arts and media management / by Stephen Langley and James Abruzzo.

p. cm.

ISBN 0-915400-99-5 : $21.95

1. Arts—Management—Vocational guidance—United States. 2. Mass media—Management—Vocational guidance—United States. I. Abruzzo, James.

NX765.L36 1992   92-5885

700'.68—dc20   CIP

CONTENTS

CHAPTER SIX

JOBS IN FINANCIAL MANAGEMENT   139

CHAPTER SEVEN

JOBS IN MARKETING, PUBLIC RELATIONS, AND SALES   149

CHAPTER EIGHT
JOBS IN FUNDRAISING, FUND GIVING AND IN SERVICE ORGANIZATIONS   165

CHAPTER NINE
JOBS IN PRODUCTION AND OPERATIONS MANAGEMENT   179

CHAPTER TEN
BECOMING INDEPENDENT   193

CONCLUSION

FORECAST FOR THE NINETIES   205

THE ARTS AND MEDIA MANAGEMENT
CAREER KIT   221

LIST OF CHARTS

ACKNOWLEDGMENTS

While it is not possible to mention everyone consulted in preparing this book, we would like to express our gratitude to
the following individuals:

For his encouragement on past two editions of this book, we
would like to thank Robert Porter, director of publishing at the American
Council for the Arts. For his research assistance on the career kit for
this new edition, we would like to thank Doug Oxenhorn, and for their
research assistance on the first edition, while they were students in the
Brooklyn College M.F.A. Performing Arts Management Program, we
would like to acknowledge Alice Bernstein, Barbara Ann Brown, Kim
Konikow, John Moore, Grace Rubin, and Gary Tydings.

For their information input and their editorial commentary we are
especially indebted to the following: Ron Aja of Actors' Equity Association,
Bruce Birkenhead of the Emanuel Azenberg producing office and profes-
sor emeritus of Brooklyn College, Janet S. Blake of Mary Tyler Moore
Productions, Ave Cohen of International Creative Management, Inc., Jeffrey
Fuerst of the Museum of Broadcasting, Kathryn Haapala of the Society for
Stage Directors and Choreographers, Jana Jevnikar of the Center for Arts
Information, Gregory Kandel of Management Consultants of the Arts, Inc.,
Ellen Lampert of the James McCallum and Robert Hudoba of Musical
America, Inc., Patricia MacKay of Theatre Crafts Magazine, Thomas
Murphy, Esq., Jack Nulsen of the Brooklyn Center at Brooklyn College,
Andrew Suser of ABC, Maureen Walsh, Lloyd W. Weintraub of MGM/UA
Entertainment Co., and Amy Wynn of the Dance Theatre of Harlem.

For their moral support and encouragement the authors wish to
thank Lorraine Abruzzo and Edelmiro Olavarria.

Finally, this book could not have been written without the authors'
many, many professional acquaintances—most notably the clients and
their associates with whom Mr. Abruzzo has worked at A.T. Kearney Executive Search; and the students and their internship sponsors with
whom Dr. Langley has worked at Brooklyn College of the City University of New York. The contents of this book reflect—as honestly and as
accurately as we could manage—the accumulated experience of two
very happy, rewarding, and ongoing careers in the arts.

INTRODUCTION

Jobs in Arts and Media Management is the only "careers" book to embrace the performing, visual, and media arts as a single industry. It is the first comprehensive guide to the job market and to career development that embraces theatre, music, dance, opera, museums, galleries, film, telecommunications, and the many types of managers and support personnel who earn a living by working at a desk behind the scenes.

This book is for managers and aspiring managers of all ages who hope to develop a career, get a better job, or switch from one discipline of the arts and media industry to another. It is also written for the growing number of bankers, brokers, lawyers and corporate executives who have decided that they want more from a job, and life, than just making money—they want to be involved in an art form that they have loved all their life. It does not, however, consider the disciplines of publishing, graphic arts, popular music, or music recording, and it avoids discussion of jobs that are primarily creative, even though some of these may require some degree of managerial responsibility. Positions covered range from executive jobs at the top to jobs in finance, marketing, public relations, sales, fundraising, fund giving, production, operations, and others you may never have known existed—you'll also find out about opportunities for becoming an independent entrepreneur. Career counselors, students, and teachers in the field will also find this a valuable resource, as will board members and managers concerned with personnel organization, staff structure, job descriptions, and job responsibilities. Any job market, after all, concerns both employers and employees.

A broad spectrum of the contemporary arts world is covered here, showing similarities between jobs in companies presenting "live" art and those in companies presenting the arts through the electronic media—as well as similarities between the commercial and the not-for-profit sectors of the industry. As artists discover that it is increasingly possible and lucrative to work in art forms that are presented live or electronically, arts managers must also understand how each operates in order to facilitate and enhance the growing relationship between art and technology. Leadership in the arts management field requires, more than ever, a broad knowledge of its diverse parts, combined with an entrepreneurial imagination that can bring those parts together.

The business of managing the arts requires a special love and dedication that goes beyond mere competence in various job skills. If art is the record of civilization and artists our true historians, then the mission of arts management must include a far-reaching sense of obligation. It must also include a sense of joy and fascination with the arts—this is an important aspect of the compensation you will receive for working in this field.

The first chapter of this book defines arts management as a profession by placing it in the context of recent history and showing how the role of the arts manager has evolved distinctive characteristics. In subsequent chapters you will learn how to plan your career, determine what kind of training you need, discover how to apply for and gain the position you want and how to move up. Then, after reading how the industry is organized, you can examine the myriad job possibilities. These are described generically, illustrating how easily skills may be transferred from one branch of the industry to another. Because most people work as employees before forming their own businesses, the options for becoming self-employed in the arts management field are saved for the final chapter. Finally, we have created a Career Kit that gives you easy access to valuable job information—a resource you will want to consult whenever you're considering a job or career change.

It is not expected that all readers will peruse this book from the first page to the last. Anxieties about job hunting run high: You may want to check out the table of contents first; then flip to the job sections that most interest you; and then proceed through the book guided by your immediate information needs. Finding a job, making a career change, or relocating is not easy. The Career Kit may be all you need to get started on the road to success. Keep this book as a reference to use when you get an offer to fill a challenging new position or, more likely, when you would like to get someone to make you such an offer. Also, use the appropriate chapters whenever you rewrite your resume, begin a job search, or prepare for an interview. If you follow our advice, you may be engaged in those activities sooner than you think!

CHAPTER ONE

BIRTH OF A PROFESSION

Perhaps your experience as a board member for an arts organization, or as a frustrated actor earning a few welcome dollars working for a theatrical press agent, or as someone trying to establish your own arts group because no one would hire you has opened your eyes to the world of arts management. Or perhaps you would like to move into arts management from a different field altogether. You have glimpsed the complex and fascinating infrastructure, invisible to the general public, that functions beyond and behind what is seen on the stage, on the film or television screen, or on the canvas: an industrious network of management leaders and employees who are facilitating the production and distribution of artistic products by, to put it as simply as possible, putting the money where the talent is.

The three basic elements that serve the creative product are talent, capital, and management. The artist evolves or expresses the basic idea—or product, if you will—and the money sustains the artist and supports the product. Management brings together these two elements.

If you have given up any artistic career goals you might have had; if you have an informed appreciation of the arts, together with a desire to serve artistic accomplishment; and if at least for the foreseeable future, you are willing to take career risks, train or retrain, earn less than you might in another career, and work longer hours than you might in another job—*keep reading!*

WHAT IS AN ARTS MANAGER?

Because this book is meant for future arts and media administrators, managers, and producers, perhaps a quick definition of those work titles is in order.

While the words *administrate* and *manage* are often used as synonyms, it is our view that a manager is a person of somewhat greater

position, responsibility, and authority than an administrator. To quote
an article about the Pentagon in the February 6, 1983, *New York Times
Magazine*: "Administration must make events march on time, have the
right people in the right places, get maximum results at minimum cost.
Management is different. It must choose directions, decide on policies,
set the targets, not for the day but for the decade." There are similar differences between executive and clerical positions. Presumably, managers and executives are paid more because they *think* rather than *do*.
Their primary function is to oversee the work of others by determining
what those others will do, why they will do it, when they will do it,
how they will do it, and for how much they will do it. Successful managers accomplish all this in a manner that increases rather than stifles
their employees. In the broadest sense a manager is any person responsible for one or more of the following activities: planning, organizing,
supervising, controlling and/or staffing.

You're right if you say that this definition makes just about anybody
a manager in some capacity, even the parent raising a child or the host
of a party. The critical difference is that some people manage well and
some don't. As you consider a career in arts management, you would
be wise to assess honestly your aptitude in regard to the four basic
management functions. Are you a person with a good reputation as a
manager? You probably are if you can answer yes to these three simple
questions:

1. Do others call upon you when there is an important job or
   assignment to be done?
2. Are you able to get others to comply with your wishes and
   requests easily?
3. Do events usually turn out as you planned them?

Yes? Then you almost certainly have an aptitude for management.
However, it is important that you genuinely enjoy being involved in the
management process, whether the goal is a successful dinner party or a
successful opening night. If you wish to become a professional, you
must also possess self-discipline. Humphrey Bogart once defined a
professional as "someone who does his job well, even when he doesn't
feel like it!"

Obviously, the more money, people, and resources a person is
charged with managing, the greater that person's responsibility and,
usually, his title and salary. However, one's ability to move from clerical

work to supervisory work and finally to an important leadership position depends not only on basic management skills and acquired knowledge, but also on such God-given qualities as vision, insight, intelligence, and energy. It also doesn't hurt to have a high degree of motivation, intellectual curiosity, taste, and a desire to contribute to the betterment of humankind.

Seeking to define the ideal qualities of an arts manager—at least in the not-for-profit sector—the landmark Rockefeller panel report *The Performing Arts: Problems and Project* (New York: McGraw-Hill, 1965) describes

> a person who is knowledgeable in the art with which he is concerned, an impresario, labor negotiator, diplomat, educator, publicity and public relations expert, politician, skilled businessman, a social sophisticate, a servant of the community, a tireless leader—becomingly humble before authority—a teacher, a tyrant, and a continuing student of the arts.

Not an easy job vacancy to fill! But it's smart to keep in mind the highest position you would like to achieve while you're picking up valuable skills and experience along the way.

Before discussing training programs and graduate degrees, job placement services and interview techniques, job descriptions and career advancement, it seems appropriate to take a brief look at the evolution of the arts and the media in this country. What is the tradition that you are about to inherit?

THE GROWTH OF THE
LIVELY ARTS IN AMERICA

The story of how the arts have been managed in America can, for the sake of simplicity, be divided roughly into two one-hundred-year periods from 1750 to 1850 and from 1850 to 1950. The third hundred years, what we will call the era of the third-century manager, is, of course, presently under way.

Prior to the middle of the nineteenth century—while the number and variety of performances grew steadily and the level of professionalism continued to improve—there was little, if any, institutionalization of the arts. There were a number of established troupes of touring actors, as well as stock theatres, music groups, and independent visual artists, but nothing like, for example, the Chicago Lyric Opera or the National Gallery of Art. Theatre business was conducted by an actor-manager, usually the leading player of the company; opera and musical events were organized by a leading singer or musician; and the visual artist sold his work out of his own studio or gallery. In other words, the business of the arts was controlled by the artists themselves. And in most cases it was a small business operated along the lines of a mom-and-pop grocery store. Real estate was cheap—you could earn back the cost of a modest theatre building with the receipts from a single week's performance. You could perform whatever you wished, however you wished, without giving a thought to royalties, fees, commissions, copyright infringements, or agents. No one received pay for rehearsal time, and performers had to provide their own costumes, wigs, and makeup. But America's industrial growth quickened by mid-century, and as the American way of doing business changed, the arts business changed along with it.

Following the gold rush in 1849, the railway industry began its incredible expansion by laying thousands of miles of tracks, linking every major city in the country by the year 1870. This growth in modern transportation, perhaps more than any other factor, drastically altered the entertainment business. Now, rather than touring alone and playing with members of the local stock company, a star could travel complete with a full cast and all the costumes and scenery that were needed. The result was a rapid, almost total decline in the number of resident or stock theatre companies. New York City was the heart of the nation's railroad network; because of that it became the city in which actors, vaudevillians, members of minstrel companies, and other performers congregated, and where a new breed of theatre managers conducted business. Starting out as booking agents who arranged tours and supplied shows for the nation's theatres, these managers were businessmen out to make a fast buck. They were neither performers nor were they socialite millionaires interested in supporting the arts. They extracted a booking fee from the theatre owners, a casting fee from the actors, and, often, a percentage of the actors' salaries. In 1896 three sets of partners joined forces to create what became the infamous Theatrical Syndicate, which by the turn of the century held a virtual monopoly on the country's five thousand theatres. By the early twentieth century the Shubert brothers replaced the Syndicate and soon exercised an even greater monopoly over the American theatre by virtue of the fact that they owned a large number of theatres and also had exclusive booking authority with those they didn't own. Their power was, however, eventually lessened by the growth of the Actors' Equity Association and other unions, the emergence of the motion picture industry, the crash of the stock market, the loss of a federal antitrust suit, and other events.

Commercial theatre had become completely centralized in New York City, and during much of this second hundred-year period, there was little else being produced. Consequently, when the Great Depression forced the closing of many theatres—or forced their conversion into movie houses—theatre circuits went down like rows of dominoes. By the year 1932 there were, at one point, only thirty-two legitimate theatres operating in the whole country!

Until the 1929 stock market crash, virtually all theatrical productions were bankrolled from the pockets of a single producer: men like Lee and J. J. Shubert, Florenz Ziegfeld, Billy Rose, Daniel Frohman, and others. After the crash, with rising costs and fewer millionaires, it was usually necessary for producers to seek out investors, or "angels," to help in financing a show. To facilitate this process an attorney named John Wharton adopted the Limited Partnership Agreement to define the rights of both the producers, or general partners, and the investors, or limited partners, and to simplify the producer's legal obligations with such agencies as the Securities and Exchange Commission. This method of producing a Broadway show is still used, although general partnerships or joint ventures are now more common. Using this method, shows are completely financed by a mere handful of individuals and/or corporate producing organizations.

While the American theatre was becoming centralized and controlled by showmen with considerable business acumen, serious music and visual arts projects were being institutionalized by wealthy industrialists and socialites. The building of the Academy of Music in Manhattan—which opened in 1854, replacing the Astor Place Opera House—was financed by a collection of socially prominent people who bought subscriptions, or shares, in the company. This entitled them to "own" boxes for the performances—not to earn profits on their investments, but just to gain admission. Such was the typical method of financing large operatic and symphonic organizations until the early twentieth century. The Metropolitan Opera was founded in 1883 mainly to satisfy a demand for boxes that the Academy of Music could not fulfill. The original organizers subscribed $10,000 each—buying one hundred shares at $100 per share—this being the cost of a single box. Those early patrons included among their numbers the Vanderbilts, Belmonts, Morgans, Rhinelanders, Goulds, and other prominent families of the day. In 1891 the philanthropist Andrew Carnegie built and endowed Carnegie Hall; others followed his example, attempting to memorialize themselves in bricks and mortar by funding arts facilities.

Just as the Depression had affected the commercial theatre, it also influenced other types of arts institutions, causing many to reorganize their business structures in order to become less reliant upon the largess of a small number of patrons. The Metropolitan Opera, for example, was purchased from its stockholders in 1940 to become a national trust. Any private or corporate contribution to a not-for-profit organization had become tax deductible—a powerful incentive for giving ever since the insidious growth of taxation following World War I. Arts institutions to this day still benefit from large gifts given by a few wealthy individuals, but they rely increasingly upon many small contributions as well as corporate and tax-levied support.

A key point to remember is that American museums, opera and dance companies, and serious music ensembles have tended to be institutionalized from their inception and have been supported by admission revenues together with, when necessary, financial contributions. Of the live arts, only the theatre and popular music started out and continued, until recently, to be financed primarily by entrepreneurs and investors hoping to make profits on their ventures.

ENTER: THE MEDIA MONSTER

In 1914 Cecil B. DeMille together with Samuel Goldwyn produced the first feature length film in Hollywood, *The Squaw Man*. DeMille made his first "spectacle film," *Carmen*, in 1915. That same year saw the premier of D. W. Griffith's *The Birth of a Nation*, by which time there were already over ten thousand movie theatres nationwide, though many of them were nickelodeons or makeshift viewing areas set up in the back rooms of stores or saloons. By 1920 there were over twenty thousand movie theatres, many of them of permanent and elaborate design. Network radio began to function in 1925, and within several years few American households were without radios. Talking pictures, beginning in 1927, redoubled movie audiences; and a generation later, starting in 1948, the advent of network television ushered in yet another media craze.

Functioning unseen during this ongoing media boom were producers, managers, and other executives whose visions, tastes, insights, and thinking—or lack of same—have probably done more to shape the world in which we live than all the presidents, generals, and diplomats of the same period. The leading movie studios were owned by men who founded them, making their power all the more absolute. Eventually, partners were taken in and after the founding moguls retired or died, the studios did go public and offered shares.

Nobody was really certain at first whether film, and then television, should be used primarily for entertainment or for educational and informational purposes. Nonetheless, a prodigious amount of work that qualifies as artistic was eventually produced. And a major reason for this—a reason that should not be lost amid all the hardware, big budgets, and corporate mergers—is the heavy dependence that the film industry and the broadcast media have always had upon artistic talent working in the live arts. Sooner or later, most leading artists in the performing arts tried their luck in the media industry. Actors, opera singers, dancers, choreographers, writers, composers, conductors—all were in demand. The NBC Symphony, for example, was formed for Arturo Toscanini in 1937; CBS sponsored live radio broadcasts of the New York Philharmonic; Leopold Stokowski went to Hollywood; Enrico Caruso and Geraldine Ferrar starred—voiceless—in DeMille's *Carmen*; actors deserted Broadway in hordes; and other talents followed during this twentieth-century update of the gold rush.

From the time that Thomas Edison began his experimentation with motion pictures in the 1870s until the creation of the private, nonprofit though government-funded Corporation for Public Broadcasting— formed in 1968 to assist noncommercial radio and television programming—the media industry was comprised primarily of commercial, profit-making enterprises, as was the theatre. But now a new type of financing was being introduced.

FOR SALE BUT NOT FOR PROFIT: THE ADVENT OF SUBSIDY

The professional American theatre remained in a precarious state until 1958 when in a momentous decision the Ford Foundation, inspired by W. MacNeil Lowry, committed $58 million dollars to assist the arts over several years and, especially, to assist theatre and dance companies. Mindful of the comparatively successful models provided by American museum, symphony, and opera institutions, the Ford Foundation gambled on its belief that the American theatre could also become institutionalized, and, as it were, legitimized. In supporting and nurturing a number of nonprofit regional theatre and dance companies, the Ford Foundation served as the impetus for substantial increases in professional activity outside New York.

A few years later, in 1965, the Rockefeller Brothers Fund published its panel report *The Performing Arts: Problems and Prospects,* which was an eloquent call for government support for the arts. In that same year Nelson Rockefeller, as governor of New York, established the first state arts council in the nation, modeled along the lines of the British Arts Council. Then-President Lyndon Johnson—still riding a wave of legislation passed in posthumous tribute to John F. Kennedy—created the twin agencies of the National Endowment for the Arts and the National Endowment for the Humanities. Although it is true that the original allocations to these agencies were small, they mandated matching allocations to any state that would equal federal money with state money. The result, predictably, was that within a single year every state in the union established a state arts council. Then in 1968, as mentioned, came the Corporation for Public Broadcasting, which also received federal support.

So the snowball began to roll: federal arts agencies, state arts agencies, city arts agencies, community arts agencies, and all the new jobs and expertise required to support this sprawling new system of subsidizing the arts. And, while tax-levied support increased each year—until the 1981 Reagan cutbacks—so did contributions from the corporate and private sectors. Not only were federal dollars generating more dollars through the "matching," or "challenge," grants system—an unusually productive expenditure of tax money—arts organizations were also hustling to raise money from other sources.

Paralleling the growth of public arts agencies was the growth of private, nonprofit arts service organizations. Theatre Communications Group (TCG), the American Symphony Orchestra League (ASOL), the Association of Performing Arts Presenters, and others not only brought arts people of similar interests together but also assisted in the process of defining the structure of the nonprofit arts world and its management needs. They helped, too, in various lobbying efforts to put pressure on legislators for increased tax support. Other organizations, most notably the Business Committee for the Arts, lobbied corporations to contribute to the arts.

THE STATE OF THE ARTS AND MEDIA
INDUSTRY TODAY

With the construction of an estimated 3,000 new theatres and performing arts centers—many on college campuses—during the sixties and seventies; with the growth of the resident theatre movement from a mere handful of companies to nearly 200; and with the even more phenomenal growth of dance companies—the 1988 *Dance Magazine Annual* lists 318 ballet companies and 358 modern dance companies in the United States and Canada, plus hundreds of other specialized dance groups—thousands of new arts administration positions have been created. Impressive growth has also been seen in the number of symphony orchestras, chamber and choral music groups, opera companies, museums, and art galleries. It was during this same twenty-year period that New York City replaced Paris as the unquestioned international hub of visual arts activity, prompting France to build the striking Centre National d'Art et de la Culture Georges Pompidou in an attempt to regain its former reputation. New York City is also the world's dance capital. And the rest of America—no longer the cultural wasteland that critics used to decry—has grown richer in and because of the arts. With the creation and artistic development of such institutions as the National Gallery, the National Symphony, the Arena Stage Company, and the Washington Opera Society, and with the opening of the Kennedy Center for the Performing Arts, the nation's capital is now both a major exhibitor and a major producer of the arts. So are, if to lesser degrees, Los Angeles, San Francisco, Chicago, Toronto, Santa Fe, Minneapolis, Dallas, Seattle, Charleston, and other cities. As the arts in America have become more established, they have also become more diversified, and, importantly, more popular, even surpassing the gate admissions for sports events.

But the greatest explosion of growth in the arts industry is reflected not, perhaps, by what has happened in the past—as impressive as that has been—but by what is happening right now. The newest theatres, concert halls, and exhibition spaces in America are not being built on Main Street but, rather, in our very own living rooms. These new stages may *look* like television screens, but they are much more than that. They are no longer owned exclusively by NBC, CBS, and ABC. They are no longer dominated by the Hollywood of yesteryear or, for that matter, the Hollywood of this year. A television screen now brings the entire range of entertainment and information into our homes.

CHART 1
A Statistical Profile of the Arts and Media Industry*

THEATRE

Broadway Theatres		37	
Off-Broadway Theatres		62	
Off-Off-Broadway Showcase Theatres and Companies		189	
Los Angeles Theatre Alliance Companies		60	
San Francisco Bay Area Theatres and Production Companies		125	
Chicago Area Theatres		30	
Chicago Non-Equity Theatres		90	
Boston League of Theatres		12	
Canadian Theatres	Equity	150	
	Non-Equity	150	
	Union des Artistes	41	
Equity Stock and Other Equity Contract Theatres		189	
Non-Equity Stock and Other Non-Equity Theatres		314	
Equity Regional LORT Theatres		85	
Equity Dinner Theatres		29	
Equity Children's Theatre Companies		65	
Road Theatres for Professional Productions (U.S. and Canada)		320	
College Theatre Programs	U.S.	1503	
	Canada	45	
	Total		3496

OPERA AND/OR MUSICAL THEATRE

Opera Companies (U.S. and Canada)			
Budgets over $1 million		54	
Budgets $500,000 - $999,999		40	
Budgets $200,000 - $499,999		52	
Budgets $100,000 - $199,999		43	
Budgets less than $100,000 (or budgets n/a)		654	
College Programs and/or Workshops (U.S. and Canada)		409	
	Total		1252

MUSIC

Symphony Orchestras (U.S. and Canada)			
Budgets over $3.6 million	U.S.	37	
Budgets $1.0 million - $3.6 million	U.S.	57	
Budgets $280,000 - $1.0 million	U.S.	124	
Budgets $135,000 - $280,000	U.S.	103	
Budgets less than $135,000	U.S.	903	
College Orchestras		158	
Youth Orchestras		257	
Choral Groups	U.S.	600	
Music Festivals	U.S.	339	
	Canada	29	
Chamber Music Ensembles (U.S. and Canada)		800	
College Music Programs	U.S.	961	
	Canada	46	
	Total		4414

DANCE (U.S. and Canada)

Ballet Companies		318	
Modern Dance Companies		358	
College Programs		266	
Miscellaneous Groups		1500	
	Total		2442

PERFORMING ARTS PRESENTING ORGANIZATIONS (U.S. only)

Independent Presenting Organizations		821	
College and University Centers		460	
Community and Civic Organizations		361	
	Total		2045

TAX-SUPPORTED ARTS COUNCILS			
U.S. Federal Agencies with Arts Programs		13	
U.S. State		56	
U.S. Community		3000	
U.S. Regional Arts Associations		24	
Canadian Arts Councils		57	
	Total		3150
BROADCASTING AND CABLECASTING			
Broadcasting Companies	U.S.	135	
	Canada	24	
Operating Cable Systems	U.S.	9300	
	Canada	651	
Cable Franchises Not Yet Built (U.S. only)		300	
Operating Radio Stations	U.S.	10,461	
	Canada	515	
Operating Television Stations (337 are public)	U.S.	1395	
	Canada	284	
College Radio/Television/Film Programs (U.S. only)		372	
	Total		23,437
FILM			
Motion Picture Theatres	U.S.	23,555	
	Canada	1007	
Motion Picture Producers/Distributors	U.S.	402	
	Canada	151	
Independent Film Companies (U.S.)		• 8000	
Major Film Studios (U.S.)		14	
	Total		25,129
VISUAL ARTS			
Museums (U.S.)	History	3350	
	Science	1206	
	Art	938	
	Other	1206	
Art Galleries	New York City	504	
	Other U.S.	1391	
	Canada	148	
College Visual Arts Programs	U.S.	1632	
	Canada	47	
	Total		10,422
UNIONS, GUILDS, AND EMPLOYEE ORGANIZATIONS (U.S.)			
	Total		65
SERVICE AND MEMBERSHIP ORGANIZATIONS (U.S.)			
The Performing Arts		535	
Broadcasting and Cablecasting		63	
Film		72	
The Visual Arts		186	
	Total		856
RECORDING COMPANIES			
	U.S.	324	
	Canada	23	
	Total		347
	Grand Total		**77,655**

*Statistics are based on a variety of 1988 and 1989 surveys and sources and, of course, are ever-changing. Where exact figures were not available, close approximations have been given. Not included here are artists' representatives and agents, who number in the thousands, and arts-related publishing companies—there are 37,500 music publishers alone.

While the film industry was hard hit economically in the years following the advent of television, this was largely because it chose to compete with television rather than to invest in it. Back lots and sound stages were sold off or rented for television production; the Desilu Studio quickly became one of the busiest in Hollywood; mergers and sellouts became commonplace. The most valuable assets retained by the studios were their libraries of films, which most had the foresight to rent rather than to sell outright for showing on television. Film production became secondary to film rental and, eventually, few new films were made without an eye to their value in the television and video-cassette markets.

It is significant that most major films are now produced by independent companies, even though financing is often provided by a major studio in return for distribution rights. Many such companies were formed by stars-turned-producers, such as Robert Redford, Jane Fonda, and Spike Lee. This has been a healthy way to get the creative process back under the control of the artists. Paramount, Warner Brothers and other former big studios are now subsidiaries of large conglomerates— such as Paramount Communications and Time-Warner—and are mainly in the business of film distribution and rental. They are also involved in the rapidly expanding telecommunications industry. Few board presidents or chief executive officers of these companies have much background in film production. Nor are they film producers in the traditional sense of that term; they do not select and develop the basic properties or scripts. Similarly, the leading Broadway theatre landlords—namely the Shubert Organization and the Nederlander Organization—are now financing numerous Broadway productions, but virtually all of their shows are first developed and staged by other producing companies.

In 1991, the major Hollywood studios continued to invest in the marketing and distribution of video cassettes. Films were made and distributed—many in studio-owned theatres. (Columbia Pictures Entertainment expanded its Loews theatres circuit while Warner Bros., Universal, and Paramount stayed in the theatre business.) Following theatre distribution, the studios manufactured and sold cassettes of their own movies to the public, and simultaneously leased the films to pay-cable operations. Then the studios syndicated their pictures to television stations or their own cable networks. So the way in which the film business is structured is again going through drastic change— this time because of home video.

The growing impact of telecommunications on artists was well illustrated by the 1987 strike by the Screen Actors Guild. Its goal was to secure for its members a share of the potentially enormous profits of film sales to cable television and video-cassette companies. Much negotiation still will be required before the economics of such matters can be hammered out, and new laws will be required to insure that profits are distributed in an equitable fashion. Considerable effort will also have to be made before live arts events can be more successfully translated into television and video programming. But the introduction of such programming has begun and has already made an impression upon both the media moguls and the media audiences. Arts programming may never have the same number of viewers as the current prime-time fare, but the demand is sufficiently widespread to give the lively arts a fighting chance of cashing in on the technological revolution.

Paradoxically, rapidly expanding video cassette recorder (VCR) sales have helped rather than harmed movie-theatre attendance—just as telecasts of live theatre, opera, symphony, and dance performances have stimulated box-office sales for live events. The Japanese have introduced "video theatres"—multiple screening rooms under one roof that seat about fifty people each and show video cassettes. The entire operation—ticket sales, concession sales, and projection—is handled by one person. The fact is that the arts and media industry today is replete with opportunity for the introduction and development of new products, companies, and markets.

THE THIRD-CENTURY ARTS MANAGER

With the sizable increase in arts activity caused by the media explosion, and with the advent of corporate and government subsidies, a new managerial support structure for the arts, together with a new entrepreneurial philosophy, has been put in place, thereby ushering in the era of the third-century arts manager—a distinctly American term in a century distinct for American achievement in the arts and media field.

Both artists and arts managers have a great deal of learning and catching up to do if they are to benefit from the opportunities at hand. While the media must learn how to allot more time to artistic considerations as well as to the processes of communication, arts people must acquire a new vocabulary, if not a new pedagogy, if the two are to become equal partners. To illustrate this point with a brief job story: Dr. Frank Stanton, who was for many years president of CBS, was once asked to serve on the search committee for a new director of Harvard's prestigious Fogg Art Museum. Asked to list the qualifications that he thought necessary for this position, he recommended that the person be able to demonstrate scholarship, curatorial experience, and a knowledge of technology and telecommunications. The last qualification, of course, is increasingly necessary as the process of museum research becomes computerized and as the ability to order instant pictures of documents and art works via satellite becomes a reality.

Tomorrow's arts manager will be an expert in his or her own art form, will possess the managerial qualities mentioned earlier in this chapter, and will demonstrate an eagerness to move into the future. A few people will have the qualifications to transcend the function and role of the arts management job and will rise to positions of leadership. They will be both humanists and generalists—people who can grasp the essence of many disciplines, who can perceive conceptual relationships, and who can relate general principles to specific problems or projects.

The management of the arts in America is no longer neatly divided between Broadway and Hollywood, or, for that matter, between what is called "commercial" and "serious" art. No longer can one expect to specialize in either live or electronic ventures, nor can one expect to settle down on one coast or the other, ignoring everything in between and outside. Similarly, textbooks, grade school and college courses, and training programs that deal with communication and with the arts can no longer ignore the interrelationships and the growing interdependencies among the various disciplines within the arts and media industry. The arts industry today is one integrated whole. A marriage has been made, perhaps not in heaven, but in the temple of technology—where viewers have already given it a high rating.

Arts management is a profession that is still in the process of being defined and is just now beginning to be understood and accepted as a necessary and legitimate field. Producers, impresarios, curators, and patrons—their functions dating back at least to the ancient Egyptians—have contributed to the evolution of the concept of arts management. Yet, only now have needs and resources combined to mandate the emergence of a professional arts manager. Many people within the arts and media industry itself still do not understand what this profession is all about, much less that a new breed of manager is in our midst. Gradually it will become clear that arts management is a viable, certifiable profession—even though it has taken several millennia of practice, experience, and accomplishment to define it.

Wherever you wish to fit into this sprawling industry, don't be overwhelmed by its size or complexity, just fuel yourself with the wonderment. Embrace the essentially facilitative role of arts management—its special responsibility to arts production and preservation, its underlying generosity of spirit—and with a little luck and a lot of hard work, the odds are that the profession will also be generous to you.

CHAPTER TWO

PLANNING YOUR CAREER

Whether you are just starting a career or assessing your future in a job market you've already entered, the sooner you come up with the answers to the following questions—answers that you will stick with—the better:

How far do I wish to go in this field? (Position)
How long am I willing to give it? (Time)
How much do I wish to earn? (Money)
What do I wish to achieve? (Goal)

SETTING GOALS AND PRIORITIES

If your goals are modest—a difficult but by no means immoral confession in this age of upward mobility—recognize that you probably do not need a graduate degree. Attach yourself to a competent professional in the specialization of your choice and, without turning another page, hand this book to the person waiting behind you at the employment agency.

It's usually difficult for a person to realistically assess his or her potential. Even aptitude tests and professional career counselors can be inaccurate. Many people with seemingly mediocre potential have gone to the top of their professions, while others with seemingly limitless potential have fallen short. Perhaps the most important success factor is, quite simply, happiness. Do you enjoy what you're doing and take such delight in it that you can't wait to jump out of bed in the morning? When that's the way you feel, you've found the right line of work. When you don't feel that way, it's time to make a change.

Assuming that you have decided to begin a new career or expand your present one, you must now consider your goals more specifically. Temper your dreams with a little common sense and write down next to each of the following items a brief indication of what you would like for yourself ten years from now.

Job Title _____

Type of Institution or

Sector of the Industry _____

Location _____

Salary _____

Major Accomplishment _____

Your answers will indicate whether your goals are modest, reasonably ambitious, or very ambitious. Perhaps you would be satisfied with a middle-management staff position with a large, established arts institution or performing company. Or perhaps you aspire to become a Broadway company manager or the executive director of an arts council. Maybe your goal is more ambitious—to become a general manager for a major performing arts center or the chief executive officer for a film company or the executive director of a leading museum. Or do you eventually wish to work independently and produce a major play or film, own an art gallery on Fifty-seventh Street in New York City, or head your own casting agency? Obviously, the higher your aspirations, the longer it will take to achieve them and the more extensive your preparations must be, both academically and professionally.

The following are all valid types of preparation that can lead you to your dream job:

1. Amateur and volunteer experience
2. On-the-job training
3. Specialized schools and workshops
4. An undergraduate degree
5. A graduate degree
6. Broad professional experience

Modest career goals may require only the first two or three of these steps, while ambitious goals will require that you fulfill all six. In other words, your goal will dictate what you must do in the next one to six years in order to reach that goal in three to ten years.

If you have the ability to place long-range goals ahead of immediate gratification, you'll be able to formulate a clear five-year or ten-year plan. Life being what it is, you'll have to compromise and modify your plans along the way; but without a clear set of priorities, you might easily find yourself right where you are now, except five or ten years older.

Let's say that your ten-year goal is to become the manager of an established symphony orchestra with a moderate budget in the Midwestern city in which you live. You hold a B.A. in music education, give private flute lessons, and, unable to secure a full-time teaching job, work as a teller at the local bank. You've always been an enthusiastic patron of the symphony and now volunteer many hours working with its subscription committee. Even though you disagree with the marketing director's strategy, you've learned a lot from him about how a symphony is managed. But you think it can be better managed. You want to expand its season, send it on tour, introduce concerts for children, and the like. Should you continue to volunteer and hope for a salaried position to open up with the symphony? Would you even be qualified if an administrative job did become available? Do you really know anything more about symphony management than what you've picked up from the very people with whom you disagree? This is a typical career crossroads for hundreds of would-be arts managers.

It is no easy matter to quit a well-paying job, to move to another city in search of experience and training, to become a student again, or to scuttle the goal of your original ten-year plan and admit to yourself that you'll never be first flute chair with the Cleveland Orchestra. Starting over is a tough assignment, but it's made a lot easier when you realize that you are not so much starting over as building on your earlier education, aspirations, and experiences. Even your work in that bank has probably been of value. If you hadn't taken all those earlier steps, you would never have found yourself in your present and deliciously challenging predicament.

After you've taken a firsthand glimpse at the field of arts administration—an absolutely crucial first step—continue your quest for new knowledge by joining as many arts management service organizations as you can afford, by reading their literature, and by attending their workshops and conferences. These activities will give you quick, inexpensive exposure to the field and will provide many opportunities to talk with experienced professionals. You may discover that it is not the right field for you, after all. But if it is still your choice, you should spend a rainy Saturday sending for brochures and applications from all the arts management, and other appropriate, training and degree programs around the country. The Career Kit includes an extensive listing of those programs.

If your determination to pursue your goal increases rather than diminishes with this process, you'll find that your priorities will arrange themselves in a logical sequence. After learning about paid internships, scholarships, tuition waivers, and student loans, quitting your job at the bank will no longer seem like the end of the world. After getting the symphony to reward your many hours of volunteer labor by paying for your trip to that arts administrators' conference, you may discover that there is a lot you don't know but that you're anxious to learn. You will have talked with people who have not only started a new career in arts management, but who have done it despite obstacles greater than your own: relocating both husband and wife, dealing with young children, having few financial resources, or going back to school at the age of fifty. If you want something badly enough, chances are you will get it—given the determination combined with a logical, long-term plan.

THE SCHOOL OF HARD KNOCKS VERSUS FORMAL EDUCATION

General principles as well as trade secrets have long been handed down from one generation to another by means of the apprenticeship method of learning. For centuries artisans, as well as artists and arts managers, have learned the fundamentals of their professions in this manner—the best of them, of course, far surpassing the achievements of their own masters.

To this day membership in many unions requires a one-to-three-year apprenticeship. If you wish to be a card-carrying electrician or a Broadway company manager, a mason or a press agent, you must usually serve an apprenticeship with one or more members of the appropriate union. Because this is the only real training many people have received, it is often touted as the only way to learn. Time and again you will hear about the importance of "hands-on experience," "working your way up through the ranks," and "learning by doing." It's an argument that is valid: Nobody becomes a manager simply by having learned some theory and been given a title. Conversely, one *may* be an effective manager without having had any formal training, and without ever having cracked a textbook.

Practical, on-the-job experience is both desirable and necessary. But the *quality* of that experience is all-important and has a direct correlation to how far you will go and how fast. Herein lies a powerful case against on-the-job training as the exclusive approach to building a career, at least if your ambitions are high.

If you are now working in the field—and in every position you hold in the future—it is imperative that you ask:
What am I learning?
Where am I learning it?
From whom am I learning it?

If you associate yourself with a person or place of employment with a poor professional reputation, you may unknowingly brand yourself with that same reputation for the rest of your career. If you are learning hackneyed, old-fashioned, and noncompetitive work habits—not to mention incorrect or unethical habits—you are obviously doing yourself great harm. Bear in mind that there are very few widely recognized masters in any field—usually only a handful, in fact. Such learning opportunities are rare.

Because the School of Hard Knocks was the only one to offer training in arts management and film and television production until the sixties, few people in the field over the age of forty, and therefore few people in leading positions today, know about recently developed alternatives. Most of them started as office boys or secretaries, and with great drive, perseverance, intelligence, and luck they have worked their way to the top. A few might have been well-educated lawyers or businessmen who came in through the side door. Most had little, if any, formal education in the arts, much less in arts management. You shouldn't be surprised, then, to find few older arts managers or media executives who would recommend formal training to you. In fact, most are proud of their "self-made" success and thereby echo the centuries-old distrust between the arts professions and the universities.

Early in the present century, however, academia began to create departments of theatre, art, and music. At first devoted entirely to history, theory, and literature, such departments eventually offered instruction in the arts and, later still, included practicing artists on their faculties. Slowly a degree of mutual respect evolved between those who were "doing it" and those who were teaching it. And now there are departments of dance, film, and telecommunications as well as several dozen degree programs—almost exclusively on the graduate level—in the area of arts management. Virtually all include some type of management internship, or on-the-job-training, to complement classroom learning. Historically, this is an unusual nod of the mortarboard in recognition of the workaday world. Just as remarkable, the workaday world has nodded back. Many descriptions for arts management jobs now specify "a degree in arts management" as a preferred qualification, especially for positions with arts councils and service organizations.

It should be obvious that considerable expertise is required of most arts managers who are now being hired for responsible positions. A high degree of conceptual and analytical intelligence is required of anyone who assumes a top-level arts management job. It should be equally obvious that few successful careers in the field are possible without experience and specialized training, and a broad-based education as well.

DECIDING BETWEEN THE COMMERCIAL AND NONPROFIT SECTORS

Whether you will function better in the commercial sector of the arts and media industry or in the nonprofit sector will likely be determined by your temperament and your world view: Are you self-oriented or altruistic? A few people have worked successfully in both sectors, but most do not. Frequently voiced complaints from people in the commercial sector include—
"It's such a cutthroat business!"
"All crass commercialism. No art!"
"It's only about getting ahead and being a star!"
"It's about ripping off the public!"

Complaints often heard from people in the nonprofit sector include—
"I'm sick of asking for handouts!"
"Why doesn't that dumb board just put up and shut up?"
"I want to do what *I* want to do, for a change!"
"To hell with art, I'm sick of starving!"

It isn't a question of which sector has greater validity—they both do. It's simply a question of which sector best suits your own particular temperament and outlook.

Compare the career choices facing you:

The Commercial Sector	*The Nonprofit Sector*
Network and/or cable broadcasting	Public broadcasting
Commercial film	Educational and/or documentary film
Broadway theatre	Resident and/or opera theatre
Popular music	Symphonic and/or serious music
Stock and/or dinner theatre	Small nonprofit companies
Galleries	Museums
Promotion	Education
Financial Speculation	Philanthropy

Do you see the differences? More important, are you more sympathetic with commercial or nonprofit choices?

Employers in the commercial sector have a monetary interest in each of their employees, each of whose salary is justified only if that employee is helping the project or firm make money. In the commercial sector the pressure, the pace, the demands, and the competitiveness are likely to be greater than in the nonprofit sector. In the nonprofit sector there is often more leniency and more concern for the employee as an individual and for the product as something more than a money-maker.

Are you the kind of person who would enjoy the razzmatazz of the commercial field as opposed to the comparatively tame, often more deliberate noncommercial endeavor? Which would motivate you the most: personal success and wealth or the furtherance of an artistic philosophy or ideal? Early in your career you will have to make a decision. No one can make it for you. In regard to your view of the commercial sector versus the nonprofit sector, however, don't be confused about an important economic reality that unites them: To make money, the commercial arts sector must produce high-quality artistic products—and to produce quality art, the nonprofit sector must also acquire money!

THE DIFFERENCE BETWEEN UNION AND NONUNION POSITIONS

All labor unions involved in the arts and media industry in the United States are chartered by the American Federation of Labor and Congress of Industrial Organizations (AFL-CIO). There are also numerous professional membership organizations in the arts that serve the functions of unions but are not chartered, such as the Dramatists Guild and the Association of Theatrical Press Agents and Managers (ATPAM). Still other arts professionals, such as filmmakers and talent representatives, have to get licenses or franchises; others must earn stamps of approval from government agencies, labor unions, and the like. Understand that no union or agency recognizes a difference between profit and nonprofit employers. Union contracts, salaries, and working conditions are negotiated in the same manner for both sectors.

Contrary to popular belief, no one can be refused a job simply on the ground that he or she does not belong to a particular union having jurisdiction over a job category. This type of "closed shop" practice was outlawed by Congress with the 1947 Taft-Hartley Law. However, gaining a job does not always mean gaining union membership. In the arts and media world it is relatively easy to get into the performers' unions and the membership associations for other creative artists because, after all, it would be too difficult and too arbitrary to devise entrance examinations that claim to measure artistic talent. So, for example, if you are hired as an actor or musician with a unionized company, you will almost certainly be asked to join the appropriate union—and, in fact, you will be obliged to do so in a timely fashion. However, this is not the case with stagehands, technicians, managers, and press agents; while you could not be denied such a position if it were offered to you, the union with jurisdiction over that job category is not required to offer you membership. This is because it is perfectly legal for unions to set annual quotas on how many new members they will accept.

According to guidelines set by the National Labor Relations Board, management cannot be unionized. This is contestable, however, and is not always followed in practice. Theatrical producers and general managers, for instance, often join ATPAM early in their careers and maintain active membership. To gain and build upon union benefits, many general managers work under ATPAM contracts—though far above minimum wage—and producers sometimes sign themselves to a company manager's contract for shows they are producing in order to earn a salary. In the role of producer exclusively, of course, they would not be entitled to a salary. Many arts and media industry executives also belong to professional peer organizations, such as the League of American Theatres and Producers; organizations of this type are formed to combine individual forces in negotiating union contracts. Other groups, like Dance/U.S.A. and the National Association of Broadcasters, are formed to help members share information, maintain and improve standards in their field, and to provide a platform from which to address government, business, media, and other segments of society.

There are many people in both the artistic and managerial areas of the arts world who do not belong to an arts union or professional association but who maintain a high level of professionalism. These include many educators, people producing the arts for rehabilitation programs of various kinds, and countless others working on the community or grass-roots level. A large number earn their livings from such activities, which is the most widely accepted definition of a professional. But if one is ambitious for wide recognition, high position, and maximum income, it is unlikely that joining an arts-related union or professional association can be avoided for long. A listing of most such groups is provided in the Career Kit.

JOB TITLES CAN BE DECEIVING

As you will see from the job descriptions in later chapters, different job titles often describe the same or very similar positions. Each branch of the arts industry has its own jargon. The differences are especially marked between the commercial and nonprofit sectors and between the public and private sectors.

Bear in mind that salary is not the only negotiable factor once you are offered a job—so is the title in many cases. Experienced employers are well aware of the fact that most people respect a title as much as, if not more than, the salary. As a consequence, a better job title may be offered in lieu of a better salary. "Office manager" sounds better than "secretary." "Director of distribution" sounds better than "salesman." "Vice-president" sounds better than "director."

Conversely, that fancy job title may really be a smoke screen created to blur the real nature of the job. This is why we strongly recommend that you speak with current employees of a prospective firm or organization—preferably with the person whom you might replace. Compare what you were promised during the interview with what responsibilities, skills, and experience the job really requires. Remember that, as much as you may want the job, the happiest and most optimistic moment ever shared by an employer and a hopeful employee is the moment of the job offer. This is analogous to a proposal of marriage— both parties have searched for each other for a long time, both are panting to consummate the relationship with a contract, both are convinced that they have an equal need for each other. Common sense is likely to be abandoned.

THE TIME FACTOR IN GETTING AHEAD

People are usually impatient to get a job, then impatient to get a raise, get a promotion, get a few more of both, and ultimately to head up the whole operation. Whether you're fresh out of undergraduate school, a tax accountant looking for a mid-life career change, or a recent retiree who wants to begin a second career, chances are that your first impulse will be to try immediately for your dream job—ignoring the lesser jobs that are probably necessary as background. Things seldom happen that quickly. Nonetheless, it may not damage your ego beyond repair if you *do* submit to a few job interviews for positions presently beyond your qualifications. Use them as learning experiences to find out what the best qualifications are for these jobs. Ask the people who interview you how you might best and most quickly reach your goals. Having been warned about employers of the School of Hard Knocks variety, you should be wary of offers to begin as a "go-fer" or as a mail room attendant. It would probably take two years for you to work up to a junior office position, and without special training, you might never graduate beyond that level. If you listen carefully and hear the clues accurately, you will probably figure out that the mystery of becoming successful can best be resolved by going back to college or otherwise retraining yourself. Why take two years to graduate from the mail room and two more to discover you've come to the end of your career line, when in half the time you could have graduated from a leading college with qualifications for a middle-management position?

In the long run at least, two years in graduate school can save you ten years on the job. And similar rules of thumb apply to other types of formal training. A one-year affiliate degree program may save you five years. Or, if you already have a graduate degree, say in economics or marketing, a few training workshops in arts management will assist you in your new specialization. So will the reading you do in the field and related areas, the performances and exhibitions you attend, the brain-picking you do among your new colleagues, and so forth. Information, technology, and the way we manage them are changing with such rapidity that the term "continuing education" is not just a marketing slogan designed to lure people back to night school—it's a necessity of life.

The best way to achieve your goals may not be the most obvious, and seldom is it the most tempting. The best way will take more time and work than you'd like. But if you return to the description of your dream job and then consider the proven ways for reaching that goal, your priorities and your course of action should become obvious.

CHAPTER THREE

COLLEGE PROGRAMS AND TRAINING OPPORTUNITIES

The claim will not be made in this book that college is the *only* way to become successful in arts and media management. There are too many exceptions, and genius can always find a shortcut. But are you *that* exceptional?

OPTIONS IN HIGHER EDUCATION: A MATTER OF DEGREES

Ordinarily, it is more prudent to increase your options in the career market with a degree or two rather than risk having doors slammed in your face later on.

If you are now an undergraduate not majoring in an arts field but are interested in an arts management career, here's what you should do:

1. Take a few arts courses that sound interesting to you.

2. Involve yourself in campus and off-campus arts or media clubs, productions, and activities.

3. Read, see, and learn about the arts as much as your free time allows.

If you are now an undergraduate who *is* majoring in the arts field and who is interested in management as a specialization—

1. Take a few courses in economics, accounting, finance, or labor relations that sound interesting.

2. Involve yourself in the administration of campus and off-campus clubs, productions, and activities.

3. Read and learn about arts management functions as much as your free time allows.

Colleges that offer graduate programs in arts management are most interested in candidates who have a good undergraduate average—usually above 3.0—and an undergraduate transcript that shows high grades in both arts courses and management-related courses, such as accounting. You might have only a few courses in one area or the other, in which case the grades become even more important. Colleges also want to see a sense of commitment to the field, a sense of purpose, and a sense of your knowing where you wish to be in five or ten years.

When you go for that all-important interview or write that letter of intent as part of your application to graduate school, let your ambition show and articulate all your highest aims. This is very different from a job interview. The graduate program director wants you to be ambitious, full of purpose, and anxious to conquer the world. These same qualities may scare a potential employer by signaling that you're after his job.

If you are not an undergraduate with an arts major, you may opt to continue on to graduate school in the field of your greatest proven strength. It may be law, economics, marketing, finance, administration, or accounting. You would probably select this option because—

1. You're not yet fully convinced that the arts field is the right one for you.

2. You wish to keep your career options as open as possible.

3. You think that you will receive a better graduate education and a more valuable degree.

We wouldn't argue with you on the basis of such reasoning, providing, of course, that your search for a graduate school has been thorough, and that it has included an investigation of arts management programs, and that this decision doesn't represent a compromise that makes you feel uncomfortable. If it feels as if it's the right decision, take it. If it doesn't, don't.

Space does not allow us to list all the management-related graduate programs in the nation, but the Career Kit does list the several dozen that specialize in arts management. For information on other types of graduate programs you should consult *Peterson's Guides to Graduate Study* (Peterson's Guides, Inc., Box 2123, Princeton, NJ 08543-2123). You will probably be interested in Book 2, which lists graduate programs in the humanities and social sciences, including the performing arts, economics, law, and mass communications. Or you may wish to consult Peterson's *American Film Institute Guide to College Courses in Film and Television*. These widely used books are updated annually with detailed and cross-referenced sources that provide ready answers to your most urgent questions regarding tuition costs, program content, financial aid, and the like. Make a list of the programs that most appeal to you, and then write off for catalogues and application forms.

Continue your research by sounding out current and former teachers whom you respect as well as current or former students of the institutions that interest you, and by reading whatever professional literature you can find. While some graduate schools will not grant interviews to potential students until after their applications have been received, most will. This technique may save you a few ten-to-fifty-dollar application fees. In any case, a personal interview with the department chairperson or program head is invaluable. It is the best way to make a strong impression and, if you are successful, the best way to land a lucrative fellowship. It is also the best way to get a sense of the campus and the faculty and students. And, if you're on the ball, you can pick up valuable tidbits regarding housing, financial aid, whom to see for what, and various other matters that may never get printed in the official literature.

HOW LONG WILL IT TAKE AND HOW MUCH WILL IT COST?

As a rule, a master of arts (M.A.) program can be completed in one year of full-time study. However, an M.A. is usually considered a mere stepping-stone to a higher degree. If research, scholarship, and further education are included in your goals, your M.A. is a good transitional experience, allowing you to expand your knowledge and search for a doctoral program that best suits your interests and needs. An M.A. will also enhance your chances of getting into such a program.

The master of fine arts (M.F.A.) and master of business administration (M.B.A.) are both considered "terminal degrees," meaning not that you will die upon completing one, but rather that you will probably not seek or necessarily need yet another degree. Hence, such programs are designed to provide a fuller education than the master's or associate degree programs. Most M.F.A. and M.B.A. degrees can be earned in two years, but it may take three. There are exceptions regarding both. Read the program descriptions closely.

The cost of earning a graduate or undergraduate degree is linked to the following major variables:

1. The time required to complete the program

2. Whether the college is a private or public institution

3. If it's a public institution, whether or not you are a resident of the state in which it is located

4. Whether or not you can earn a scholarship or fellowship

5. The availability of low-cost housing

6. Your qualifications for financial assistance—often determined in part by your parents' income level if you live at home, or by your own income level as of your last filing with the Internal Revenue Service

As everybody knows, college education is expensive these days. But it is still not out of reach for people who are bright and resourceful— even if financially destitute. Private colleges, generally considered the most prestigious, are more expensive than public colleges, meaning state-, city-, or community-supported institutions. Our advice is to examine both public and private programs. You may discover that with a fellowship or scholarship you can get a free education at an expensive ivy league college, or you may discover that the low-tuition public university offers a better program for you. Don't judge the catalogue by its cover! Don't judge the program by its address!

You will see that many private colleges now cost about $20,000 per academic year and that many public colleges cost less than half that amount. If you are given substantial financial aid, the cost differences are meaningless. What is most meaningful to the school is your background—your academic record, your test score results, your life experience, your articulated commitment to your field, and your character references. Lacking outstanding qualifications, you will soon learn that you must pay full dollar for your education—if you are accepted in the first place. But—and this is a big *but*—don't get discouraged or sell yourself short. Don't let a few rejections discourage you from applying elsewhere. Remember that what you put into the selection of a college program and what you get out of it are directly related. More often than not, *you* are the special ingredient that will mean success—not the teacher, the college, the program, or the address.

The best news for well-qualified students, at least through the nineties, is that they are in a buyer's market. The baby-boom generation has now passed its third decade and federal cutbacks in aid to education have discouraged many who are eligible for college from applying. Most colleges, graduate schools especially, are aggressively competing with each other for promising students. If you are accepted into several programs, you will be in a strong position to negotiate even more financial assistance than you were originally promised. Don't be afraid to dangle the acceptance letter from one college in front of the dean or chairperson from another college.

Other than scholarships, which are outright gifts of money granted by a college, a high school, or a charitable organization; or fellowships, which usually require the student to teach or conduct research, the main types of financial aid are—

1. Student loans—the number of low-interest student loans provided by the federal government has been sharply reduced, but a college or a private bank can still assist you in securing a loan;

2. Full or partial tuition waivers granted by the college— similar to scholarships;

3. College work-study assistance.

Work-study assistance is a program in which a college will pay you an hourly wage—higher for graduate students than for undergraduates —for working in a campus office or an approved off-campus agency. Sometimes coordinated by an urban corps office or a city-run cultural agency, these programs make it possible for students to be placed in jobs with nonprofit arts institutions or agencies, thereby gaining valuable experience while working through college.

Of course, there is always the possibility of taking some other job to pay for your education. One comparatively painless way of doing this, especially if you're single, is to secure a live-in position as a domestic, which would provide room and board as well as a small salary. Or you may decide to take a full-time job and study on a part-time basis. The important thing is to begin your studies. Even if you have sufficient resources for only the first year or the first semester, begin. Make a start. If you impress the faculty favorably and learn the ins and outs of securing financial assistance or finding employment, chances are good that you will find a way to continue.

GRADUATE PROGRAMS IN ARTS MANAGEMENT

The list of graduate programs in the Career Kit should enable you to select at least half a dozen to contact directly for more detailed information. The points to examine most closely when making your choice include—

1. The basic thrust of the program: for example, theatre management, community arts management, public policy and the arts, museum management, management of non-profit institutions;
2. The amount of field work or internship opportunities offered—more is usually better; and
3. The number of arts-related courses—this means courses specially designed and taught for majors, as opposed to courses picked up from other departments, smorgas-bord-style, in which you would find yourself in class-rooms with economics, law, hospital administration, or other majors, being taught by instructors who have little or no interest and background in the arts.

Start there. Do not concern yourself initially with tuition cost or the location of the college. When you receive a full catalogue, look closely at the faculty, the course descriptions, and the internship sponsors. A sizable faculty, either full-time or adjunct, with professional arts credentials is a plus, as are internship opportunities with a wide range of off-campus professional arts institutions and performance companies of high reputation. Using this criteria, you will probably narrow your choices down to two or three programs. Then arrange for interviews with the program directors and apply, negotiating for the best financial assistance.

Bear in mind that new programs are developing every year, and existing ones may be discontinued or redesigned. Tuition rates also change with inflation. You may wish to consult the latest edition of *Survey of Arts Administration Training*, prepared by the Center for Arts Administration, Graduate School of Business, University of Wisconsin at Madison and published by the American Council for the Arts, 1 East 53rd Street, New York, NY 10022. This listing is updated every two years.

INTERNSHIPS AND APPRENTICESHIPS

Many individuals, companies, and organizations in the arts and media field are willing to take on interns or apprentices, even if they are not associated with college or training programs. There is nothing to prevent your approaching someone for whom you'd like to work and asking if they would accept you on this basis. Of course, you risk being used as a go-fer, and the experience you gain may be minimal. Internships offered through formal training programs have the advantage of providing supervision, utilizing only the most reputable organizations, and setting up guidelines that the organization must follow.

The list of internships and apprenticeships given in the Career Kit includes only formal, well-established, ongoing programs. The ideal situation is one that combines classroom learning with practical, on-the-job experience under the guidance of a recognized professional. As mentioned before, virtually all graduate arts management programs offer internships as part of their required course of study. But there are alternatives. Aside from the list in the Career Kit you may also want to consult the trade papers related to your field of interest—*Variety, Back Stage, Billboard, Business Screen*, to mention a few—in which you may find apprenticeships and similar opportunities advertised by both established and incipient organizations in the arts and media industry.

WORKSHOPS, SEMINARS, AND INFORMATION CENTERS

There are literally hundreds of short-term training programs, workshops, seminars, conferences, and continuing-education opportunities related to arts and media management. Many of these are conducted annually by service organizations, associations, or colleges. Others are one-time programs presented to satisfy a need or to explore a trend. For example, Theatre Communications Group has sponsored a week-long conference on "Computers and the Arts," which resulted in a publication on the subject, and New York University has sponsored a three-day seminar on "The Arts and Cable Television." All such events are open to everyone on a first-come, first-served basis.

The Career Kit lists only established training programs that are offered yearly. Each is described briefly; but keep in mind that the focus for a session may change to accommodate new trends and developments. Also included in the Kit are the leading service organizations, which may not sponsor workshops but do publish newsletters and otherwise serve as excellent sources of information for the most recently announced special training opportunities.

CHAPTER FOUR

GOING AFTER THE JOB

One of the greatest feelings in life results from being offered an attractive job unexpectedly. The phone rings, you're invited to lunch, the offer is made, and suddenly your career has taken a giddy turn upward. This scenario can happen, and, in fact, if you manage your career well, it *should* happen. Success, after all, means being in demand. However, this chapter assumes that you must take the more usual approach and conduct a job search. This will entail—

1. Assessing your qualifications
2. Networking
3. Checking out job listings, services, and agencies
4. Composing your resume(s)
5. Sending out broadcast letters or information releases
6. Conducting a direct-mail campaign
7. Going to interviews
8. Following up

Experts estimate that it takes one month of searching for each $10,000 in salary you wish to receive. Conservatively, you can plan on a three-month job search for a $30,000 position. If you are seeking a significant salary increase, hoping to make a career change, or dealing with unusual circumstances, the search will probably take longer. The message should be clear: Plan well in advance.

If you are graduating in June, your job search should be in full swing by January. If you realize there is no growth potential for you in your present theatre company or symphony orchestra, start your search at the beginning of the season so you can have another position waiting at the end of it. Put time on your side and avoid being forced into taking a job for purely economic reasons. Consider it this way: For every month you are not working, you are losing the equivalent of 8 percent of your salary. If you are in the $20,000 bracket, not working for two months represents a loss of about $3,000.

ASSESSING YOUR QUALIFICATIONS

Perhaps the job seeker's most common mistake is to apply for the wrong position: a job for which he or she is either under- or overqualified. If you are not being invited for interviews or are being interviewed and not getting the offers, make a comparative study of your qualifications and the job descriptions. Ask yourself—honestly and realistically—if there are not noticeable gaps between your actual skills and those required in the job descriptions. Take a look at your competition—the people who *are* getting those jobs—and find out what their qualifications are. Ask your colleagues and, perhaps, a few of your former teachers to assess your chances for getting certain positions. You may not like everything you hear, but if there is a consensus of opinion among such people, you should reassess your immediate career goals. This will be far less damaging to your ego than a continuing series of turndowns.

No matter how you construct your resume, if you have never raised funds, no one will hire you to run a fund-raising campaign. Face it and, perhaps, apply for a lesser job in the development office. On the other hand, perhaps you have been a successful fund-raiser for the American Heart Association, but your first love is classical theatre and you apply for a lesser-paying position with a Shakespeare festival. The size of your current salary may discourage a potential employer from even inviting you for an interview. In that case the problem is easier to solve because it's a simple task to deemphasize accomplishment, but it's impossible, without lying, to fabricate accomplishment.

As you assess your qualifications, keep in mind that virtually every potential employer is looking for a specialist: a person with a particular mix of qualities and skills to fill a particular job. It's fine to be an all-around arts administrator, except that "all-aroundness" can seldom be marketed. Ideally each broadcast letter and resume that you send out should be tailored to fit a specific job opening. When this is not possible, your resumes should be targeted for such job categories as fund-raising, marketing, or press relations, in each of which you may have employable skills. Write separate resumes to illustrate separate skills. You cannot be the answer to *all* the employer's prayers—only to one of them.

Your search may take many directions, but each must be clearly defined and focused. Always, however, honestly and carefully compare your abilities and accomplishments with the demands listed in a job description. If the match is good—and includes just enough challenge to give you incentive—then go after the interview. If not, be honest with yourself and keep searching.

NETWORKING

In every cliché there is an element of truth. Take, for example, Its not what you know, but whom you know. If this were entirely true, both education and a systematic approach to a job search would be unnecessary. Yet it is undeniably true that your professional and personal contacts can often help in building your career. It has been said that the only time you should let everyone know of your plans is when you're looking for an apartment or a job.

Using the advice in this chapter, you can transform your skills and accomplishments into a resume or a broadcast letter that invites interest. But such tools will still be only impersonal pieces of paper. They can never be as powerful as—or open as many doors as—a recommendation from a well-connected professional associate or personal friend.

Networking, in the broadest sense, is the sharing of ideas, interests, and solutions. Every profession uses networking. It is the oral tradition that complements methodology and practice. In the arts, networking is often used as the first means of job recruitment. If a museum is looking for a new public relations director, the director will call friends at other museums and arts organizations for suggestions. After a formal job advertising campaign, the director will again call contacts who may know the applicants under consideration. For these reasons networking—or the development of personal contacts—is crucial to a successful career. This is especially true in the professional arts world, which is a comparatively small and close-knit community of colleagues.

How do you get plugged into the network? Begin when you're in school. Your professors almost certainly will have contacts in the field, especially if they supervise internships or field work or serve as consultants to professional organizations. Tell them about your career plans; ask for advice and suggestions about possible job openings; give them updated copies of your resume. Teachers are always interested in the growth and development of their students. College professors receive numerous announcements about job openings and are usually delighted to make referrals. They may also offer objective advice, which can be difficult to get from other people. Because you spent a lot of time and money on your college education, it would be foolish not to continue taking advantage of that network of information, no matter how long ago you graduated.

Classmates should also become a part of your network. The so-called old-boy network, or clubism, has worked for centuries for the alumni of the Ivy League schools. It is now common practice for graduates of arts administration programs to use their alumni network to enter the work force. Make it your business to obtain the names and current positions of other graduates from your college program and to contact those who may be helpful—even if you've never met. Just mentioning that you are a fellow alumnus should always get you in the door. Alumni associations, college affiliate groups, and others are composed of working professionals. Join them.

Visit the professional arts organizations in your community and try to become acquainted with their managers. The typical arts management career includes numerous positions in different cities. The general manager of the local ballet company may be on the other side of the continent running an arts center in a few years—just when you're applying for a job there.

Start a name and address file immediately and continue to augment and update it. Make brief notes next to each name—especially for those people whom you rarely see—including spouse's name, birthdays, where you met, and other personal notes that you may use when you next meet. Such a resource is literally worth its weight in gold when you are job hunting or when you are in a position to hire someone yourself.

An effective professional network requires continuing attention. Bear in mind the following:

1. Don't make unreasonable or overly frequent demands upon your contacts, however well you may know them.

2. One good turn deserves another; reciprocate!

3. Maintain your reputation by keeping your contacts informed about your abilities and accomplishments.

4. Treat any recommendation, lead, or job offer very seriously; it represents a large professional favor.

5. Do not pursue offers that don't interest you. This infuriates people who have spent time promoting or interviewing you.

6. Thank your contacts for leads and suggestions and keep them informed about your progress.

Sad to say, the level of courtesy these days is very low. Few people bother to say thank you or to keep in touch with former friends and associates except when they need a favor. Why not increase your visibility, maintain your reputation, and demonstrate your integrity by becoming the exception to this unfortunate norm? Quick phone calls to congratulate other people on their accomplishments, short notes, or even greeting cards are sound investments in your future. Don't overdo the amenities, but don't forget them either.

THE COURTESY CONTACT MERRY-GO-ROUND

Now, having stressed the importance of using a personal network when looking for a job, we must add a warning about certain dangers and delusions inherent in this approach. Networking can easily become a dead end and a time-waster.

For example, your father, Aunt Tilly, or best friend knows the chairperson of the board of the local ballet company or of Time-Warner or of whatever. You let it be known that you are looking for a job, and so your contact mentions your name to that chairperson, who agrees to see you as a favor. You arrange an interview and are given the royal treatment: a private meeting in a plush office, coffee, polite questions, and interesting advice. Then you're informed that there are no openings at the moment. At best, this influential chairperson may arrange for you to meet one of his or her influential colleagues, merely to avoid sending you away empty-handed. You are thereby deluded into thinking that you are making progress when, actually, you are no closer to your goal.

The next week you have another "noninterview." It is just another courtesy extended as a favor to someone else. But because you're being ushered into the most important executive offices in town, you are lulled into a false sense of hope for imminent employment; therefore, you neglect sending out resumes and broadcast letters and checking the want ads.

How can you recognize the difference between a meaningful contact and the beginning of the courtesy contact merry-go-round? Ask yourself:

Am I even remotely qualified for a job with this organization?
Do I want to work with this organization?
Is this person in a position to recommend me for a job?
Is this the best time to exploit this contact?

If your answer to any of these is no, you could be headed for disappointment. Yet meetings with celebrities and VIPs are always difficult to turn down. Go ahead, but keep your expectations very low and your questions very specific. Ask the VIP to arrange for you to meet someone lower down on the staff, someone who supervises an area or department in which you have employable skills. Ask—though the VIP may not even know—what specific openings exist within the organization. Think about the VIPs likely contacts in the profession at large and ask for a specific referral to a company or person for whom you'd like to work. Be appreciative of the VIP's time, show your seriousness by being informed and prepared, but don't grovel or appear foolishly impressed. Compliment the VIP by questioning and by listening intently as opposed to talking. If you manage to present yourself as bright and capable, the VIP may well take an interest in you and make a serious effort to promote your career. For many VIPs who can boast high salary, position, and achievement, helping others on the way up may provide a special satisfaction. Other VIPs may get their kicks from boasting and showing off—you must learn early to be a good judge of ego and character.

CONSULTING JOB LISTINGS, SERVICES, AND AGENCIES

There are over thirty thousand nonprofit arts organizations in the United States and Canada and thousands more in the commercial sector. Many of these have a constantly changing staff; new companies are formed every day; new projects that require new leadership and staff are organized. How do you find out about them? The most popular method of learning about job openings is through printed job announcements and placement listings. These may appear in the classified section of newspapers, in trade magazines, in professional association newsletters, in direct-mail announcements, or on the bulletin board in your office or dormitory.

Study the list of professional associations in the Career Kit and join the ones that are appropriate for you. Most national associations have regional and state chapters, and membership includes a subscription to a newsletter that may list job openings. Many such associations operate a job referral or placement service. Most also run an annual conference and offer workshops and seminars. If there is a guest speaker or another member of the association whom you'd like to meet, mail a short note to that person a few weeks prior to the event. Explain that you'll be at the conference and would like a few minutes of his or her time. Don't include your resume, and don't mention that you're looking for a job. Just introduce yourself casually. When you meet in person, the other party will almost certainly remember you and feel sufficiently complimented by your note to give you some time, if not a few job tips as well.

If you're interested in a job in the commercial sector, check out the trade papers on a regular basis. Those of primary importance are listed in the Career Kit. In addition to the professional associations that offer job listings and placement services, your college or university may also operate career counseling and/or placement services, often at no charge to you or your next employer.

An employment agency, on the other hand, receives a fee based on a stipulated percentage of the first year's salary, provided that the person recommended by the agency is hired. Sometimes this fee is split between the employer and the employee. There are thousands of employment agencies across the country; every city has a few. Some specialize in a particular industry, such as data processing or insurance, and some in a particular profession, such as accounting. Others are general agencies, which handle jobs in any profession or industry. However, few but the largest arts and media organizations are likely to list positions with such agencies. For one thing, the nonprofit groups can't afford—or prefer to avoid—paying the required fees, and, for another, job advertising through professional associations and direct mail is the standard practice in this industry.

Getting a job through an agency may offer certain drawbacks. Remember that an agency only makes money if it places you. Thus, it is less interested in finding a job that suits you than in simply getting you *any* job. If you receive many calls and interviews through an employment agency, be very definite about defining your job objectives to each prospective employer. You must realize that an agency may circulate your resume all over town, making it difficult or redundant for you to conduct your own job campaign and making it dangerous if your present employer doesn't know that you're looking. And be certain that you register only with reputable agencies. Each state has a chapter of the National Employment Association that will provide you with a listing of the approved employment agencies in your area.

Search firms are consulting companies that are retained by a corporation, on an exclusive basis, to assist in the recruitment of senior level executives. Search firms are often called "recruiters" or "head hunters" because their work entails identifying the successfully employed executive and matching that executive to their client company. Corporations have used outside search for over forty years and recently the corporate executives on nonprofit boards have been turning to search firms to fill senior level nonprofit management openings. The major orchestras, museums, theatres and dance companies often use search firms when filling their executive director and senior management positions.

Search firms fees are calculated at 33 1/3 percent of the starting compensation. The fees are paid by the company, never the job applicant, and therefore the firm works on behalf of the company, not the job seeker. You should send your resume to executive search firms, but don't expect them to help you find a new job. Try to include executive search consultants as part of your network. If you receive an inquiry from a recruiter—either unsolicited or as a result of your own efforts— treat the contact as you would any job interview. Arrange a personal interview, even if your are not sure the position is of interest, and begin to establish a rapport with the recruiter.

A.T. Kearney has an arts management and broadcast practice that fills executive level positions for major nonprofit and commercial arts and media corporations, in addition to its extensive corporate practice. Other large search firms also work with cultural institutions as do arts management and fundraising consulting companies. For a list of executive search firms and their specializations, consult the *Directory of Executive Search Firms* published annually by Executive Recruiter News, Fitzwilliam, New Hampshire.

COMPOSING YOUR RESUME(S)

When searching for a job, your first goal should be a personal interview. You must sell yourself during this interview. While a resume will almost certainly be requested at some time, the resume alone will not get you a job.

1. A resume has no intrinsic value, no magical power—you and you alone are the living document.

2. A resume is as likely to lose you an interview as to get one for you.

3. A resume can easily become an unnecessary crutch during an interview.

There are a lot of myths surrounding the importance of resumes, and there are many contrasting views about how to write one. Because a resume reflects an individual, no single model or method can be right for everyone. Your resume is about you, and, following some general guidelines, you must write it. Certain resumes serve as a curriculum vitae or vita, which presents a straightforward statement of a person's educational and professional credits. The primary function is to provide information required for, among other things, personnel and promotion files for employees, biographical listings, or obituaries. The resume that is sent out as part of a job search, however, should be written quite differently. It must be a sales pitch.

Just for a moment compare your resume to an advertising supplement like that found in a Sunday newspaper. The purpose of the supplement is simple—to get the customer to phone the store and order the advertised merchandise, or, better still, to visit the store and buy other items as well. Because these advertising enclosures are expensive, they must be concise. Choices about the content, format, and layout must be made carefully in order to project the desired image. Also, the places in which the supplement will appear are chosen based on marketing research, with different products and copy presented in different publications—in New York City, for example, more expensive merchandise may appear in the *Times*; bargain store items in the *Daily News*.

Now consider your resume. Its purpose is to get you a personal interview. To the reader the format, style, and copy represent your image. The content should be designed with specific markets, or employers, in mind and must be based on logical criteria.

A resume will get you an interview only if it contains information about your experience and accomplishments that an employer thinks will be useful to his or her organization. It should project an image of you that fits the image of the organization. Therefore, your resume must clearly delineate experience, education, and training relevant to the job opening and to the organization. Remember that it is a sales pitch, an advertisement, for a *specific* set of your skills—one ad cannot promote everything in a department store. Be selective, and, based on your research about the job and the organization, target the content of your resume as directly as possible.

Look at the fictitious resume for Jane J. Smith (Chart 2) and notice the corrections. She has apparently made every mistake possible; yet, ask yourself how many similar mistakes appear on your current resume. Now lets reconstruct Ms. Smith's resume.

From the Top

Why bother to head your resume with the word "resume"? Your covering letter has already mentioned what is enclosed, and if the person reading the resume can't tell by the format what it is, we recommend that you don't apply for the job!

Personal Information

List your full name, home address—mailing address, if different—and telephone number. Don't forget your zip code and telephone area code. If you are not easily reached at your home telephone number, give a number where a message can be left or consider using an answering service during your job search and list that number. If you are employed and your present employer doesn't know you're looking for another position, do not include your business address or telephone number.

Do not include your age, height, weight, sex, marital status, number of dependents, or ethnic origin. It is illegal for an employer to make any hiring decisions based on these factors, and they may very well be used to your disadvantage. For example, if you are married and have three children, a prospective employer may assume that you can't afford to take a particular job because it won't pay enough to support your family. But that is for you to decide after the interview, the offer, and salary negotiations. You are usually in competition with many other qualified applicants, and an employer may grasp at any criteria for limiting the number of applicants.

Do not include a photograph with your resume or have one superimposed upon it.

Job Category, Objective, Career Goal

Some resumes show a job category directly below the person's name, such as "general manager" or "press agent." Others give a brief description, in capsule form, of the person's employment or career goal. Both invite the quick disposal of the resume into the wastebasket; unless, that is, the career goal has been written as a carbon copy of the job description. This may be fine for individually prepared resumes, but it is not advised for a general resume. It is simply too easy to unwittingly disqualify yourself from a potential job. For example, Ms. Smith states that her objective is "a marketing position with a major sym-

---

CHART 2
RESUME

Jane J. Smith   Age: 34
1000 Appalachian Way   Marital Status: Single
Naples, New Jersey   Height: 5'9"
400-2000 Weight: 130

Professional Objective: a marketing position with a major symphony orchestra.

Education:
1961-65   Naples High School (Diploma)
1965-69   New Jersey College (B.A.in anthropology)
1969-71   Yale University (M.F.A. in Theatre Administration)
1980-   Columbia University Ph.D.
          (in progress)

Professional Experience:
1974-76   Field Consultant, NJ Arts Council
1976-78   Consultant, Media Metro, Inc. NYC
1978-82   Marketing Assistant, Naples Opera Co.
1982-   Director of Marketing, NJ State Symphony

Other Activities:
1967-69   College Orchestra, Press Liason
1970-71   Coordinator, Concert Series
1975-80   YWHA Womens Softball League
1981-   Columbia Women For Peace (Dir.)

Hobbies:
Fencing, traveling, skating, needlepoint

References:
Dr. John Doe, Chairman of Music, NJ College
Mrs. Flo Right, Music Director, Wayne Symphony
Ms. Beth Gould, Director, Trenton YWHA

---

phony orchestra." By doing this she disqualifies herself from work with presenting organizations, theatres, arts councils, recording companies, and television stations; and she may be soft-pedaling her skills in public relations and promotion. Employers are usually swamped with resumes and look for any reason to reject as many as possible. If, however, you feel compelled to give a career objective, keep it broad, avoid flowery language and hyperbole, and write something like this:

To apply and build on my ten years of experience in nonprofit arts through a challenging leadership position with a major arts organization.

Yet, why fall into the trap that ensnares so many actors by "typecasting" yourself?

Education

For job openings in which your education may be of paramount importance— academic and arts council positions, for instance—place these credits next. Otherwise, lead off with your professional experience. If your major areas of study make sense in relation to the job you're seeking, mention them. If they don't, simply name the degrees you received.

When listing your educational credits—and any others—always arrange the items in reverse chronological order, beginning with the most recent. If you don't wish your age known, omit graduation dates. Do not include your grade point average or class standing, although you may indicate "cum laude" or "summa cum laude." Then follow your college degrees with relevant seminars and workshops. Leave out the names of your high school, grammar school, summer camp, and flying school.

A word about Ph.D. degrees. They are very valuable and often necessary for college, arts council, and museum positions. But sometimes there is a backlash against a doctoral degree. Even though you worked very hard for that Ph.D., consider omitting it from your resume if it is not required within the job market of your choice. Also, avoid placing the words "in progress" after a degree. This may cause the employer to wonder, "How can Ms. Smith work for me and complete her degree at the same time?"

Professional Experience and Employment History

This is by far the most important section of your resume and requires the greatest attention. It will tell the employer how suitable you are for the job opening—providing, that is, that you *sell* it as well as tell it. Think again about that newspaper ad. Simply to state "Field consultant, New Jersey Arts Council" is comparable to simply stating the name of a product. It may be fine if the ingredients and qualities of the product are so well known that their praises need not be sung. But are your qualities that well known? If not, you must list not only your current and former positions, you must also define them and praise them. Define them by stating the responsibilities. Praise them by stating your accomplishments.

You may select from a variety of formats for this section of your resume. The most common is a chronological listing, in reverse order, of paid positions, titles, organizations worked for, and dates of employment. Remember to underscore, italicize, or otherwise set off the job titles so that they are easily seen and understood. For organizations not commonly known, include a short description. Two examples in different formats:

9/87-present   VICE-PRESIDENT, Ampersand, Inc.
                 (A commercial consulting firm for
                 the performing arts)

EXECUTIVE DIRECTOR,   Grand Opera House, 9/87-present
                        (A multi-arts presenting
                        organization in Wilmington, DE)

The second format is preferable because it emphasizes the position rather than the dates.

After each of your most recent positions or after those you wish to highlight as most appropriate for a particular job, state your responsibilities and accomplishments. Herein lies your sales pitch. Keep in mind that an employer wants to see success and results and wants to believe that you will earn your salary many times over.

After listing your title, briefly describe your responsibilities. Be honest and to the point. Then sell yourself with a powerfully worded description of your accomplishments in that job.

Instead of

designed a subscription campaign for seven mainstage productions

aim for something like:

designed a subscription campaign that increased sales by 60% and the number of subscribers from 250 to 500

What if your campaign was a failure? Don't mention it! Perhaps you bought and set up a computer system for your film distribution company. Did it increase record-keeping accountability, save money, or increase rentals? Or was it a white elephant that eventually sat idle in the corner? Never mention a pet project that turned out to be a dud. If you're asked to talk about it at an interview, it will be painfully clear at least to the employer that you're a dud!

Refer to the jobs chapters in this book which describe your specialization; read them to understand the skills and qualifications that are most sought after by employers. This will stimulate your memory and help in writing the descriptions of your own positions, responsibilities, and *accomplishments* in your resume. Again, we stress the importance of describing your accomplishments.

It is not enough to say that you were a program director for a community arts council, for example. You must be specific. Did you increase the number of performances? How many were there when you began, and how many when you left? Did you work within budget and, perhaps, even save your organization some money? How large a staff did you supervise? Did you develop innovative programming? You may be able to transform something as nondescript as this:

PROGRAM DIRECTOR, Amani Arts Council, 1981-87
Directed the performing arts series for community high schools, churches, and parks. Responsible for all arts activities throughout the county.

into this:

PROGRAM DIRECTOR, Amani Arts Council, 1981-87
As program director for the third-largest arts council in the state, I was responsible for—

- Programming sixty concerts per year that involved local talent and booking professional stage performers and international talents, such as Peter Nero, Yehudi Menuhin, and Julian Bream
- Supervising a staff of three administrators, a staff of two technicians, and a volunteer support staff of fifteen
- Controlling an annual budget of $200,000

Selected accomplishments during my two years in the position:

- Formed a statewide booking consortium that reduced per-performance fees by 18%
- Remained $2,000 below budget for the first year and $4,000 below for the second year while increasing the performances by 50%
- Increased audiences by 60% through the use of public service announcements on radio and by writing and placing human interest stories in local newspapers
- Formed a standing committee of volunteers to assist in concert production and fundraising activities

You may not want to write such a detailed description for each job you've held, but when assembling your job history, you should document your responsibilities and accomplishments as fully as possible. Then select the best items for the *particular* resume you're writing. In fact, keeping a job history should be an ongoing activity. It's easier to keep a current file or record of your chores and achievements than it is to reconstruct events, facts, statistics, and dates after you've left a job. Ask yourself this: If your company folded, if you were laid off, or, heaven forbid, if you were fired tomorrow, how easily could you get the information you need to compile an effective new resume? Be on the safe side: Keep an updated file or diary and then, when the time comes, pick and choose the facts you need to impress a particular employer for a particular job.

Remember to be selective and to make your former positions sound as impressive as possible. Perhaps the program director described above also answered correspondence for the arts council president; took turns on the office switchboard; and hauled out the trash every day—these facts need not be included in a resume or mentioned in an interview.

The format for presenting the facts on your resume is not as important as the content. But do use short sentences and a staccato style to bombard a future employer with your accomplishments: You may indent and number the items or use asterisks, plus signs, or other symbols to facilitate readability. Three or four real accomplishments are more powerful than a rehash of your job description.

If your job history shows a logical progression from advertising director to marketing director to vice-president of marketing, for example, then your resume should be organized chronologically, listing the most recent position first. But not all careers move sequentially. You may have worked as an artist before deciding to pursue an arts administration career, or you may have held a variety of jobs in the arts: performer, teacher, technician, and administrator. If this is the case, your professional experience should be organized using the functional resume format.

Instead of leading off with a statement about your career objectives, begin by summarizing your qualifications in the form of a preamble:

Qualifications: Ten years of successful marketing and promotion experience. Includes directing a national marketing campaign for a major book publisher, as well as sales and promotion for two nationally recognized arts institutions. Extensive experience in board committees, volunteerism, group sales, and direct mail.

This statement must attract attention and focus your skills in a specific direction. It should tie together pertinent experiences, however diverse, with a common thread. Follow your preamble with something like this:

Selected Accomplishments

- Increased profits for trade-paperback sales division through a direct-mail campaign. Reduced operating costs by 55% and increased volume by 80%.
- Designed an identifying look for a national opera company through logos, campaign copy, slogans; and redesigned brochures, programs, and posters. This campaign won a regional advertising award.
- Developed a direct-mail sales campaign for a cultural organization that netted $400,000 over three years and increased the donor list by 250,000.
- Led conferences, seminars, and workshops for management staffs on marketing an organization. Designed written materials for follow-up and practical applications.

This marketing specialist may have had little experience working directly with an arts organization, but the accomplishments are highlighted in such a manner that they may be attractive to such an organization. It could be that some of the accomplishments were achieved when the applicant was a board member, a special project director, or a consultant. That in no way diminishes their importance.

The accomplishments section in a functional resume is followed by a chronological work history. For example:

Work History

1988-present	DIRECTOR OF MARKETING, Newton Books, NYC
1982-1988	DIRECTOR OF MARKETING, Chicago Lyric Opera, IL
1978-1982	CONSULTANT, Media Metro, Inc., NYC
1973-1978	MARKETING ASSISTANT, New Haven Opera, CT
1972-1975	FIELD CONSULTANT, Connecticut Arts Council

The field consultant position may have been on a per diem basis, and the Media Metro position may have been a door-to-door salesperson for a cable television company. The functional format is designed to emphasize accomplishments rather than sequential work history. This approach may be a great advantage to many job hunters, particularly those changing careers.

At this point in both a functional resume and a chronological resume, you should list your college degrees if you did not list them above your work experience.

Other Activities

This section, like the others, should include only items that will strengthen your chances of getting an interview. List your professional affiliations and any offices you've held, but do not list fraternities, sororities, and other social, political, or religious affiliations. If you have served on boards for nonprofit or commercial organizations, list those here, as well as your service on panels and advisory boards. But keep this section brief, sensible, and to the point.

Hobbies and Extracurricular Activities

Here you may be tempted to list your professional or avocational experiences in the arts as a performer or in some other creative capacity. The slightest hint of an active artistic career in your resume will sound the death knell for an interview. And keep that type of activity out of your work experience section! An employer may suspect that you would rather perform on stage, direct films, or whatever, than manage an office. Many competent arts administrators find it difficult to secure new positions because they insist on listing their performances, creative awards, and even reviews in their resumes.

As a rule, hobbies and other activities do not belong in a resume. If you happen to know that the museum director to whom you've applied for a job collects Italian wines, and you, too, are an oenophile, perhaps you should mention it. Otherwise, keep your personal interests out of your resume.

References

Many people list the names and addresses of references at the bottom of their resumes. But suppose your reference is a lifelong enemy of the person receiving your resume? Or perhaps the person you've listed is so well known in the field that everyone who receives your resume calls that reference? This may be so annoying that your "good reference" will start sounding less than complimentary about you when asked for an opinion for the umpteenth time.

Omit references on your resume. You may even omit the phrase "References furnished upon request." This is understood. So, if asked at an interview, be prepared to supply references. By the time you are asked, you should be able to identify someone who would be regarded favorably by your potential employer. During the interview you should also be able to sense which people or organizations the employer dislikes. It is permissible to ask if you may phone the employer's office the next day to provide reference names and phone numbers. This will give you an opportunity to select your references carefully and to prepare them in advance of their being contacted.

Gaps in Work History

There are many circumstances that can cause a gap in your work history: pursuing an independent project, returning to school, having a baby. If the gaps are frequent, they may cause employers to think that you can't hold a job for very long. The functional resume format will help to minimize them, but you must be prepared to explain gaps during an interview.

If you left a job in June of 1986, traveled until March 1987, and began a new job in May, you could list your employment as follows:

1987-88   General Manager, XYZ Company
1981-86   General Manager, Opera, Inc.

Lying In Your Resume

There is a difference between the above technique and lying about degrees, accomplishments, affiliations, and positions. If it is not found out immediately, your lie may be discovered at the interview or during a reference audit or even after you've been hired. Remember that you can only kill your reputation once.

Format

As with a newspaper advertisement, your resume must first invite someone to read it. The format should contain a generous amount of white space. It is better to use two pages than to overcrowd one page. The copy should read easily and never contain long paragraphs of wordy prose. Think of your resume as just one of several hundred that an employer receives—like one advertisement buried in that bulky Sunday newspaper. Use different type styles and sizes, and whatever else you can think of to invite the reader to read on.

Color, Size, and Type of Paper

A small, nonprofit arts organization—the kind that reuses old press releases as scrap paper to cut stationery costs—may easily be turned off by an expensive-looking resume. The organization may feel that you would be uncomfortable in such comparatively impecunious surroundings or that you're simply not very cost-conscious. However, if you are applying for a position as the corporate grants officer with a Fortune 500 company, you may want to use gray, 100 percent rag paper with a border around the text. In other words, base such choices upon the type of position and organization you're pursuing. But never use pink, dark brown, or other artsy paper or ink. They are distracting and appear juvenile—and they don't reproduce well on copy machines. You are safe with white, buff, or gray paper, and blue or black ink. Also, stay away from onionskin paper, glossy stock, or cardboard-weight paper, which doesn't fold well in an envelope. Use 8 1/2" x 11" paper; legal size has a way of sticking out of files, and monarch size is too personal.

Typed, Typeset, or Photocopied

A resume typed on a high-quality electric typewriter is always perfectly acceptable. Using a dual-pitched machine with different elements can afford a varied style and make the copy visually appealing. Or, you may use a word processor. You can then easily and inexpensively have the original version of the resume photocopied. Laser printers are ideal.

Typesetting is an expensive process and must be done by a professional. Typesetting will give you access to hundreds of different typefaces and can give a very polished look to your resume, but the big drawback, aside from the cost, is that your resume is then fixed in place; if you wish to alter it, you must begin the expensive and time-consuming task all over again. Furthermore, a typeset resume is usually reproduced by the hundreds, which indicates to a potential employer that it is being circulated all over town.

Regardless of the format you select, make certain your resume is typed or set *perfectly*: no strikeovers, erasures, skipped spaces, wrong dates, or misspellings.

There is a story about a public relations director who, during a day of frustration over his job, prepared a resume on the office word processor and had it delivered by a messenger to the city's leading search firm. The head hunter read the resume, circled "liason" in red, and had it returned to him by messenger. The next day a corrected resume arrived with a covering note that read, "I wrote the word 'liaison' two hundred times on the blackboard!"

Ask friends to proofread your resume before you send it out. Be consistent in style and spelling. *Nonprofit* is not hyphenated. *Liaison* has two *i*'s. *Commitment* has only one *t* in the middle. Your good shoes and interview outfit will remain unworn in your closet if you represent yourself with a sloppy or careless resume.

Now, lets return to Jane J. Smith and see what her resume looks like after the advice in this chapter (Chart 3). Notice how her new resume

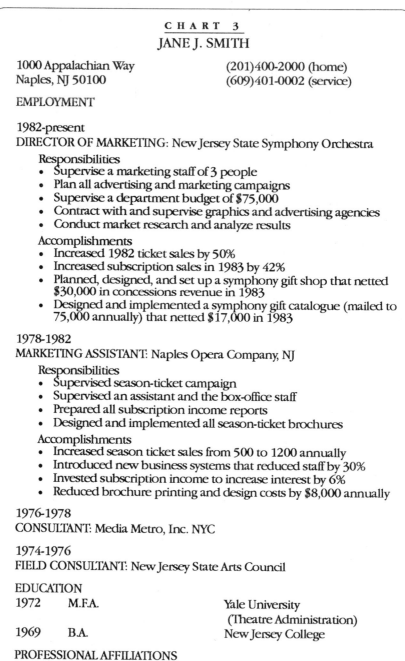

CHART 3

JANE J. SMITH

1000 Appalachian Way · · · · · · · · · · · · · · · (201)400-2000 (home)
Naples, NJ 50100 · · · · · · · · · · · · · · · · · · (609)401-0002 (service)

EMPLOYMENT

1982-present
DIRECTOR OF MARKETING: New Jersey State Symphony Orchestra

Responsibilities
- Supervise a marketing staff of 3 people
- Plan all advertising and marketing campaigns
- Supervise a department budget of $75,000
- Contract with and supervise graphics and advertising agencies
- Conduct market research and analyze results

Accomplishments
- Increased 1982 ticket sales by 50%
- Increased subscription sales in 1983 by 42%
- Planned, designed, and set up a symphony gift shop that netted $30,000 in concessions revenue in 1983
- Designed and implemented a symphony gift catalogue (mailed to 75,000 annually) that netted $17,000 in 1983

1978-1982
MARKETING ASSISTANT: Naples Opera Company, NJ

Responsibilities
- Supervised season-ticket campaign
- Supervised an assistant and the box-office staff
- Prepared all subscription income reports
- Designed and implemented all season-ticket brochures

Accomplishments
- Increased season ticket sales from 500 to 1200 annually
- Introduced new business systems that reduced staff by 30%
- Invested subscription income to increase interest by 6%
- Reduced brochure printing and design costs by $8,000 annually

1976-1978
CONSULTANT: Media Metro, Inc. NYC

1974-1976
FIELD CONSULTANT: New Jersey State Arts Council

EDUCATION
1972   M.F.A.   Yale University
                                      (Theatre Administration)
1969   B.A.   New Jersey College

PROFESSIONAL AFFILIATIONS
APAP (Member and Marketing Workshop Coordinator)
American Association for Ethics in Advertising (Board Member)
American Symphony Orchestra League

speaks specifically to an employer looking for a marketing expert—
such an employer couldn't afford *not* to interview her—while the first
Ms. Smith's resume would have been thrown into the wastebasket!

THE COVERING LETTER

After you have composed a focused, accomplishment-filled resume,
or resumes, you are ready to respond to various job announcements
and openings. This often entails mailing out your resume, in which
case it must be accompanied by a covering letter.

Remember to learn as much as you can about the position you are applying for and fashion your resume to respond to the position. (If you are
not applying for a particular position send a broadcast letter.) Choose
from your arsenal of skills and experiences to construct a compelling set
of reasons why a prospective employer would call you for an interview.
When you send the resume, use an equally powerful cover letter.

The cover letter will introduce your resume, tell why you are writing and for which position you are applying (sometimes employers are
hiring for more than one position simultaneously). Use the cover letter
to your advantage: it is your opportunity to "speak" directly to an
employer. In many instances, a well-written, eloquent cover letter has
made up for a lack of direct experience and has led to an interview.

A few other points to remember about the cover letter:

1. It should be one page, not longer, and like the resume,
   should not look crowded on the page (plenty of white
   space).

2. It is a business correspondence and should maintain a business tone and format.

3. Use either your personal stationery or a simple bond paper
   and attach your resume to the letter. Do not use your
   present employer's stationery. It leads one to think, "If she
   is using her present employer's letterhead to get a new job,
   she may do the same when she is working for me." Also,
   think of the embarrassment if the letter and envelope is, for
   some reason, returned to sender.

4. It is an opportunity to say something more personal that
   may be inappropriate in the resume (for example, "I have always enjoyed the work presented at Ensemble Studio
   Theatre and . . ." or "some of my fellow alumni from
   Columbia University have worked on your staff . . . etc.")

CHART 4
The Covering Letter

Mr. John Doe
Executive Director
The New Symphony Orchestra
Newtown, PA

Dear Mr. Doe:

Enclosed is my resume which describes my qualifications for your organization's position of Director of Marketing.

As noted in the resume, in my present position I have been responsible for a substantial increase in earned income for the San Jose Symphony. As a member of the management committee, I have contributed to the overall planning of the organization. Over the last three seasons, I have also taken on increased responsibilities and now manage the audience development and public relations functions.

I am very challenged by my position and my present employer is not aware that I am applying to you. However, this opportunity, to work for an organization with such a talented conductor, Maestro Mester, whose work I have followed for years, is too compelling not to pursue. My former classmates from Binghamton speak highly of the management team of the New Symphony, which is all the more reason for my interest.

I will be travelling east to visit my family the week of June 8, and could be available to meet with you, if convenient.

I will call your office next week to follow up. Thank you for your interest and for keeping this correspondence confidential.

Sincerely,

Jane J. Smith

Encl.

---

5. Use the cover letter to direct the reader to the specific points on your resume which most directly apply to this position: "You will notice that in my previous position I was responsible for all government grant applications while serving as booking director."

Be sure to mention your accomplishments early in the letter. Remember that employers want professionals who can make money for, or add other value to, their organization. That you have "always been interested in marketing" or "looking for a change" is not good enough. And stress confidentiality, if that is an issue. It will avoid a compromising situation with your present employer and add some value to your application (It implies that at this point, you don't want to jeopardize the great job you now have).

When dozens or sometimes hundreds of resumes are received for a position, they may not be carefully read. Cover letters may also suffer the same fate. By composing a short, clear, neat, businesslike letter which meets the criteria we have set out above, you will further increase your chances for getting a job interview. A sample cover letter is shown in Chart 4.

THE BROADCAST LETTER: AN ALTERNATIVE TO RESUMES

A broadcast letter differs from a covering letter in that it is not accompanied by a resume. If a resume can be compared to a newspaper advertisement, a broadcast letter can be compared to the direct-mail approach for soliciting magazine subscriptions. You know the tactic: A personalized letter is sent that introduces you to the contents and style of a magazine, inviting you to sample it. You don't receive a copy of the magazine, just a point-by-point description. The pitch usually begins something like this:

> Because you are a person who enjoys the great outdoors, we think you should know about the advantages of reading *Outdoor Life*

It then goes on, in telegraph style, to itemize the benefits of the magazine and closes by inviting you to sample a copy in your home.

The broadcast letter is based on the same principle and is written in the same style. Your opening sentence responds directly to the precise requirements of the job sought:

> Because you are looking for a marketing director with several years experience in the performing arts, you will be interested in my accomplishments. For instance, as marketing director for the San Diego Opera, I have:

Then go on to list, in short sentences or in bullet form, five or six accomplishments that also respond to the requirements of the position. *Limit the accomplishments you list to those.* You may, however, include a sentence about your education if it is relevant to the position. Finally, stress your desire for a personal interview. You may even take the initiative and state that you will phone the following week to arrange an appointment. When you call and are requested to send a resume, ask if you may deliver it in person at the time of your interview.

Remember that your first objective is to get that interview, and if an employer shows interest in you based on your broadcast letter, seeing your resume should wait until you meet in person. Use every possible tactic, without, of course, seeming difficult or rude, to secure the interview without using a resume and answer any questions the employer may have about it.

Each letter of this type will be different. Each will respond specifically to the qualifications requested by the job description, making it virtually impossible for the employer *not* to interview you. In fact, because so few applicants take the trouble to write a broadcast letter, your application may stand out above all others—even without a resume! Chart 5 provides a detailed illustration of a broadcast letter.

The broadcast letter should not include classes you taught, ensembles you conducted, committees you served on, or any other activities not directly related to that job description.

THIRD-PARTY LETTERS

The third party letter can serve as a broadcast letter when confidentiality is an issue. If you are employed and your boss doesn't know you are looking and applying for positions you can ask someone, a friend, professor or colleague (but usually not a peer at work) to write a broadcast letter for you (the third party is writing). It should read something like this:

Dear _____:

It has recently come to my attention that an acquaintance [former student, former employee, colleague] of mine is seeking a challenging new job in the marketing field. This person's accomplishments include:

Continue with the list of accomplishments from your own broadcast letter, rewritten in the third-person singular. Then the third party concludes.

If these qualifications interest you, and I believe they will, please contact me, and I will arrange for you to meet this promising marketing expert in person.

Sincerely,

Third party letters can also be letters of reference. After an interview a prospective employer may not contact your references. Excellent references from respected persons in the field (or from funders or artists, etc.) may just be the element that distinguishes you from the competition. After an interview (for a position you are sure you want)

CHART 5
The Broadcast Letter

JOB OPENING: Music Program Director for a state arts council. To direct music programming activities for the state. Includes providing technical advice on concert setups, evaluating grant requests, working with sponsors and performers, representing and articulating the music policies of the council to its constituents. B.A required, advanced degree preferred.

Your response should be as follows:

Dear _____ :

Because your job listing for a Music Program Director appears to describe a specialist with my exact qualifications, I believe that I may be the person you are looking for.

As concert chairperson for State College and manager of a contemporary string ensemble, I have—

- Insured smooth technical operations for a sixty concert annual schedule by personally overseeing backstage operations;
- Evaluated booking requests, negotiated artists' contracts, and participated in consortium-booking arrangements, totalling over $60,000 of bookings per year;
- Established a record of excellence for sponsorship, recognized by an annual ACUCAA award; and
- Led workshops and seminars on music programming and spoken frequently as a representative of state College and the community arts council.

I hold a B.A. in music and an M.F.A in arts administration from State University.

Because I am frequently out of my office due to the requirements of my present position, I will phone your secretary next week to arrange an interview at your earliest convenience.

Sincerely,

call your references and ask them to write a letter of reference. Be sure to tell the reference about the position and its requirements and how you are qualified for it. It may be a great deal to ask from a reference so play this card sparingly.

CONDUCTING A DIRECT-MAIL CAMPAIGN

While there are usually hundreds of arts management openings being announced or advertised at any given time, there are even more that are not widely publicized. Some perhaps have been open and unfilled for many months, while others are just being contemplated by an employer. This vast, unknown job market can be tapped by means of your own direct-mail campaign.

The strategy here is to target your market and saturate it. Begin with an honest self-evaluation of your skills and interests. What do you do best and what do you like doing best? What sector of the industry could best use someone with your qualifications? What particular type of position are you most qualified to hold?

Now compose a broadcast letter, cover letter and resume, or have someone write a third party letter similar to the samples given for Jane J. Smith. Because this is a general mailing aimed at unknown positions, the content cannot be targeted as specifically as you would like. Nonetheless, limit the content to a specific job category. Use business-size stationery and envelopes, and don't forget to include your full address and phone number on the letterhead! It's amazing how many people merely print an address on the envelope, which gets discarded, and don't think to put it on the letter or even on the resume itself. And be certain, too, that your full name appears typewritten below your signature; nobody will phone you if they can't decipher your name.

Because office addresses and the names of managers and directors are always changing, compile your mailing list from the most recent information available. Go to the library and consult the annual directories for the professional organizations in your field of interest; or you can purchase such lists from professional associations. Mail your letters to the chief management person in the organization—unless that is the position you're after yourself, in which case write to the chairperson or president of the board. Although such names are public information, you may not be able to obtain private or personal business addresses for them. If you cannot, mail the letter to the organization and mark it "personal."

If you have access to a word processor, you'll be able to personally address each letter on your list. Otherwise, if the mailing is a large one, the salutation "Dear Sir or Madam" will have to suffice. Send out fifteen or twenty at a time and follow-up with phone calls. Remember, getting a job is partly a numbers game, so do everything possible to put the odds in your favor.

INTERVIEWING

Your first contact for an interview in response to your resume, broadcast letter, or information release will probably come through a phone call from the manager, director, staff person, or from the member of the search committee who will be interviewing you. This initial contact is very important in establishing a good impression of yourself. If you happen to be in the middle of a party; if you have just awakened; or if you are preoccupied in any way, avoid a lengthy conversation and ask if you may call back. If you use a telephone answering machine, be certain that the message you record is simple and straightforward during periods when you're conducting a job search. Many people find background music and cute messages to be offensive. If you answer the phone yourself and the caller wishes to conduct a telephone interview, exercise caution. This technique is only used to prescreen applicants in order to eliminate as many as possible. You will never get a job offer through a phone call alone. If the caller insists on this procedure, which is common if you live in another city, try to schedule the call for the best time possible. Then prepare as you would for a personal interview. During the call try to secure a personal interview. Don't offer to send additional information, and don't answer questions about salary.

Should you be invited to travel to another city for an interview, clear up the question of reimbursement right then. Such reimbursement is standard. Reach an understanding on costs for travel, meals, and lodging. Confirm this in a short letter, summarizing the conversation and the reimbursement agreement. This is appreciated by professionally run organizations. If the organization hesitates to pay your expenses, it may indicate that its interest in you is lukewarm at best. Try at least to obtain partial travel coverage. Rarely should you assume all expenses yourself.

Be Prepared

Preparedness is a concrete and demonstrable way to impress your potential employer. It says—

1. You really care about the organization and the job.
2. You are inventive and intelligent enough to research the organization.
3. You are industrious and can work on your own.

When you set up the interview by phone, ask the caller to send you a press kit, the latest annual report, a foundation proposal, some reviews, old programs, catalogues, and anything else that may be helpful. What you cannot get in this manner, get from the library. You can acquire information on nonprofit organizations from the National Endowment for the Arts and/or the National Endowment for the Humanities, or from the appropriate state arts agency. Most of the information held by such government agencies must, by law, be made available to anyone who requests it.

Find out about the organization through your own network. Perhaps an actor friend has worked at that theatre or a former classmate is now living in that city. Construct a profile of the organization:

- Size, scope, point of view, artistic mission
- Financial situation: earned and unearned income, audience size, long-term debt
- Type of community: cost of living, other cultural and entertainment outlets, climate, economy
- Board members: names and occupations
- Size of staff and staff turnover
- Reputation in the community and the profession
- Personal traits and habits of the person(s) who will be interviewing you

Organize a set of notes, including questions you wish to ask, and bring it to the interview. You may refer to the notes, further illustrating your preparedness. This should relieve any nervousness you feel by giving you something specific to talk about.

Punctuality

Make every possible effort to be on time. Allow time for traffic jams, subway breakdowns, and wrong directions. It's much better to sit in a nearby coffee shop for an hour before your appointment than to sit in downtown traffic for an hour after missing it. However, should you be late, apologize quickly and forget it.

What to Wear

Always dress for an interview in a manner that most closely suits the image of the organization. You should certainly know enough about your prospective place of employment to know if its executives wear standard business attire or jeans. Generally, however, it is better to overdress rather than dress down. Always appear neat and clean. And avoid flamboyance and eccentricity, which may work in favor of performers at auditions, but seldom for managers at interviews.

Beginning the Interview

Start with a firm handshake and a smile and establish eye contact. Then survey the room with a quick glance. Avoid—

1. Being seated on an overstuffed chair or sofa; this will probably place you physically below the interviewer's eye level, making you feel subservient rather than equal;

2. Having the light from a window or lamp shining in your face; or

3. Accepting refreshments, especially of an alcoholic nature; being made to feel too much at home can easily put you off guard.

If the interviewer is holding your resume and has focused attention on it, you're in trouble. Get the interviewer to react to *you*, not to your resume. Take command and win the person over. Say something like, "Yes, I can tell you much more about that in my own words," or "My resume just touches on the things I accomplished in that position."

If you find yourself in a situation in which the interviewer is constantly being interrupted by phone calls, colleagues, or secretaries, ask whether it would be more convenient if you were to return later in the day. The interviewer will usually get the hint and pay attention to you and respect you a little more. The same tactfulness should also be displayed when you encounter a person who is obviously feeling ill or otherwise out of sorts. Remember that everyone has bad days. If either party at the interview isn't having a good day, the conversation should be postponed.

Focus

You will meet a number of interviewers who are unprepared or who are distracted by the events of the day, or who have misplaced your letter or resume, forgotten your name, or even forgotten the reason you are standing in front of them! Always greet the person by stating your full name, even if you're meeting for the second or third time. If he or she doesn't seem to light up with your reason for being there, find a casual way to refresh the person's memory. Then ask questions and get the interviewer to do most of the talking. Use your prepared notes and keep the focus on the job area in question. For instance, "I notice that your federal grants account for 30 percent of your total income. What are your plans against anticipated reductions?" or, "How have you achieved such a large membership compared to the other museums in the city?"

As for yourself you must be prepared to answer the following questions:

What can you tell us about yourself?

Why would you want a job like this?

Why would you leave your present job?

Where do you see yourself five years from now?

Mold your answers so they touch on important and salient points related to the job opening. Don't wander from the subject or offer extraneous information. Above all, don't ask questions about salary, benefits, and vacations. These are inappropriate at this time.

Among the questions you should be prepared *not* to answer are:

How much are you making at present?

What do you think is a fair salary for this job?

How much do you need to earn?

You can easily parry such questions by saying, "Although I expect to be paid what I'm worth, money isn't my biggest concern at this point," or "I'd rather not discuss salary until you have a clear picture of what I can do for you." Only talk about compensation after an offer has been made. At that point you will know the employer wants what you've got, and you can negotiate from a position of strength.

More Don'ts

Don't try to solve the problems of the organization. It's presumptuous to believe that in one hour you can come up with a solution to a problem that the management has been grappling with for two years. Offer opinions if requested to, but don't be dogmatic or glib.

Don't name-drop. It won't impress any secure person and will only serve to expose your own insecurities. Besides, not everybody is loved in this business, and name-dropping can easily backfire.

Don't argue with the interviewer. You can never win. Don't gossip about or bad-mouth anyone or any organization. Never discuss your personal life except in the most general terms, and never talk religion or politics.

You may be asked to talk about your weaknesses and bad points. Minimize these by phrasing them in positive terms: "I'm sometimes too hard on myself," or "I have a tendency to let my work consume my personal life."

Don't linger after the interview is concluded; don't overstay your welcome. If an offer is made, you may be wise not to accept it immediately—unless it comes at the end of several interviews and some honest soul-searching, and with a clear understanding on both sides regarding the terms of your contract. The job offer places you in a strong position and you should take advantage of it. You may, for example, wish to give your present employer the opportunity to make a counteroffer. Or perhaps you interviewed for another, more desirable position and can now use the concrete offer to elicit the offer you would prefer. If you are reasonably certain that you will accept the job, you may give a conditional yes when the offer is made, subject to mutual agreement of terms once they have been put into writing.

At the end of the interview, thank the interviewer, express again your interest in the job, and leave on a positive note with a second firm handshake.

FOLLOWING UP

Immediately after your interview, write a short follow-up note that restates salient points made at the interview, adds information you forgot to mention, confirms your interest in the position, and thanks the interviewer. Don't be apologetic, overly thankful, effusive, or sentimental. Keep the note businesslike, polite, and brief.

If the interviewer is an easily accessible person, you can also follow up with a phone call to keep in direct contact—not with a secretary, but with the boss. Call with the information on references; call to provide other information you might have promised during the interview. Don't be a pest, but do be aware that many job seekers have beat out their competition by showing the greatest interest and enthusiasm for a position.

This is also the time to ask for a few friends and colleagues who are known by the interviewer to phone or write on your behalf.

SECOND INTERVIEWS

When the position is an important one, you may be called back to meet other management leaders in the organization. While this indicates you are even closer to an actual offer, take the following advice:

1. If you've decided after the first interview not to take the job, save everyone's time and decline it right then.

2. Demonstrate at the second interview that you've done further research and thinking about the organization and its leaders since the time of your first interview.

3. Without seeming overly self-confident, allow yourself to relax a little, to smile more, and to otherwise show that you'd make a good team player. Remember that a first interview is likely to concentrate on your professional skills and qualifications, whereas the second interview is often requested in order to take a closer look at you as a person.

4. Be wary of multiple interviews. They could be a sign that the organization doesn't know what its looking for and is really using these interviews to get free advice.

EVERYTHING IS NEGOTIABLE

If you have researched the position and know the field, you should have an idea about the salary that will be offered. Let's say that the job is listed at $25,000 to $35,000. The organization will probably begin by offering you the lower amount, and you will feel that you deserve the higher sum. Everything is negotiable, and don't forget that there are more items to the compensation package than the salary.

If you're single, a large portion of your salary will be withheld for tax purposes, and even if you have dependents, that salary deduction can still seem enormous. Consider certain nonsalary items that may be more advantageous to you and to the company. Discuss and negotiate the following:

1. Medical and dental benefits

2. Sick days and personal days

3. Vacation time and holidays

4. Moving and relocation expenses

5. Professional membership, affiliation, and education cost reimbursement

6. Business travel reimbursement

7. Conference attendance expenses

8. Periodic promotion and salary reviews

9. Personal expense accounts—business entertaining, etc.

10. Use of a company car, or local transportation reimbursement

Most of us are not in the arts for the salary alone. Salaries in general are lower than in other fields. Some organizations will not be able to meet your salary demands without upsetting the pay structure of the entire staff. But you may still come out ahead by negotiating the right combination of benefits. Even nonprofit organizations must contribute to FICA unemployment insurance, and worker's compensation funds. These payments are based on your salary. You could remind your prospective employer of this and show, for instance, how it can be less costly for the company to offer you an expense account and a somewhat lower base salary than you are seeking.

Unless you are self-incorporated and file your own income taxes and deductions, or unless you are being hired as a consultant, you should not agree to work for a straight fee or to be paid under the table. Some small businesses may offer to pay their workers in this manner in order to save money for themselves and to give their employees increased take-home pay. If this seems tempting, despite the fact that it is illegal, consider that if you are injured on the job, you will not be covered by workmen's compensation; and if you are fired or the job ends, you will not qualify for unemployment insurance. Both you and your employer may also face legal charges from the Department of Labor and/or the Internal Revenue Service.

If you keep the above negotiating points in mind, you will be able to reach the best possible compensation package. After spending so much time and effort to secure a job offer, it would be foolish to accept it blindly.

Job Offer

After a job offer is made and you have accepted it, ask for a contract or letter of agreement from your new employer. This can be a simple letter which contains information on salary and benefits. It should also state your responsibilities and goals for the position (sometimes the job description is attached) and some indication of when your performance will be reviewed and when you will be eligible for a raise. For senior level positions, severance packages are also included sometimes. After you have received the written offer you are ready to resign your current position.

Resigning and the Counter Offer

You should offer your resignation to your immediate supervisor in person and accompany it with a letter of resignation. The letter is important because it usually becomes part of your personnel file and proves that you left on good terms from the position. Don't use this letter to complain, but rather to thank your employer for the opportunities afforded you and to indicate that you are leaving to pursue a "more challenging position" or to enter "a field more directly related to long term career goals." Also, you should indicate any vacation time or other accrued benefits owed to you and when your last day of work will be. Keep the letter brief and formal.

Sometimes your employer will ask you to reconsider your decision and offer you more money or an enhanced position to stay. Counter offers are very flattering. In effect, a counter offer puts you in a position to play one offer against the other. But be warned: first, you have already accepted a position, so you are forced to go back on your word; second, your current employer now has doubts about your loyalty.

You should ask yourself the following questions: Why did it take your resignation to get you what you think you deserve for this position? Will this counter offer satisfy you in the long term? Has your employer made you an offer just to keep you until he or she can find someone to replace you?

The best solution is to take a new job because it offers you the compensation and career path you want and deserve. Then, no counter offer can be acceptable to you.

CHAPTER FIVE

HOW THE ARTS AND MEDIA INDUSTRY IS ORGANIZED AND WHAT THE TOP JOBS ARE

The first chapter provided a history of the arts and media industry in America from the economic viewpoint; this chapter describes how the industry as a whole is structured and how its various components, or sectors, are organized. Emphasis is placed on corporate organizations, because that is where the majority of management jobs are to be found. After a consideration of unincorporated as opposed to incorporated business structures, we will look at the differences between the commercial and the nonprofit sectors and also discuss their similarities. Finally, we will survey the specific types of arts and media organizations in terms of particular organizational needs, executive leadership, and common career paths.

You will begin to see that in many cases job titles, functions, and qualifications within different organizations are similar and, therefore, that many job skills are transferable from one sector to another. In almost every case, there is a nonprofit counterpart for each commercial arts organization: regional theatres are nonprofit ventures, and Broadway productions are almost always commercial enterprises; public television stations are nonprofit, and local network affiliates are commercial corporations. Furthermore, there is sometimes a close relationship, if not an interdependence, between the nonprofit and the commercial companies: a theatrical property may be developed in a nonprofit regional theatre and end up as a commercial release on cable television; or the funding office of a commercial business corporation, together with the funding office of a nonprofit foundation, may jointly support the work of an individual artist whose paintings are sold by a commercial gallery and eventually end up hanging in a nonprofit museum. So, while clarity demands that we examine each branch of the arts and media industry separately, bear in mind that each part relates to the whole. (See Chart 6 for an overview.)

CHART 6

SENIOR MANAGEMENT JOBS AND FUNCTIONS IN THE ARTS
AND MEDIA INDUSTRY

Organization Type	Commercial Theatre	Small Nonprofit Performing Companies	Large Nonprofit Performing Companies and Centers
Leadership	Producer(s)	Board of Trustees	Board of Trustees
Top Management	General Manager	General Manager or Executive Director	Board Chair, President, and General Manager or Director
Product Development	Producer(s)	Managing or Artistic Director	General Manager and/or Artistic Director
Finance	Producer, with General Manager and Accountants	Business Manager or Controller and Fundraiser	VP or Director of Finance, Business Manager and Development Officer
Marketing and Promotion	Press and Advertising Agents	Press and Promotion Director	VP or Director of Marketing or Audience Development
Operations	Company, House, and Production Stage Managers	House, Tour, Stage, and Technical Managers	Director of Operations and House Managers

Independent Film, TV, Cable and Radio Companies	Large Network TV, Cable Corporations, and Film Studios	Medium-to-Large Museums	College or University Arts Centers
Owner or Executive Producer	Board of Directors and Stockholders	Board of Trustees	Board of Regents or Trustees
Owner, Producer, or Executive Director	Board Chair, President, CEO and Subsidiary Division Presidents	Board Chair, President, and Director	President, Arts Dean, and Center Director or Manager
Owner, Producer, or Director of Programming	Division President, VP, or Director of Creative Development	Chief Curator, Director of Research and Acquisitions	Dean, Center Director, and Department Chairs
Owner, with Business Manager or Controller	VP or Director of Finance	Treasurer, with VP or Director of Finance, and Development Officer	College Budget Director and Center Business Manager
Sales, Distribution, and Franchising Directors	VPs for Sales, Marketing, and Distribution	VPs or Directors of Membership and Marketing	College Admissions Director and Center Promotions Manager
Unit, Traffic, or Studio Manager	VP or Director of Operations, with Unit, Studio, or Traffic Managers	Facility Manager, Registrar	College Buildings Director, and Center, House, and Stage Managers

UNINCORPORATED COMPANIES, ASSOCIATIONS, AND PARTNERSHIPS

Everyone is free to acquire a space, hang up a sign, and declare "open for business." In fact, this is a common occurrence in the arts world, although the vast majority of such businesses fail due to insufficient capital, lack of sound legal and financial advice, or because the market for their product is too small or even nonexistent. Nonetheless, many artists, as well as entrepreneurial arts managers, begin an unincorporated company, often because they failed to gain corporate employment or because they preferred to be their own boss. The unincorporated company, whether individually or jointly owned, is financed exclusively by the owner(s), who enjoys full decision-making powers and considerable freedom from various legal regulations, excluding the tax laws. However, these owners also assume full personal liability, which means that all their personal assets may be attached in order to settle any debts incurred by their business dealings. Few people are willing to take this risk for very long.

If you are employed by an unincorporated individual or company, be certain that you are covered by worker's compensation, unemployment insurance, social security, and other standard types of insurance. Some of these businesses, as well as small incorporated outfits, may offer to pay their workers under the table. This is an illegal arrangement that saves the employer money and gives the employee increased take-home pay but leaves the employee without such protection as health insurance, worker's compensation, and unemployment insurance. Even if you initiate direct legal action to claim such benefits, you may still be out of luck.

One type of unincorporated business structure used in the commercial arts world that insures legal protection for the investors and requires accountability of its principals is the Limited Partnership Agreement. This is an especially effective arrangement for attracting investors for Broadway shows and independent film projects; it is also offered to attract investments in race horses, gold mines, and other highly speculative ventures. The general partners, or producers, control these ventures fully. The limited partners—also called investors, or angels—only lose money or earn money by sharing in the losses or profits according to the amount of their individual investments. Again, each project financed in this way is a separate legal entity; neither the investments nor the jobs related to them are guaranteed if the project is a flop or comes to an end.

CORPORATIONS

A corporation as an entity is legally separate from the lives of its officers, shareholders, or participants; the corporation has perpetual life unless it is legally dissolved. The three basic, and most common, types of corporations in the arts and media industry are defined below; these definitions vary somewhat as stipulated by the laws of the state in which a business is organized. Most people who earn their living in the arts and media industry work for one of the following types of corporations:

A Private Corporation

All corporations must have officers and a board of directors. In the most simple arrangement only two people may fill the roles of president, vice-president, secretary, and treasurer. Often these people are close relatives, and usually the president-treasurer is the top executive for the business while the vice-president and secretary may be merely a figurehead, as is the case with many stock and dinner theatres, small recording companies, independent publishers, and for most talent and advertising agencies. Other private corporations are operated as partnerships in which a small number of people share the company's assets and liabilities. This arrangement is often used in the operation of art galleries, large talent agencies, and production companies. Of course, private corporations may involve private investors who are not partners, officers, or directors in financing independent theatre and film projects.

A Public Corporation

This type of corporation offers shares to the public through the stock market and conforms to additional regulations, such as those of the Securities and Exchange Commission. Its board of directors and officers are elected or ratified by vote of the shareholders, who also may share the profits in the form of dividends. The price of the shares of these corporations may fluctuate and is affected by the profits and assets of the company. This arrangement is common for commercial television and radio networks, film studios, and large publishing and recording companies.

A Not-for-profit Corporation

This is a corporation that is prohibited by law from distributing any of its assets as profits per se. It may offer salaries and pay its bills like any other business, but it may not award dividends of any kind to its participants. It has gained nonprofit and usually tax-exempt status from the appropriate federal, state, and local agencies. This structure is utilized by virtually all noncommercial ventures and institutions in the arts and media industry.

Large commercial arts organizations—which are either private or public corporations—include such well-known companies as Sotheby's, Time-Warner, and CBS. Large, not-for-profit arts corporations include the Kennedy Center, Lincoln Center, the Metropolitan Museum of Art, and National Public Radio (NPR).

COMMERCIAL ARTS AND MEDIA CORPORATIONS

William Paley, the late founder and former chairman of CBS, was once asked by a newly appointed station manager, "Well, what do you want? Do you want ratings? Revenue? Profit? Community service? Image? What do you want from this television station?" Paley answered, "I want all those things." (Interview with Van Gordon Sauter, *New York Magazine*, January 23, 1984).

People often think that the only purpose of companies in the commercial sector of the arts and media industry is to make money. And certainly a shareholder in CBS is interested in maintaining dividends and watching the stock price rise. But Paley's mandate to his station manager is much closer to reality. Leaders and managers in both the commercial and nonprofit sectors of the arts and media industry must maintain broad interests and diverse goals in order to operate successfully.

If earning profits is not the only mission of a commercial organization, it is certainly the primary one, and unlike income earned by a nonprofit organization, these profits are subject to taxation. A publicly held corporation, like CBS, Inc., is actually owned by its shareholders: individuals, other institutions, pension funds, trusts, etc. Shareholders may participate in open shareholder meetings (although they rarely do) and may vote for directors through their shares (or give their proxies to others). Shareholders also may receive a part of the profits of the corporation in the form of dividends. Also, the value of the shares of a public corporation fluctuate based on numerous factors, including the company's profitability and its potential for making profits. Individual outside shareholders, however, have little say in policy making.

The policy-making authority and control of a public corporation rests largely with its board of directors. This group, composed of the senior management and outside directors (usually elected by senior management), is organized into committees: executive, finance, audit, compensation, etc. The executive committee is usually the powerful operating group of the board (and in many ways is similar to the non-profit corporation board). The board can hire and fire a Chief Executive Officer, even if that person is himself a member of the board.

Once again, CBS is a fascinating case study. In 1986, the president and CEO, Thomas Wyman, was fired by the board of directors, and a powerful private shareholder and board member, Laurence Tisch, assumed that position. Following this internal "takeover," the magazine division was sold, as was the prestigious Records Division (to SONY). The sales of these assets and others increased the company's capital, thus increasing the book value of its shares and ultimately its market value. CBS also cut costs throughout the remainder of the corporation—most noticeably by firing reporters in the well-respected News Division—and created an atmosphere throughout the Broadcast Group that put maximizing profits as the primary goal. In many ways, CBS was responding to the competition and its environment. ABC and NBC had both been bought by nonmedia corporations (ABC by Capital Cities, and NBC by GE, as part of GE's purchase of RCA); and CBS itself had had to fight off Turner Broadcasting, which had made an unsuccessful attempt to take it over.

The commercial media business is even more complex and intertwined. Once dominated by the three networks, it now includes dozens of television broadcasting networks, such as TNT and Fox Television, regional networks, and religious broadcasting networks. At the same time, the stronghold that the three networks held over prime-time broadcasting has lost to the endless choices of special cable programming channels, "shopping channels," ethnic programming, and video text service companies. Furthermore, with video cassettes making up a larger portion of the viewing audience, movie libraries and the rights to those properties have become increasingly valuable.

With the advent of cable systems, satellite broadcasting and the increasing number of viewing choices, the television industry has radically been altered. And so has the film industry.

Today, the commercial media corporations are giant conglomerates with varied interests and holdings in film companies, television and radio broadcasting, recording companies, cable programming and broadcasting, newspaper chains, and book and magazine publishing. By integrating these interrelated industries, corporate giants like Capital Cities/ABC, Inc., Time Warner Inc., and Paramount control the products and the delivery systems.

These conglomerates consist of numerous companies, each headed by a president who reports to a group president, who in turn reports to a division president. Managing this operating division is a corporate staff consisting of the chairman and chief executive officer, the president and chief operating officer, division presidents, and executive vice presidents overseeing centralized staff functions such as legal, treasury, stock holders' relations, communications, etc. Chart 7 outlines the companies and divisions of Capital Cities/ABC, Inc. Each of the companies listed has presidents, with those of the television and radio stations holding the title of president and general manager. For acquired companies in the publishing group, the chairmen have retained their titles, and in the newspapers division the presidents have the additional titles of publisher.

The division presidents, or production chiefs, of large broadcasting networks and film studios make basic decisions that are really megabuck gambles about which programs or properties will be produced and/or financed. Despite the availability of sophisticated marketing data, a high percentage of such decisions are based upon the executive's intuition. The ability to read the market is of major importance to the success of management and production throughout the commercial arts world—on Broadway as well as on television, in the art galleries as well as in publishing.

While the success of a nonprofit organization is properly judged by how well it fulfills its stated, nonpecuniary mission, a publicly owned corporation is judged according to the daily stock quotations for the company, which can create considerable job stress. Executives of radio, television, or cablevision corporations have the additional stress of responding to the program rating polls as an indicator of policy decisions. It is little wonder, then, that such executives can easily lose sight of the quality, integrity, and value of the artistic products. Film studios often consider scripts only of the specific genre that their market research indicates will appeal to their target audience. Multiple endings may be tested on preview audiences to determine the final cut of a movie. The mindless subject matter of many sit-coms is ample evidence that artistic compromise is frequently the price paid for increased ratings.

CHART 7

STRUCTURE OF AN ORGANIZATION: CAPITAL CITIES/ABC, INC.
(1989)

Corporate

- ABC Television Network Group*
  - ABC Entertainment
  - ABC News and Sports
  - ABC News
  - ABC Sports
  - ABC Television Network
  - ABC Communications

- Broadcast Group*
  - Television Stations—East – 4 Stations
  - Television Stations—West – 4 Stations
  - National Television Sales
  - Video Enterprises
    - ABC Distribution
    - ESPN**
    - Arts & Entertainment**
    - Lifetime**
  - Broadcast Operations & Engineering
  - Radio
  - ABC Radio Networks
  - Radio Stations—Group I –9 Stations
  - Radio Stations—Group II –7 Stations

- Publishing Group*
  - Specialized Publications
    - Fairchild Publications*
    - Institutional Investor
  - Daily Newspapers –7 Newspapers
  - ABC Publishing – 7 Companies
  - Weekly Publications

NOTES:
*=President also holds corporate position and title
**=Partially owned by corporation.

Happily, there are at least a few leaders in the industry who trust artistic quality—these individuals usually have a background in the creative areas of the business. For example, Norman Lear, head of a successful television production company, began in television as the creator/producer of "All in the Family." And there *are* producers who give their managers, directors, and designers full artistic control. Ultimately, though, profit determines the life or death of a property in the commercial sector. There are no patrons and no subsidies to help keep even the highest artistic success in the theatre or on the screen.

Certain functional responsibilities in large corporations are handled by professionals in specific disciplines who may not be people with a background in the arts. Corporate controllers, human resource managers and tax attorneys may not have any special interest or background in an art form. The skills required of them are dictated solely by the exigencies of the business situation as are their management decisions. A corporate controller for an entertainment company is probably a specialist in finance and cost control, trained in a business school and holding a CPA, with prior experience in public accounting.

As one gets closer to the art itself, a specific knowledge of the art form is needed. For instance, marketing, as a measure of audience response and manipulation, requires an understanding of the product. It would be an asset for the marketing director of an opera company to know a great deal about opera and about the artists who create and interpret an operatic work. However, there is a tendency in the commercial sector to value specific functional skills more than knowledge of an artistic product.

The theory is that if you can market toothpaste, you can market any consumer good, including television programs. The commercial media business is just that—a business. And the executives who now run it, like Laurence Tisch, are "corporate managers" who operate as if the media business is no different from running a hotel or manufacturing an appliance. The head of NBC came from a financial position in the operating division of the parent company, GE, and one programming chief of ABC television quipped that it's probably an advantage that he has no experience in prime-time programming!

Although companies in the commercial sector must pay taxes on their profits, they may lessen their tax liabilities through write-offs and deductions related to the cost of doing business. Herein lies another difference between the commercial and not-for-profit sectors. By investing in the development of talent and artistic products, a commercial company may actually reduce its costs by reducing its tax burden. The nonprofit company, on the other hand, must finance such development out of precious operating budgets. Film companies may spend millions of dollars optioning properties, developing scripts, hiring consultants and conducting market research. Few nonprofit arts organizations are able to invest on this scale, although the production opportunities they provide to artists on a smaller scale are, ironically, vital to the health of the entire industry.

The commercial sector of the arts and media industry runs the gamut from small, struggling stock theatres and film companies to huge broadcasting networks and film studios with multimillion-dollar budgets. You may be the general manager of a dinner theatre who lives in a mobile home that doubles as a dressing room at show time, or the CEO of a film studio who lives on a lavish estate and owns a private plane. More likely, you will have a position and a life-style somewhere in between. But wherever you work in this sector, you will rarely forget about money, though you may forget about art.

NONPROFIT ARTS AND MEDIA CORPORATIONS

A nonprofit or not-for-profit corporation—the terms are used interchangeably—is not necessarily one that doesn't earn revenue over its expense or one that is unbusinesslike. It simply means that the equity of the corporation, its assets, cannot inure to its board members, managers and directors of the company. For example, the considerable revenues earned by A Chorus Line are not shared by the board members of the nonprofit New York Shakespeare Festival, which produced the show. Rather, they are maintained by the corporation and used to support other projects. Furthermore, if a nonprofit corporation is dissolved, its assets must be turned over to another nonprofit organization. The pictures hanging in a museum cannot be distributed among the board members if the museum closes its doors forever.

When goals are formalized through the creation of a not-for-profit corporation, several basic rules of operation are established:

1. None of the profits may inure to the benefit of any private individual.

2. The officers and employees of the nonprofit corporation may, of course, receive salaries, and these may be increased with the budgetary growth of the corporation.

3. Control rests with a board of trustees rather than with an individual producer, manager, or owner.

4. The organization may not lobby for changes in legislation.

In the academic world most arts programs, facilities, and centers are operated under the not-for-profit seal of a college or university. Most civic arts groups and agencies function under the legal umbrella of municipal or government protection, as do those in the public education system. In these cases the arts program executives are appointed by the academic administration or by elected political officials.

The trustees of a nonprofit corporation are nominated and elected by the current board, maybe upon the recommendation of the general manager and/or artistic director. The only exception to this is when a nonprofit organization is first formed, at which time the board is hand-picked by the organizers of the venture. In the arts field some ongoing companies have been the inspirations of specific, individual artists or entrepreneurs, such as Joseph Papp, Twyla Tharp, Tyrone Guthrie, and Martha Graham. A founding artistic director usually commands unquestioning support from board members because they are, after all, enthusiastic believers in the founder and his or her company. It is when the founding artistic director leaves the project that the board must make its most important decisions, starting with the hiring of a new artistic director.

A board of trustees is most effective when it is comprised of committed individuals from the community who share a deep interest in the artistic work of the organization. Historically, board members have come from the upper social classes. Today boards retain influential people, but most have also added members with various kinds of professional expertise and connections. Board members are expected to contribute their time, knowledge, connections, influence, and money to the nonprofit organization without receiving salaries or honoraria.

Robert Crawford wrote in his book *In Art We Trust*, "The basic role of the board of trustees for a not-for-profit professional arts institution is to provide through its actions and its efforts the best possible environment conducive to the fullest implementation of the artistic purpose of the institution, consistent with prudent management." (Published by

FEDAPT, New York, 1981) The specific structure of the board is established in its bylaws, and decisions are reached through a vote when a quorum is present. Most boards have an executive committee—which often consists of a president, vice-president, treasurer, and secretary and a number of standing committees and members-at-large. Typical responsibilities of a board (and committee within the board) are—

1. To make and/or approve policy (executive committee and full board)
2. To hire artistic and managerial leadership (executive committee and search committee)
3. To develop long-range planning (planning committee)
4. To approve and monitor the budget (finance committee)
5. To raise the unearned income needed (fundraising or development committee)
6. To promote ticket sales and raise other earned income (marketing committee)
7. To nominate new board mèmbers (nominating committee)
8. To volunteer personal time and services for special events (volunteer or special programs committee)
9. To approve large capital expenditures and leases (executive committee and full board)

Other committees, whose responsibilities are self-explanatory, would be education, public relations, endowment, legal, acquisitions, and programming. The number of trustees that comprise a board is determined by the constitution of the organization and varies from a mere handful to many dozens.

All of the above committees work with the executive director, the artistic director, and often with staff managers on the many aspects of the organization. When fully utilized, board members can provide volunteer leadership, professional expertise, and valuable insight into the personality of a community.

A board chairperson is elected by the other board members and is vested with whatever powers are specified in the bylaws. It is usually assumed that the chairperson is the most important figure in the whole organization, since this position appears at the top of any organizational chart. In reality, he or she may not be the most active or influential member of the board, perhaps having been elected for qualities of neutrality or passivity. Usually, however, the chairperson is the chief communicator, who informs the executive management of board decisions and informs the board of management actions, problems, and accomplishments. The chairperson must also, on occasion, represent the organization to the outside world and, conversely, serve as a conduit for communications from outside the corporation.

If you presently serve on a board of trustees or ever consider doing so, you should know that a trusteeship is more than just an honorary position—it carries very real fiduciary and legal liabilities. If a trustee's actions can be proven to be negligent, prosecution is a possibility, depending on state corporate laws. In many states the law holds that a board member of a nonprofit corporation is legally required to act "with that degree of diligence, care, and skill which ordinarily prudent men would exercise under similar circumstances in like positions." If actions to the contrary can be proven in court, then the trustee is held personally liable to share losses or damages with the other trustees, unless he or she has previously submitted a written statement of dissent for inclusion in the appropriate board minutes or unless, suspecting an illegality, he or she has notified the state attorney general's office. Trustees in all states are forbidden by law from realizing any personal financial gain from their positions, although they may receive per diem fees or expense reimbursements.

COMMERCIAL THEATRE

The commercial theatre is largely composed of—
Broadway productions
Off-Broadway productions
National touring productions
Bus-and-truck productions
Stock theatre productions
Dinner theatre productions
Industrial shows

In each of these categories an individual producer or packager acquires the rights to a theatrical property, raises the necessary capital, and hires the managerial and artistic personnel. Although anyone who owns the rights to a property may become a producer, only those with long experience are likely to be successful. Among the small number of producers who have enjoyed repeated success over many years are

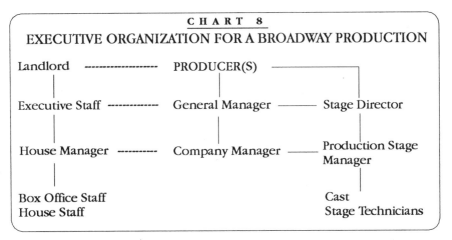

CHART 8

EXECUTIVE ORGANIZATION FOR A BROADWAY PRODUCTION

Landlord — — — — PRODUCER(S)

Executive Staff — — — General Manager — — Stage Director

House Manager — — — Company Manager — — Production Stage Manager

Box Office Staff
House Staff

Cast
Stage Technicians

Emanuel Azenberg, Alexander H. Cohen, Morton Gottlieb, Elizabeth McCann, Nelle Nugent and David Merrick.

A Broadway producer—as shown in Chart 8, which outlines the executive organization for a Broadway production—is forced to work in close partnership with a theatre landlord. The Shubert Organization, the Nederlander Organization and Jujamcyn, Inc. own most of Broadway's thirty-seven theatres. These landlords often contribute to the financing of a show and provide the theatre facility as well, through a complicated licensing procedure that involves a large rental fee based on box-office income and on services and personnel provided by the landlord. The landlord may share some advertising costs for a show and, if provided for in the licensing agreement, has the right to evict the show from the theatre if ticket sales fall below a specified point for a specified time period.

A general manager in New York commercial theatre is an independent specialist who is often incorporated and may maintain a permanent office and staff. The general manager earns a livelihood by handling virtually all the business supervision for specific productions when he or she is hired to do so by a producer. In effect, the general manager is an executive producer. On behalf of the producer, the general manager is responsible for negotiating theatre licenses, setting up the production staff, accounting for the finances, and dealing with the theatre landlord or the landlord's executive staff. The general manager may work for a single producer or manage a number of different productions simultaneously. Many producers have been general managers themselves and some function in both roles for their shows. Many producers were also at one time company managers or press agents. This is a common career path and a proven way of learning the business.

A company manager on Broadway and on the road is contracted to the producer but reports to the general manager and is hired to insure the smooth day-to-day running of the production and its cast. The company manager is also accountable for the box-office receipts and daily expenditures, including payroll. The landlord's counterpart is the house manager, who must supervise box-office, ushering, and other house personnel employed by the landlord. So the company and house managers have different bosses but work together and must reconcile any differences regarding staff, operations and box-office receipts.

Since the advent of not-for-profit theatre companies, more and more plays have been developed in the noncommercial sector before being produced on Broadway. With production budgets at $1 million to $4 million, there is little room for experimentation on Broadway; as a result, the Broadway theatre is becoming increasingly dependent on film companies and cable television companies, many of which help finance a theatrical production in return for the rights to adapt and distribute it.

National touring companies, also called first-class touring companies, are organized and controlled by the producer of the original Broadway production. These companies play the large theatres in such cities as Boston, Philadelphia, Detroit, Chicago, Los Angeles, and Washington. After audiences for these tours diminish, the bus-and-truck rights are sold to a packager, who then organizes tours of smaller cities for shorter engagements. American Theatre Productions and CAMI Theatricals, Inc., are among the largest of such packagers. Eventually, the rights to a recent Broadway hit, assuming it was an original property, are sold to a play publishing company, such as Samuel French or Dramatists Play Service, which, in turn, licenses the property for production in stock, dinner, community and amateur theatres around the country and in foreign nations.

Off-Broadway theatres are rented to producers on a "four-wall" basis, which means that the landlord provides nothing more than the theatre facility. Both commercial and not-for-profit productions are presented Off-Broadway, *The Fantasticks* being the longest-running example of the former. Many Off-Broadway employees—including actors, directors, company managers and stage managers—are unionized, although salary scales are considerably lower than on Broadway. Other employees, including stagehands, technicians, designers, box-office personnel, and house managers are usually not under union contract. These factors, combined with the Off-Broadway tradition of mounting smaller productions in smaller theatres, make it possible to produce a play Off-Broadway for about one-third the cost of a Broadway production. Financing is usually raised from private investors through the device of a Limited Partnership Agreement, as is the case on Broadway. Most Broadway producers and landlords belong to the League of American Theatres and Producers, while the comparable Off-Broadway association is the League of Off-Broadway Theatres and Producers.

Stock and dinner theatres are categorized by Actors' Equity Association according to the type of entertainment they produce—musical, dramatic, indoor, outdoor; by whether or not they maintain a resident acting company; and by the amount of their potential weekly gross. Virtually all stock theatres operate on a seasonal basis, summer or winter, whereas dinner theatres may either produce their own productions or buy them from a packager. While administrative salaries are low, the opportunity to learn is considerable and certainly makes for valuable entry-level experience for someone seeking a theatre career.

Industrial shows promote or demonstrate a product or line of products. They are presented by the manufacturer at sales conventions, trade shows, world fairs, and the like. Most "industrials" are planned by the manufacturer's advertising agency, which hires a theatrical producer or packager to produce them. This is similar to the process by which manufacturers and others hire an advertising agency to produce a television commercial.

Everybody in the commercial theatre, it seems, dreams of working on Broadway. For all its problems and failures, or perhaps because of them, arriving on Broadway is far from impossible if you have the right background and enough perseverance. Broadway executives are impressed by a resume that includes experience with leading Off-Broadway, stock, and regional theatres: They are more impressed by the school of hard knocks than by college credits, although a combination of both is gaining favor. Starting as an intern, secretary, or administrative assistant with a producer's or landlord's office is a good beginning after you've earned some experience in another branch of the theatre business. As you become acquainted with the most active professionals in this rather small community of workers, seek out an apprenticeship with the Association of Theatrical Press Agents and Managers (ATPAM), which will mean several years at a good salary assisting an ATPAM company manager, house manager, or press agent. The greatest opportunity for such employment, both for apprentices and union members, exists with the touring companies, because most ATPAM members simply prefer not to travel.

ATPAM, which is a small union, recently announced that it would severely limit the number of apprentices it would accept. Furthermore, apprentices are required, after a specified amount of employment over a two- or three-year period, to pass a written exam. ATPAM's jurisdiction covers all Broadway and first-class touring productions as well as most major road theatres in the larger cities. This means that all company managers, house managers and press agents employed by such theatres must be ATPAM members. A general manager, on the other hand, need not belong to the union, although most do, or did at one time.

NONPROFIT THEATRE

The nonprofit theatre is composed of—
Resident theatre productions
Off-Off-Broadway and showcase productions
College and university productions
Civic and community theatre productions
Children's theatre productions

However, some stock theatres and Off-Broadway productions are presented under nonprofit status, and a number of children's theatre companies are for-profit ventures.

Resident theatres are nonprofit organizations that maintain an ongoing management staff and sometimes an acting company that is under a season-long contract to present a season of productions. Many are professional in that they use union performers and are members of the League of Resident Theatres (LORT), an association that, among other functions, negotiates a basic contract with Actors' Equity on behalf of its theatre members. The eighty LORT theatres around the country include the American Conservatory Theatre in San Francisco, Washington's Arena Stage, the Actors Theatre of Louisville, and Circle in the Square in the heart of Broadway in New York City. Measured by the number of people employed, weeks of work, and the number of performances given, LORT theatres represent the single largest segment of the theatre industry. Managerial and artistic standards are high in these theatres and the salaries offered for professional management positions are competitive with those offered in other types of nonprofit arts organizations. In addition, there are about 150 nonprofit professional theatre companies that do not operate under a LORT contract.

Annual operating budgets for LORT theatres range from about $60,000 to over $7 million. The LORT theatres employ middle managers in the areas of fundraising, marketing, finance, operations, and, sometimes, educational and touring programs. Management positions with a theatre company require the same kind of specialized experience required of managers with symphony orchestras, and with ballet and opera companies of equivalent size. The salaries offered by these various performing arts companies are competitive, and jobhopping among them is common.

The "producer" of a LORT theatre is called a producing director. This person, who reports directly to the board, has total responsibility for the artistic and managerial decisions affecting the company's operations. Ideally, the board, which has the authority to hire and fire a producing director, will select an individual whose artistic philosophy and achievements they respect. The board then relinquishes the realization of that philosophy to the producing director, who must accomplish the artistic goals of the theatre within a framework of financial accountability. The producing director in a regional theatre, therefore, must often combine the knowledge and abilities of both a general manager and a stage director; he or she must also possess an artistic vision and philosophy that can sustain the work of the theatre—not just through one production, but through a series of productions over a number of seasons.

Given the scarcity of people who qualify as outstanding producing directors, it is common for LORT theatres—and many community, civic and amateur theatres—to divide the artistic and managerial responsibilities between two persons, an artistic director and a managing director or general manager. Both report to the board and, in theory, have equal authority. (See Chart 9.) In this configuration, the managing director is responsible for all nonartistic decisions, such as marketing, budgeting, staffing, long-range planning and fundraising. The artistic director is responsible for selecting plays, casting, choosing directors, and managing key technical personnel. This relationship is, of course, complicated by the fact that every artistic decision has an impact on management and vice versa. In practice, these two executives must

---

CHART 9
EXECUTIVE ORGANIZATION:
A LORT THEATRE BUDGETED OVER $1 MILLION

Board of Trustees

Artistic Director -------------------------------------- Managing Director

Finance Director	Marketing Director	Development Director	Company Manager
Accountant	Press Agent	Associate	Road Manager
Box-Office Staff	Subscription Manager	Staff	Educational Programs Coordinator
Staff	Group Sales Manager		
	Staff		

---

work very closely together—something that is almost as difficult to achieve as finding one person who is qualified to do both jobs.

Off-Off Broadway productions are works presented in theatres with less than one hundred seats. In these productions, as well as in the showcase and workshop productions that are produced for very limited runs in Off-Off Broadway theatres, the actors work for car fare or a very small stipend. There are hundreds of such productions each year. Most are organized by a single producer or, perhaps, by a playwright or an actor who becomes a producer so that his or her work can be seen by the public. The ongoing Off-Off Broadway theatre companies, such as Ellen Stewart's LaMaMa Experimental Theatre Club and Miriam Colon's Puerto Rican Traveling Theatre, have boards of trustees and several paid staff people who perform artistic and managerial functions. Budgets for these companies are astonishingly small and the tenure of paid personnel is often quite short.

Most civic and community theatres utilize volunteers instead of paid staff. Board members often perform staff functions, and whatever income is raised or generated is usually spent on production expenses and on hiring a professional director or professional guest artists for leading roles.

There are hundreds of college and university theatre companies that present works with student casts and faculty directors. However, there are also professional companies, such as the Yale Repertory Company in New Haven and the American Repertory Theatre in Boston, that are supported financially by a university but employ professional actors and staff, with some of these positions also being filled by students. The largest of these theatres, such as the two mentioned, are members of LORT and function in a manner similar to other LORT theatres, except that the university administration usually replaces the function of a board of trustees.

A wide variety of children's theatre companies flourish across the country. Most are run by a small administrative staff and, as do community theatres, depend on volunteers. Some of the higher-quality childrens' theatre productions come from LORT companies that have established special productions that may tour in local schools, sometimes statewide; these companies often have their own administrative and technical staffs as well as separate boards of advisors. Most companies that hire professional actors belong to the Producers League of Theatre for Young Audiences (PLOTYA).

Career paths in the nonprofit theatre can be traced up through the management ranks from assistant or secretary to managing director. It is possible to begin in a middle-management position if you have business skills in payroll, bookkeeping, marketing, or accounting. Most LORT theatres have internship programs and will often hire people for assistant positions directly from college and arts management programs. Developing your skills and expertise in a particular area, such as fundraising or business management, will make you more valuable and give you more upward mobility. The route to managing director positions in nonprofit theatres is well established. LORT managers usually move from small theatres to larger ones, and/or from a middle-management job to managing director, after a tenure of two to five years in a position. The network is so tight and job reputations so well known in professional theatre that any exceptions to this are noteworthy.

Although theatre in this chapter has been discussed in terms of methods of producing in the commercial and nonprofit sectors, there is no actual dividing line in terms of employment opportunities. Many people have worked in both commercial and nonprofit theatre, although this is much more common for artists than for managers. And in the management field, it is easier to move from the commercial sector to the nonprofit sector than the other way around—perhaps due to the persistent myth that commercial theatre is tougher and more aware of the nickels and dimes than the nonprofit theatre. But don't kid yourself. No theatre in America is about to catch fire because somebody is burning money!

OPERA

Opera is logistically the most complicated of the performing arts to produce. It requires organizing a symphony orchestra, a chorus, and a ballet company and necessitates the production capabilities of a large theatre. For these reasons opera is also the most expensive to produce of all the performing arts. For example, the cost of a season of four fully staged productions of only two performances each can easily exceed $500,000. The 1983 annual budget for New York's Metropolitan Opera Association was in excess of $70 million, by far the largest budget for any nonprofit performing arts company in the nation.

Most opera produced in this country takes place on college and university campuses, which serve as an excellent training ground for young singers, directors, musicians, composers, and conductors. However, in addition to New York, other cities, such as Boston, Washington, Dallas, Houston, Santa Fe, San Francisco, Seattle and Chicago, can boast major professional opera companies. With very few exceptions, most notably the Broadway production of Gian Carlo Menotti's *The Consul* and *The Telephone* in the 1950s, opera is produced by nonprofit organizations.

The trade association that represents the professional nonprofit opera field, OPERA America, lists almost 100 companies as members, including several from Canada and South America. Each has an annual budget of over $50,000 and each performs staged productions annually. Companies affiliated with OPERA America are categorized as full members or as correspondent members, the latter being the smaller companies with fewer productions.

As with symphonies and theatre companies, the size of the opera company staff and the degree of decentralization of the management is proportional to the size of the operation—the more productions there are, the larger the budget and the staff. Furthermore, in companies with budgets under $100,000 there is more direct involvement in the day-to-day operations by the members of the board.

Many opera companies are headed by one person, a general director or managing director, who has ultimate control over both the artistic and management decisions. This is the same role as the producing

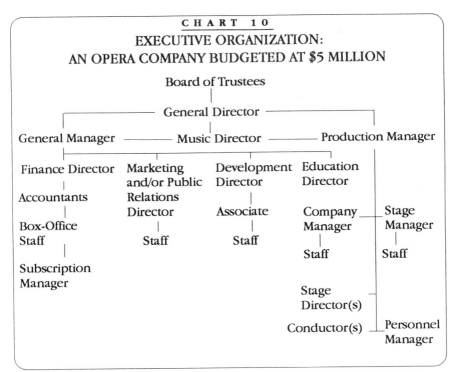

CHART 10

EXECUTIVE ORGANIZATION:
AN OPERA COMPANY BUDGETED AT $5 MILLION

director in nonprofit theatre companies. The Michigan Opera Theatre, the New York City Opera, and the Charlotte Opera, to name a few, are presently headed by general directors. The position is a highly specialized one. It requires strong managerial skills combined with artistic instincts and a vast knowledge and understanding of opera repertoire, singers, conductors, directors, designers, as well as many other aspects of opera production and performance. (Chart 10 shows how a fairly large opera company may be structured.)

Most general directors begin their careers in the artistic area of opera. Beverly Sills, former general director of the New York City Opera, had an illustrious career as a singer; Robert Driver, general director of the Syracuse and Indianapolis opera companies, began as a stage director. The knowledge and experience required for the job are such that one cannot become the general director of a sizable opera company overnight. Some have, however, begun in opera or music management, such as Sir Rudolf Bing, former general manager of New York's Metropolitan Opera; and Terrance McEwen, former general director of the San Francisco Opera, who was a record company executive. Because there are comparatively few opera companies that offer full-time, salaried employment, the competition even for entry positions is keen. Experience in college or community opera would be an asset, as would specific business skills in accounting, marketing, or development.

SYMPHONY ORCHESTRAS

Symphony orchestras are the oldest and most established of America's performing arts institutions. They are also the most numerous. There are over fifteen-hundred symphony orchestras in the United States and Canada. Even small cities with populations of less than fifty thousand have symphony orchestras, and some larger cities can boast of having four or five. With the exception of a few orchestras that are formed for specific projects or exclusively for recording purposes, most established symphony orchestras that perform the classical repertoire are nonprofit organizations. And almost all of these are members of the American Symphony Orchestra League (ASOL), a membership and service organization.

The salaried leadership of a professional orchestra is shared between a music director, who is usually the conductor, and the general manager—or executive director, managing director, or president (See Chart 11). Both report to the board of trustees and each has specific areas of responsibility, similar to the directors of theatre and opera companies. The general manager of an orchestra obviously must have strong management skills, particularly in major orchestras that have large budgets and a management staff of over fifty people. In the smaller orchestras, such as urban and community orchestras, the general manager assumes most of the management functions with only volunteer assistance from board members. Because so many management decisions are based on the length of a musical piece, the number and types of musicians required, rehearsal demands, and the requirements for guest artists, the orchestra manager must also have a good working knowledge of the classical orchestral repertoire. Although not directly responsible for choosing repertoire or hiring soloists, the general manager's input in such areas is often sought out and valued. Knowing, for example, that it is more expensive to rehearse and perform a Mahler symphony than an early Haydn symphony can greatly simplify programming discussions and translate more readily into budgetary decisions.

The general manager, or executive or managing director, is also the chief spokesperson for the orchestra. Because it is common for the

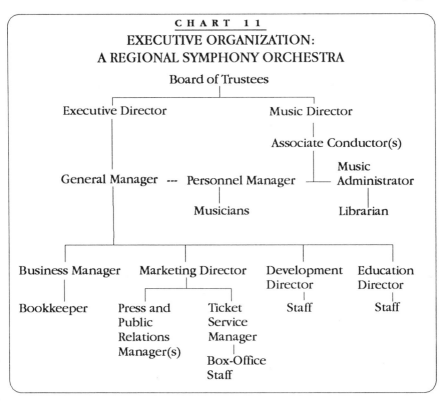

CHART 11
EXECUTIVE ORGANIZATION:
A REGIONAL SYMPHONY ORCHESTRA

Board of Trustees

Executive Director   Music Director

Associate Conductor(s)

Music
General Manager --- Personnel Manager   Administrator

Musicians   Librarian

Business Manager   Marketing Director   Development   Education
Director   Director

Bookkeeper   Press and   Ticket   Staff   Staff
Public   Service
Relations   Manager
Manager(s)
Box-Office
Staff

music director to be away from the city for up to half of each year—performing with other orchestras or opera companies—the general manager becomes the representative of the orchestra to the community, the press, the funders, the union representatives and the board.

An important management position unique to symphony orchestras is the personnel manager, sometimes called a contractor. This position requires a person who can supervise the musicians and represent them to management. The personnel manager must also organize auditions, hire extra musicians when needed, monitor management's compliance with union contracts, and serve as liaison with the music director and the general manager. The personnel manager in small organizations is a member of the orchestra who is paid extra for undertaking these management responsibilities. He or she must know musicians and understand their concerns, and must be an able negotiator.

There are two other positions unique to symphony orchestras that also require specialized musical knowledge and artistic ability as well as administrative know-how: music administrator and music librarian.

The music administrator is responsible for the day-to-day music-related decisions and works closely with the music director regarding rehearsal scheduling, soloist contracting, and program planning. The administrator also works with the general manager on budgetary, planning and operational matters. Typical duties of this job include planning program and subscription series, engaging guest conductors and soloists, scheduling rehearsals, making contingency plans for all performances, and finding last-minute replacements when individual artists are unable to perform.

The music librarian in a small orchestra is usually one of the musicians. In a larger orchestra, the position of librarian is a full-time administrative job; responsibilities include renting and purchasing music parts and scores, controlling the costs for such expenditures, organizing and maintaining the music library, and supervising assistant librarians.

As the size and complexity of an orchestra's management increases the general manager concentrates more effort on long-range planning, fund-raising, board-related duties, and community relations. When that occurs the position title is elevated to executive director (or president) and a day-to-day operating position, also called general manager, is created between the executive and the staff. This requires that much of the routine supervision of the organization be delegated to an orchestra manager or operations manager. A number of management positions below that of the general manager require a strong knowledge of classical music and repertoire. This is less important for people in fund-raising and finance, but essential in areas such as marketing, operations, and music administration.

In earlier days much of the management personnel for orchestras was drawn from the musicians themselves, but the current generation of symphony orchestra managers is entering the field directly from a management track. There are two typical career paths: beginning as a general manager or executive director of a small orchestra and gradually moving to larger orchestras, or beginning in an entry-level position with a larger orchestra and being promoted within the organization. Those who have been successful in following the latter route have usually developed a mentor relationship with a managing director as well as contacts on the board level. In either case, the careers of most symphony managers have been helped along by the American Symphony Orchestra League. ASOL concentrates much of its efforts on training, career development, and placement in the field. Younger symphony managers are emerging from the seminars, regional workshops, and fellowship programs offered by ASOL, and from graduate arts management programs. Through these training forums people are learning the principles of orchestra management and are developing personal contacts with experienced managers and board members. ASOL also acts, informally, as a referral service for boards and managers, sometimes suggesting candidates for openings that may not even be public knowledge. During the annual ASOL conference, a great amount of interviewing and hiring takes place.

MODERN DANCE AND BALLET

Both modern dance and ballet companies present dance on stage, usually with live or recorded musical accompaniment, and both require similar management support. However, individual companies can vary greatly depending on the dance idiom being presented and the size of the company, its budget, the length of its season(s), the amount of touring it may do, whether or not it operates a school or education program, whether its staff and artists are employed year round or part-time, and what special projects the company may undertake in such areas as film, television and cablevision.

Modern Dance

Modern dance has experienced unparalleled growth over the past several decades. There are now hundreds of incorporated companies and many more unincorporated companies and solo performers in the field. Unfortunately, comparatively few companies are able to offer a year-round living salary either to their artists or to their administrators. Although artistically diverse, most of the so-called emerging modern dance companies have very similar management structures—or lack of same. Most represent the vision of a particular artist who leads the company both artistically and managerially. If incorporated, these groups begin with a "paper board"—or trustees who are friends of the artist and who lend their names to the papers of incorporation, but who do not control artistic policy or influence the management of the company. Such boards seldom contribute financially. Rather, the entire administration is likely to be handled by the founding artistic director. Some companies have existed for many years in this manner, recruiting dancers for secretarial and part-time office work.

Because small modern dance companies are usually in a state of growth or crisis, there are frequently openings for administrators. Entry into the management ranks in the modern dance field requires a belief in, even a passion for, the particular aesthetic of a given company—a passion greater, perhaps, than that required for any other performing art. For this reason, and because their artistic careers are comparatively short, many former dancers have become dance managers.

Perhaps the most pressing problem faced by small dance groups is that of keeping the company together—a necessary condition for artistic accomplishment and growth. Among other considerations, this may involve scheduling the right number of employment weeks in the right period of time to guarantee that the artists can collect unemployment insurance between engagements. Or it may require that the company manager sell presenters not only public performances by the company, but also "residencies," during which a company remains at a campus or community center for a number of days to offer special classes and lecture-demonstrations, thereby lengthening its term of employment.

A recent development in the management of small dance companies has been the formation of consortiums in which several small companies hire the services of the same general manager, fund-raiser, press agent, accountant, or a group of these specialists. If the giants of the performing arts industry, such as Lincoln Center and the Kennedy Center, can provide certain services for their performing constituents, a similar type of centralized support should be, and is, possible for small companies, even if they do not share a facility in common. Several firms —such as Pentacle/Danceworks, Inc., in New York City—now offer a wide range of management services to small dance and other performing arts companies.

Once a company earns the critical acclaim and audience support necessary for budgetary growth, professional management must be introduced. This often begins with the expansion of the board and its greater involvement in policy, planning, and fund-raising. The general manager probably supervises all administrative functions with the assistance of outside agencies that specialize in booking, financial management, and advertising. As managing a company becomes more demanding with the increase in its activities, more staff must be added in the areas of development, business management, marketing, and operations. The general manager—or, now, the executive director—concentrates on long-range planning and board development, and delegates routine management chores to staff members. The founder-artistic director is thus freed to develop the company artistically and to choreograph new works. Theoretically, the structure becomes bilateral in terms of authority, with the executive director's status equivalent to the artistic director's—a situation often found in symphony orchestra, opera and theatre company management. In practice, however, the artistic director usually has veto power over the executive director. This happens because the company strongly identifies with the artistic director and the veteran board members retain their original allegiance to the founder-artistic director. To illustrate this, imagine that an impasse between the manager and the founder of the Paul Taylor Dance Company is resolved by firing Paul Taylor. Obviously, such radical action is rarely taken.

The ultimate crisis occurs when the artist who founded a company retires or dies—this is especially traumatic when the company bears the artist's name. Only a loyal company and a strong board can sustain such a loss, as was accomplished after the death of Jose Limon, who had founded a company bearing his name. The Joffrey Ballet, Martha Graham Company, and Alvin Ailey Dance Theatre are currently facing such a challenge.

Ballet

Modern dance companies are concentrated in the nation's larger cities, but many smaller communities can boast the cultural asset of a civic or regional ballet company, usually supported and run by a board of trustees. The board hires an artistic director who recruits and trains dancers, sets classical dances, or creates new works for the company. Many regional companies operate a ballet school that is owned by the artistic director or by the nonprofit corporation; many also operate in-school programs that give employment to the dancers and encourage local funding for the company.

While the majority of dance companies are minimally staffed, the major companies—such as the Joffrey, Eliot Feld's Original Ballet Foundation, the Alvin Ailey American Dance Company, the American Ballet Theatre, the Dance Theatre of Harlem, the National Ballet of Canada and the San Francisco Ballet—maintain ongoing operations that employ dozens of administrators, technicians and artists on lengthy or year-round contracts. Their engagements include national and international tours and an annual season in New York or in their home city. With budgets in the millions, large unearned income goals and high production costs, these companies require sophisticated management and active board members. Development, marketing, finance and operations become separate departments, each with managers, staff and board involvement. Ideally, the executive leadership is shared by a strong artistic director and a proven executive director, who together are able to sustain and give vitality to a complex artistic enterprise without stepping on each other's toes.

Dance/U.S.A. is the professional association of the major modern dance companies and the large ballet companies. It provides a forum for the managers and artistic directors to discuss mutual problems and common issues and acts as an advocate on the national level for increased support and touring opportunities. Regional Dance America, formerly the National Association of Regional Ballet (NARB), has a membership of small-to-mid-size civic and professional ballet companies. Both associations have annual conferences and some regional meetings and are good sources of information for job openings and trends in the field.

PRESENTING ORGANIZATIONS AND PERFORMING ARTS CENTERS

A presenting organization hires live attractions and presents them to a community. All but a few operate as nonprofit corporations. There are four types of presenting organizations:

Independent presenters or promoters

Community and civic presenters

College and university presenters

Presenting-producing organizations or performing arts centers

If one takes a low figure and estimates that there are two thousand presenting organizations nationwide that offer an average of twelve performances annually, then this branch of the industry is responsible for 24,000 live performances each year, involving symphony orchestras; opera, theatre, and dance companies; rock groups; circuses; and acrobatic acts. They also present soloists—singers, instrumentalists, poets, mimes, puppeteers, comedians, and one-person shows—and many sponsor film series. Presenting organizations provide performing groups and individual artists a touring circuit, which allows them to increase their performance seasons, often to a year-round schedule. Equally important are the opportunities for artistic growth that touring provides for incipient companies and developing artists who lack the resources, reputations, or levels of accomplishment that would enable them to perform in the major houses of our largest cities. Columbia

Artists Management, Inc., a leading talent and booking organization, has made a particular contribution to the field through its Community Concerts Guild, which is a national network of presenters who book young and often unknown talent into small concert halls, where volunteer committees sell tickets and thereby provide audiences.

Even though almost all presenting organizations operate on a nonprofit basis, many of the soloists, popular music groups, bus-and-truck tours, and guest artists function as for-profit entities. The nonprofit groups that are presented, of course, also earn fees and, sometimes, a percentage of the box-office income.

Independent Presenters and Promoters

Independent presenters and promoters are really impresarios who seek to earn their livings from their booking activities. Most work out of a permanent office but seldom own a facility; rather, they rent a hall or performance space as needed. Most are small, low-budget outfits that have little if any support staff. The independent presenter arranges performances with the owners of the performing space or with another presenter, such as a performing arts center. For this the independent presenter receives a fee or commission based on the performance fee. Other independent presenters operate within a particular city and usually reserve certain dates in the performing halls available to them. They then bring in and present the performing artists or groups. In these cases, the presenter pays the group a fee that is expected to be more than covered by box-office receipts. This type of presenter must also pay for the support staff—box-office, security, house-management, and technical personnel—as well as advertising and publicity costs, and earns a profit only after all such expenses are covered. The element of risk is considerable.

Community and Civic Presenters

Community and civic presenting organizations operate in much the same manner, except that they are nonprofit corporations and can supplement their ticket receipts with unearned income from their fund-raising efforts. The typical community presenting organization is run almost completely by volunteers, usually members of the board, who wish to import certain cultural events into their community. Perhaps a number of citizens are interested in bringing the great ballet companies to a community that is too small to support its own company. Typically, they form a board, raise money through special events, receive a grant from the local arts council, and then negotiate with a booking agency to present a dance series. The volunteers rent a hall and then contract with a local public-relations or advertising agency or try to sell enough tickets themselves to cover the cost of the event. As such groups become more successful, they hire paid staff, beginning with an executive director or general manager. The board continues to raise unearned income and to participate in special activities, while the general manager assumes other managerial duties.

Some community presenters have raised enough money to purchase an old vaudeville or movie theatre. With the support of local government and the blessing of local business, these restored theatres are operated by the presenters, who also rent them to outside groups to earn additional income. There are a number of well-known renovation projects that are now regarded with great pride within their communities—the Grand Opera House in Wilmington, Delaware; the Ohio Theatre in Columbus, Ohio; and Symphony Hall in Newark, New Jersey, are just a few examples. In these and in similar cases, a nonprofit corporation is the part-time presenter for the facility and the full-time landlord. The executive director of such a presenting organization is responsible for the artistic decisions involving the booking of events and the rental of the facilities, as well as the day-to-day administrative duties. The executive director reports to the board and may supervise a staff of three to twenty or more people. (See Chart 12.) The service organization for restored theatres is the League of Historic Theatres.

Executive directors of presenting organizations must be very familiar with performing arts groups and artists in order to understand which are most appropriate for their community. A presenter once booked an African dance group into his center, which happened to be a very conservative, religious community. Because he had never seen or read about the group, he was not aware that both the male and female dancers performed topless! There are many other more subtle judgments that the executive director must be able to make in order to best satisfy the cultural tastes of a given audience. The position also calls for the skills and experiences required of managers in other types of nonprofit arts organizations: the ability to work with a board, to hire and supervise staff, to represent the organization to the community, to develop budgets and stay within them, and to work with the board in raising unearned income.

College and University Presenters
College and university presenting organizations, which use the campus theatre or auditorium as a performance space, are usually

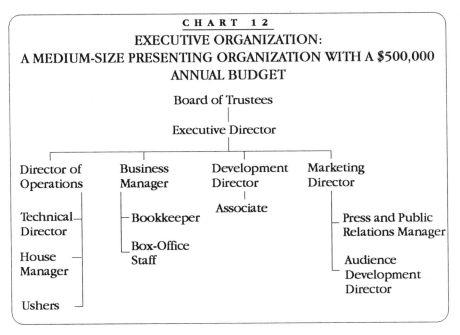

CHART 12
EXECUTIVE ORGANIZATION:
A MEDIUM-SIZE PRESENTING ORGANIZATION WITH A $500,000 ANNUAL BUDGET

Board of Trustees

Executive Director

Director of Operations · Business Manager · Development Director · Marketing Director

Technical Director · Bookkeeper · Associate · Press and Public Relations Manager

House Manager · Box-Office Staff · Audience Development Director

Ushers

headed by a member of the faculty or administration who books and supervises the presentation of film and lecture series and one or more performing arts series. A large college or university with a very active series of events, such as Brooklyn College, Stanford University, and Dartmouth College, employs a full-time director and a permanent staff (See Chart 13). In all cases, the events that are booked have to be coordinated with the performances of the university's music, theatre, and dance departments; because the demand for the campus theatre or auditorium is usually high, animosities can easily arise among the factions vying for space. This may be complicated by the fact that the director of the professional series must usually book events a year or two in advance. Whoever holds this position, then, must be realistic about the diverse needs of an academic community and must be able to accommodate them. The director may also have to answer to a faculty-student advisory committee that has the authority to suggest and to veto programming decisions.

Some campus presenters operate out of an academic department, others out of a dean's office or the student union. Most are ultimately responsible to the college president. When the cash flow from a series is substantial, it may represent one of the president's few sources of unencumbered or unrestricted funds. Also, a professional arts series has a highly visible public-relations factor that can strengthen or weaken cam-

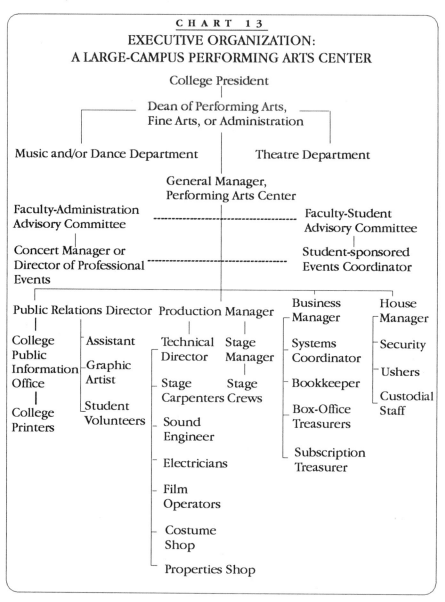

CHART 13

EXECUTIVE ORGANIZATION:
A LARGE-CAMPUS PERFORMING ARTS CENTER

College President

Dean of Performing Arts,
Fine Arts, or Administration

Music and/or Dance Department | Theatre Department

General Manager,
Performing Arts Center

Faculty-Administration Advisory Committee ---- Faculty-Student Advisory Committee

Concert Manager or Director of Professional Events ---- Student-sponsored Events Coordinator

Public Relations Director | Production Manager | Business Manager | House Manager

College Public Information Office | Assistant | Technical Director | Stage Manager | Systems Coordinator | Security

Graphic Artist | Stage Carpenters | Stage Crews | Bookkeeper | Ushers

College Printers | Student Volunteers | Sound Engineer | Box-Office Treasurers | Custodial Staff

Electricians | Subscription Treasurer

Film Operators

Costume Shop

Properties Shop

pus-community relations. While the presentation of a distinguished artist adds to the college's luster, the presentation of a rock group that attracts an audience of drunken or drugged teenagers does not! Hence,
the interest and input of the college administration is important, although it may not always be appreciated by the manager of the series.
The service organization that represents college and university pre-

senters, as well as many community and commercial presenters, is the Association of Performing Arts Presenters, headquartered in Washington, D.C.

Presenting-Producing Organizations or Performing Arts Centers

Large, successful presenting organizations that own or lease their own facility sometimes produce as well as present events. The Victoria Theatre Association in Dayton, Ohio, used to produce a series of plays during the spring and summer, bringing in guest directors, designers and actors. During the remainder of the year, it presented the Dayton Contemporary Dance Company, the Dayton Ballet and other arts events. The Brooklyn Academy of Music (BAM) is a presenting-producing performing arts center that has enjoyed long success in presenting ballet and dance companies. BAM has also served as producer of its own resident theatre company for several seasons and oversees the Brooklyn Philharmonic's operations; it has also been the producer of The Next Wave, an annual festival of performance art.

The largest presenting organizations are the performing arts centers: Lincoln Center, The Los Angeles Music Center, and the Kennedy Center being the big three. These organizations are operated as nonprofit corporations, with their own boards of trustees; they serve as landlords, presenters and producers, while also accommodating a number of constituent performing arts companies. (See Chart 14.) Constituents of the Kennedy Center include the National Symphony Orchestra and the Washington Opera Society. The Kennedy Center also produces or coproduces new plays and revivals, which it then moves to other theatres and sometimes to Broadway; it also books into its halls a wide variety of touring attractions, making it a presenting-producing organization. Lincoln Center, Inc., is a holding company that oversees the land and buildings that make up the complex: the Metropolitan Opera House, Avery Fisher Hall, the Vivian Beaumont Theatre, the Performing Arts Library of the New York Public Library, the Juilliard School, the New York State Theatre, and the parking facilities. It produces the Mostly Mozart Festival, and the summer outdoor festival of Lincoln Center, and is involved in television projects, including the "Live From Lincoln Center" series that is broadcast on PBS.

Lincoln Center, Inc., raises funds through its board of trustees and through a united corporate fund-raising campaign, some of which funds go toward the general operating cost of the complex and some of which are distributed to its constituents. The Lincoln Center board,

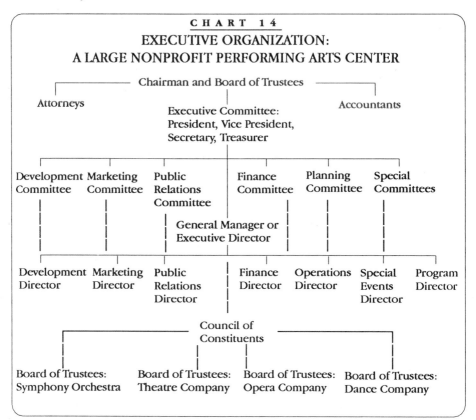

CHART 14

EXECUTIVE ORGANIZATION:
A LARGE NONPROFIT PERFORMING ARTS CENTER

Chairman and Board of Trustees

Attorneys

Executive Committee:
President, Vice President,
Secretary, Treasurer

Accountants

Development Committee   Marketing Committee   Public Relations Committee   Finance Committee   Planning Committee   Special Committees

General Manager or
Executive Director

Development Director   Marketing Director   Public Relations Director   Finance Director   Operations Director   Special Events Director   Program Director

Council of
Constituents

Board of Trustees: Symphony Orchestra   Board of Trustees: Theatre Company   Board of Trustees: Opera Company   Board of Trustees: Dance Company

through its chairman and its president, oversees the policy of the center. There is also a council composed of representatives from its constituents: the Metropolitan Opera Association; the New York Philharmonic; the New York City Ballet; the New York City Opera; the Juilliard School; the Vivian Beaumont Theatre Company, which also operates the Mitzi Newhouse Theatre; the Chamber Music Society of Lincoln Center; the Lincoln Center Institute, which is the educational arm of the Center; and City Center, Inc. The latter is itself a holding company for the State Theatre and rents space to the opera and ballet companies in residence there. City Center also presents other arts events and rents the hall to outside tenants. In some ways Lincoln Center, Inc., is a nonprofit corporate conglomerate. However, it is important to understand that the constituents are independent, nonprofit corporations, with their own boards of trustees, and each is largely responsible for its own operating and program-related fundraising. In the early days of Lincoln Center there was concern, especially in regard to fundraising, that the efforts of the Center would conflict with those of its constituents, but this had not proved to be the case. The most glaring problem until recently was the operation—or lack of it—of the Vivian Beaumont Theatre. Notably, this was the only facility at the Center that was not built to house an established performing arts company. The creation of a new, strong board, as well as an artistic management team has neatly solved that problem.

In general, the large performing arts centers have had a positive impact in helping to foster high standards and achievements in, and to bring national attention to, the performing arts. While most top-level managers in a large performing arts center are recruited from outside, middle-level positions are often promoted from within or are open to qualified applicants with the necessary experience and training. Most performing arts centers sponsor administrative internship programs that provide good short-term training but seldom guarantee a job at the end of the internship.

MUSEUMS

This country has over five thousand museums, making it the largest single category of arts organizations. Some are very small, operated only by a board and volunteers with no paid staff. Yet the number of management positions and the employment possibilities within the museum system are vast.

Museums are more than buildings with paintings in them. As defined by the Association of Art Museum Directors in its 1972 pamphlet, *Professional Practices,* a museum is "a permanent, nonprofit institution, essentially educational or artistic in purpose, with a professional staff, which acquires objects, cares for them, interprets them, and exhibits them to the public on some regular schedule." The museum profession encompasses much more than art museums like the Museum of Fine Arts in Boston or the National Gallery in Washington, D.C. In fact, only about 15 percent of the five thousand museums are art museums. Others include history museums, representing 50 percent of the total; and science museums—including zoos, botanical gardens, and arboretums—representing 18 percent of the total. The remaining ones, from the greatest in number to the least, are general museums, specialized museums, park museums, visitor centers, and children's museums.

As institutions, museums are like symphony orchestras in that they are typically among the older, more established arts organizations.

Many were founded during the last century by influential citizens who supported them financially and who eventually donated their own collections. Thus, many museum collections were built from the estates of these founding patrons. Most museum buildings and facilities are owned by the museum corporation or housed in buildings leased by the corporation from a city or local government. More museums have endowments than any other type of arts organization, and their boards are usually larger with members serving for longer periods of time. These factors, in addition to the fact that the primary mission of most museums is to preserve and exhibit works of the past, explain the generally conservative policies and management styles in the museum system.

The size of a museum staff depends upon its budget and the scope of its activities. A small museum may have only one employee, a generalist who manages all aspects of administration, acquisition, exhibition, and conservation. Some of the larger museums have hundreds of employees, much more than most other nonprofit arts organizations. These museums have departments of finance, fundraising, marketing, public relations, and operations, with managers and staff carrying out duties similar to their counterparts in orchestras, and in theatre and opera companies. Museums also have specialized management positions unique to the field, with responsibilities specifically related to the type of collection or the particular focus of the museum. These positions include the following:

Curator: responsible for the interpretation of collections through acquisitions, exhibitions, catalogues, lectures, and writings

Conservator: responsible for the care, preservation, and repair of objects in the collection

Exhibition designer: designs and oversees the installation of the exhibits

Education director: in charge of programs designed to enhance public understanding of the collections, such as lectures, art classes, field trips, and tours

Registrar: organizes, documents, and otherwise keeps track of objects in the museum

Research director: oversees visiting researchers using the collections, in-house or field research sponsored by the museum, and special educational research programs

Collections manager: works with the conservator in

maintaining a catalogue of the collection and oversees the
moving and storing of museum items

Director of acquisition: works under the museum director
and board acquisition committee to coordinate the purchase
or acquisition of new items, often using consultants or independent agents, and helps to search out, suggest, and/or
acquire objects either on a permanent or loan basis

The top-ranking management person, responsible for overseeing
the staff and executing the policies set by the board, is the director. This
is the most common title for the chief museum executive, although
president and *executive director* are also used. The museum director
reports to the board and manages the organization. Responsibilities of
the job include hiring staff, budgeting, fundraising, marketing, long-
range planning, serving as the liaison with the community and government agencies, and maintaining professional contacts in the field
through personal associations with other museum leaders. The director must also provide artistic leadership. It is essential that the person
have expertise and experience in the particular focus or subject matter
of the museum. In fact, the director's interest in a particular type or
style of art can influence the focus of the museum. Consequently, a
museum known for contemporary art, for example, will seek a director
whose expertise is in that area. A historian, as director, will influence
the research and collections of a particular history museum. The ideal
museum director will impart an artistic vision and provide leadership
in program development as well in management areas. In art
museums, expertise is usually gained through a curatorial position.
Curators of large collections usually have, in addition to curatorial
responsibilities, management duties: supervising a staff of assistant
curators, controlling exhibition budgets, working with board committees, preparing grants, speaking to the membership, and participating
in conferences as a representative of the museum, to name a few.

There are many museums connected with universities and colleges. These are often part of the art department and fall under the control of the department chairperson, or they may be operated by the office of the president or the dean of fine arts. The director must usually
hold advanced degrees and have a reputation supported by scholarship, lectures, and publications.

Entry into the field of museum management may begin in college,
where internships and work-study positions are often available in the

campus museum or gallery. Most communities have a museum of some kind; in smaller cities these may have only one full-time staff person, who usually welcomes volunteers or docents to assist with tours, exhibitions and openings. Expertise or knowledge in the particular holdings of a museum is obviously helpful, but there are many entry-level positions in public relations, membership, accounting, and development that do not require such specialized knowledge. Several graduate programs have a concentration in museum management and several offer degrees in museology or museum management. In addition, there are dozens of seminars, workshops, courses, and classes offered by museum associations and management assistance organizations. (See Career Kit.) The American Association of Museums, one of the nation's largest professional arts associations, sponsors an annual conference with attendance in the thousands. There are also many smaller associations designed to meet the interest of science and history museums, and these often have regional affiliates. Such organizations should be contacted when considering a career in museum management.

ART GALLERIES

A gallery is a space that exhibits art works for the purpose of selling them. Most galleries exhibit the works of living artists: paintings, drawings, sculpture, photographs, and so on. Galleries also exhibit craft items, such as ceramics and textiles. There are three ways in which a gallery can be organized: on a commercial, privately owned basis; on a commercial, cooperative basis; and on a nonprofit, cooperative basis.

The purpose of a commercial gallery is to earn profits for the owners and investors through the sale of art works, although some wealthy individuals support the operation of a commercial gallery as a tax shelter and actually hope to lose money. The commercial gallery is operated by a dealer, who is often the principal owner. (See Chart 15.) He or she has managerial and artistic control of all gallery operations. The dealer makes a profit through commissions on sales, but is much more than a salesperson. Successful dealers not only attract potential buyers, but also control the market for certain art works, influencing the value of the works and having a direct impact on the careers of the exhibiting artists. The dealer becomes, in effect, a personal agent or manager for a select number of artists. His or her personal tastes can often influence the artists, and as the artist's works are sold, the dealer

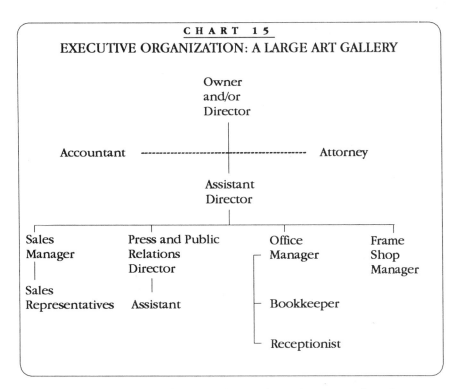

CHART 15
EXECUTIVE ORGANIZATION: A LARGE ART GALLERY

Owner and/or Director

Accountant ---------------- Attorney

Assistant Director

Sales Manager | Press and Public Relations Director | Office Manager | Frame Shop Manager

Sales Representatives | Assistant | Bookkeeper

Receptionist

can often demand a specific type of work from the artist. Thus the dealer can choose which works of the artist will be exhibited and sold. By promoting and providing for the artist, a dealer maintains control over the work. By setting prices, the dealer also influences the market value for the work. The most successful dealers have not only chosen good works to exhibit and sell, they have also had a part in determining which works are "good" and therefore "valuable." Dealers often serve a function similar to managers of performing artists. They guide the careers of promising artists, support artists and their work—sometimes providing them with stipends—and provide both artistic and business advice.

It requires capital to own and operate a gallery, to invest in artists and their works. Rent, maintenance, insurance, entertainment, promotion, and staff expenses can add up to a tidy sum. In some cases the gallery owner is a wealthy individual or a professional from an unrelated field. When this is the case, the owner hires a gallery director to manage the business. The director provides the expertise and management for the owner, who supplies the financing. The dealer-owner or the gallery director clearly must have experience and knowledge at least in a particular art form and period, must be able to recognize the potential of an artist and know how to help in developing that potential, and must understand the art market and have contacts with potential buyers. The successful gallery director is also an accomplished salesperson.

There is no clear path to becoming a gallery director. Some of the established directors have built their careers and businesses through the successes of artists whom they have discovered. Others began with money, or with contacts with monied people, and have developed a knowledge of the business. Taste, good business skills, sales sense, and entrepreneurial flair are important ingredients. Some curators and other museum professionals, attracted by higher salaries, have made a successful career move into gallery management. Often, however, these professionals have had to give up the research and scholarship connected with museum work.

By way of combating the tremendous power that private galleries and dealers exert within the art world, some artists have joined together to operate cooperative galleries. In the cooperative gallery, or artists' co-op, the control exerted by the dealers' personal tastes is replaced by a committee composed of the members of the co-op. This committee decides the policy of the gallery and also chooses the works that are exhibited. In small cooperative galleries the artists are also responsible for the management and maintenance of the gallery. In large co-ops a gallery director is hired. However, it is the board or membership committee that decides policy. Some cooperatives are for-profit organizations and some are nonprofit. Nonprofit cooperative galleries cannot sell the work of their artists directly. However, they do help to promote the work and assist in arranging for sale of the work away from the premises of the gallery.

The larger galleries, both independent and cooperative, have a full professional staff, which reports to the director. The positions, as illustrated in Chart 15, are similar to those in museums, having similar titles and job descriptions, and requiring similar skills and training. Works of art must be cared for and handled properly, and exhibitions must be professionally conceived, designed, and executed. The successful opening of an exhibition requires the effective management of publicity, press releases, personalized invitations; and the ability to involve art critics and supporters. Openings often become media events, complete with live performances, catered food and beverages, and glossy promotional material. Large galleries employ professional services to accomplish this. The sale of art also requires good marketing and selling techniques, which must be accompanied by careful accounting and record-keeping and appropriate administration of copyright and other contractual obligations between the gallery, the artist, and the buyer.

COMMERCIAL RADIO STATIONS AND TELEVISION NETWORKS

Through the eighties, the broadcast industry was dominated by the three major networks: CBS, ABC, and NBC. These companies, which are owned by large entertainment and communications corporations with diverse interests in film, publishing, recordings, news and other unrelated businesses, captured home audiences through their prime-time schedules and their sports and news programs. They also had a significant impact on local radio and television through their owned and operated stations—called O & O's—in the major markets, meaning in the larger cities.

The networks purchase programs from independent producers; buy or rent movies from film companies; sometimes participate in the financing of movies and serial entertainments; produce sit-coms and soap operas as well as news and documentary programs; cover national events, such as presidential elections and space launches; and broadcast national sporting events, such as the World Series and the Olympics. Networks supply these programs nationally to their own stations and to affiliated independent stations called network affiliates. In the larger markets—a market is roughly determined by numbers of households with television sets in a specific geographic area—all three major networks have affiliates. There may also be stations affiliated with other networks, such as Fox. In small markets served by only three or four broadcast channels there may be only one or two affiliate stations.

Networks provide prime-time and special-events programming to their affiliates without charge. They also provide publicity, marketing expertise, and other services designed to help stations maintain and increase their audiences. Networks work hard to keep their affiliates happy, satisfied and loyal. In return, the networks get viewers. In commercial broadcasting the more viewers there are, the larger the audience share and the more competitive and valuable the advertising time. It is advertising revenue that supports commercial broadcasting and earns profits for the owners or stockholders of its stations and networks. Each advertising minute during a network program such as the evening news or the World Series may be sold for $100,000 or more. If a situation comedy or adventure series is watched by a substantial percentage of the viewing audience, advertising time becomes more valuable and the program will generate greater profits. If that audience share is small or diminishes, the program will lose money and will be cancelled or dropped from the schedule.

Each network is organized differently, although the functional areas are basically alike. These may be summarized as follows:

Programming: purchases and produces programming, and is organized into departments or divisions for such areas as news, sports, special events, weekly series, movies

Station management: provides support services, including financial planning and legal services, to the managements of the affiliate stations

Marketing and public relations: supplies advertising and promotion for network programming

Sales: sells time to national advertisers, works with advertising agencies and clients who use broadcast advertising

Research: provides documentation to assist programming and marketing decisions, to determine advertising rates, and to assist affiliates

Finance and administration: provides general management of the network corporation; coordinates relations with other corporate entities and government agencies; oversees legal affairs and obligations; supervises fiscal planning and control; and offers support in these areas to the O & O's

Upper-management positions in the networks are among the highest-paying of all positions discussed in this book. Vice presidents can earn over $100,000 per year and, in addition, usually receive bonuses and stock options. Such positions are very competitive and are held by the sharpest, most experienced executives in the industry. There seem to be two general career paths that lead to heading up a network division: one involves developing a strong business or legal background and holding a position such as chief financial officer or corporate counsel; the other involves working up through one of the programming divisions of a network. Top managers for the network corporations are frequently recruited from management at the station level. Executives in network sales have come from advertising and sales positions at local or independent stations, from other industries such as packaged or consumer goods, and from advertising company positions. The most important credential is clearly the sales ability, not the prior experience in broadcasting. Entry positions at a network often exist in the areas of accounting, sales and research. These positions do not require prior experience in broadcasting, although it is always an advantage to learn all you can about the field of your choice. There are numerous cases of secretaries who have been promoted to entry-level management positions. For management-track positions, networks offer very competitive starting salaries and can attract graduates with M.B.A.s or degrees in communications or broadcasting. The networks hire interns and have formal intern programs from which they recruit entry-level management talent. On the corporate level the networks employ hundreds of administrative and management staff people. They all have personnel departments that are responsible for entry-level hiring and for many of the internal promotions. Within such a large corporate structure one's career can develop and progress very nicely because the networks and large broadcasting corporations look within to promote. This policy encourages professional growth, is good for morale, and makes the corporation attractive to the best people.

The networks also recruit from their own television stations and from other stations around the country. A typical career path to a middle-management position with a network or a corporate management position in broadcasting would be from an independent or affiliate television or radio station. Many of these positions, except for technical and engineering jobs, require similar skills and experience so that career changes from radio to television or vice versa also occur.

There are numerous broadcasting networks other than the big three. These include the Madison Square Garden Network and the Hughes Television Network, which broadcast sporting events; and there are also those that specialize in religious and other types of programming. Some networks provide programming to independent stations. Because most networks are modeled after the big three, they have similar management departments and functions.

INDEPENDENT COMMERCIAL RADIO STATIONS AND TELEVISION STATIONS

Independent commercial radio stations and television stations are as varied in management size and structure as the audiences they serve.

An independent station in a large metropolitan area may have separate departments for programming, sales, finance, and engineering, each with department heads and staff. (See Chart 16.) In smaller stations the station manager may also be the program manager, who has a secretary to keep the financial records; or the general manager may also be an owner or part-owner of the station. In any case, the general manager is the top person in the organization, reporting to the stockholders in a public company or directly to the corporate headquarters if the station is owned by a network.

The general manager is responsible for the proper business management of the station: hiring personnel and developing a staff, supervising short-term and long-range planning and fiscal management, and serving as liaison to the community, the Federal Communication Commission (FCC), and the broadcast industry. In addition, the general manager has ultimate authority and influence over the programming of the station. This, in effect, gives this executive both management and artistic control, like the general director of an opera company or the executive director of a museum. An effective general manager in broadcasting must understand the format of the station and its market, and be able to translate this knowledge into policy and programming that earn profits. This requires a background and training in broadcasting; in fact, it is very rare for a general manager to arrive at this position from a different field. The career path to the job is usually from the technical engineering area, the sales area, or from an announcing position. As with symphony orchestras and theatres, general managers move from the smaller companies to the larger ones, supervising progressively larger staffs, budgets, and programming schedules.

The FCC, the agency that regulates the broadcast industry, defines four principal areas of radio and television organization, as reflected in Chart 16: general and/or administrative, sales, technical, and programming. Positions in sales and promotion, as well as those in business management, utilize skills that can be learned in other fields. A controller for an opera company or arts council, for example, would have skills that are transferable to a television station. Likewise, someone who has sold advertising for souvenir programs or managed ticket sales for concerts could transfer those skills to a position in sales or promotion for a radio station. Some positions, however, are unique to broadcasting. A traffic manager, for instance, is responsible for tracking programs and commercials on a second-by-second basis; also for

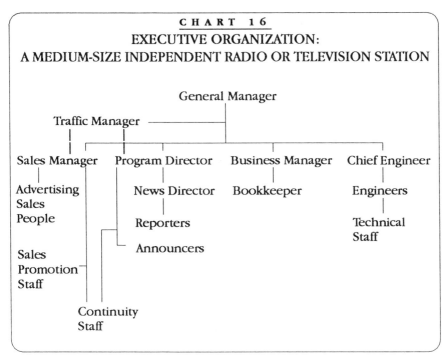

C H A R T 1 6

EXECUTIVE ORGANIZATION:
A MEDIUM-SIZE INDEPENDENT RADIO OR TELEVISION STATION

scheduling announcers and other on-air assignments and for working with the sales department to schedule the placement of commercials. A program director collaborates with the station manager and the sales manager to select programming that will increase audience share and conform to the policy of the station. Most radio stations have specific formats and are identified with a particular programming emphasis: all news, all classical music, easy-listening music, all talk, or whatever. The program director must know the medium as well as the format of the station. Radio program directors usually begin as announcers or disc jockeys. Most colleges have a radio station and many also have a television station where students can gain on-air experience that can lead to programming positions.

In small radio stations the general manager takes on the responsibilities for sales and sometimes even programming. In some stations the sales manager is also an announcer, which can be advantageous because the element of celebrity stimulates advertising sales.

In both radio and television there is a direct relationship between the market size and the size of the administrative staff. Small radio stations, serving a market population of less than ten thousand, may have as few as six full-time employees, including technical personnel; whereas a television station in one of the larger markets will employ over one hundred people.

The positions that are most scarce and most sought after in radio and television are the on-air and programming positions. The glamor of performing and the promise of fame and fortune are big motivating factors. Anchor people for a network O & O become celebrities and can earn over $500,000 annually just for reading the news. On the other hand, there are often openings for salespeople in the advertising departments that go unfilled for lack of job seekers. In fact, this is one of the best entry positions in broadcasting. A new sales representative will be trained in the operation of the station and learn about its programming, and will be in contact with the research department and interact with the continuity and traffic managers as well. More important, success in sales is easily and clearly documented. Overshooting sales quotas receives immediate recognition, not only from the sales manager but even from the general manager of the station. Since sales people usually are compensated by commissions, the successful sales people can directly influence their salaries from the day they begin work. Also, a salesperson with a record of success can be promoted within the station and has a greater chance of moving to another station. In short, though less glamorous than other areas of broadcast management, positions in sales are probably the best for short-term success and long-term career advancement in commercial broadcasting.

PUBLIC BROADCASTING

Public broadcasting is the generic term for noncommercial and educational radio and television. A distinction should be made, however, between the national organizations that help support public broadcasting stations and the stations themselves.

Public broadcasting became firmly established in 1968 when the United States Congress passed the Public Broadcasting Act, which created the Corporation for Public Broadcasting (CPB). The purpose of this quasi-independent, nongovernmental agency is to help in the development and support of noncommercial radio and television stations. It is a service organization that provides research, programming, libraries and information, as well as assistance in building stations. It also makes grants: to nonprofit broadcasting stations that meet its criteria; to producing organizations that present programming proposals;

to the Public Broadcasting Service (PBS); and to National Public Radio (NPR). CPB's funding criteria excludes stations that have a small staff and very limited programming and audience potential, as well as those with religious, political, or special-interest programming policies.

National Public Radio, established in 1970, supplies programming to its nonprofit member stations and to others that are licensed through colleges, universities and municipalities. With studios in Washington, D.C., and a sizable staff, NPR is able to produce such programming as "Morning Edition" and "All Things Considered," which would be beyond the means of independent nonprofit stations. By raising the programming quality of such stations and by offering other kinds of assistance, NPR has become a potent force in the growth of public radio broadcasting throughout the nation. Chart 17 illustrates the actual organizational structure of NPR as it was in 1982.

The Public Broadcasting Service, like NPR, is an independent nonprofit corporation that also receives funding from the Corporation for Public Broadcasting. PBS provides programming and services to independent nonprofit television stations. Aside from producing and coproducing its own programming, PBS also obtains programming from member stations. For example, WGBH in Boston, WNET in New York City, and WQED in San Francisco produce original programs that are supplied to other stations through PBS. Or PBS may purchase programs from nonprofit producing groups, the best known being the Children's Television Workshop (CTW), which has produced "Sesame Street" for many years. PBS also obtains programs from independent producers and from other broadcasting systems, the most notable being the British Broadcasting Corporation (BBC), which produced "I, Claudius" and "Upstairs, Downstairs."

CPB, NPR and PBS together provide many of the same services for the nonprofit broadcasting stations as the networks do for their commercial affiliates. An important difference, however, is that affiliates do not pay for the network programming they receive, whereas nonprofit stations are billed for their NPR or PBS air time. These national organizations, then, are dependent upon their individual member stations, and also serve as advocates for their members in the halls of government and with major corporate and foundation grantors. The larger the membership of an affiliate, the greater its clout.

Public broadcasting stations are organized as nonprofit corporations and are controlled by a board of trustees. Some are independent

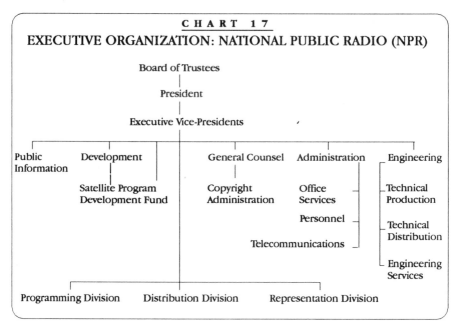

CHART 17

EXECUTIVE ORGANIZATION: NATIONAL PUBLIC RADIO (NPR)

Board of Trustees

President

Executive Vice-Presidents

Public Information

Development

Satellite Program Development Fund

General Counsel

Copyright Administration

Administration

Office Services

Personnel

Telecommunications

Engineering

Technical Production

Technical Distribution

Engineering Services

Programming Division   Distribution Division   Representation Division

nonprofit organizations while others, as mentioned, are licensed under the aegis of a college, university, or municipality. All are monitored by the Federal Communications Commission and must abide by its regulations in order to satisfy the license renewal requirements. Neither NPR nor PBS own or operate their own stations, as do the commercial networks. There are, however, a number of nonprofit broadcasting networks—or clusters of stations that are operated by a single nonprofit corporation—such as the Minnesota Public Radio Network and the Maine Public Radio Network. For the most part, however, the public broadcasting stations are separate and independent. Some subscribe to membership with NPR or PBS, and some do not, though both types may purchase programming from the national organizations. All nonprofit broadcasting stations also produce their own programming—which they are required to do by the FCC—in order to serve the needs of their specific communities. Clearly, the viewers of WGBH in Boston are different from those in Tempe, Arizona. Through their programming departments, nonprofit stations provide programs of local interest, such as local news programs, a community affairs series, or a health and science series produced in cooperation with the local hospital.

Nonprofit stations are organized in the same way commercial stations are, except the nonprofit stations do not have an advertising and sales department. In fact, they are prohibited from selling advertising time, and the amount of public recognition nonprofit stations give to corporations for their support is regulated. So, just as in other non-profit arts and media organizations, public broadcasting stations must raise funds from government, corporate, foundation and individual sources. On-air fundraising appeals are also an important method of generating contributions for many nonprofit stations. Major corporations and foundations have become interested in supporting PBS programs that have wide appeal and large audiences. Instead of directly advertising their products, the corporations receive benefits through an association with the program. Just as Texaco has been associated for many years with the Saturday radio broadcasts from the Metropolitan Opera, Exxon and IBM have associated their corporate identities with quality arts and science programs on public television, and many foundations have supported programs that reflect their interests in science, education, the arts and other areas.

The general manager for a nonprofit broadcasting station reports to the board of trustees and is responsible for station management and programming. He or she also represents the station to the community and to CPB, as well as to PBS or NPR. While the manager is not responsible for making a profit, there is a financial obligation to balance the annual budget and to provide sufficient funding for projects, programming and growth. The general manager hires and supervises the staff and works closely with the board, which is ultimately responsible for fundraising.

Career opportunities and financial rewards are not as great in public broadcasting as they are in the commercial sector, mainly because there is no ownership of public stations and no possibility of equity or a share in the company. Furthermore, nonprofit stations by their nature can never be cash-rich or profitable. General managers for nonprofit stations, like their commercial counterparts, must know television— the technical, programming, and on-air aspects. Therefore, it is unlikely that general managers in the broadcasting field will come from another area of the arts and media industry. Rather, they usually move from the small public stations to the larger ones. They may also move to general manager from a middle-management position in public radio or television, such as director of development or business manager. Because of the monetary rewards, there is more career movement from the non-profit to the commercial sector rather than in the reverse direction.

CABLE TELEVISION SYSTEMS

Cable television is a rapidly growing area within the arts and media field, despite competition from video cassette recorders and satellite discs. Small companies are still being started by entrepreneurs who perceive an open marketplace, while large corporations are entering the industry by purchasing already existing cable systems: For example, Time Warner owns American Television and Communications Corporation (ATC) one of the largest multiple system operators in the country. Newspaper chains are purchasing systems and bidding on franchises for new systems while religious organizations, among others, are forming programming networks to take advantage of unused cable television channels.

Performing arts organizations are welcoming the proliferation of cable television and the opportunities it provides for the programming of symphonies, jazz, opera, theatre and dance, just as in earlier years the advent of movies, records, and television was hailed as a boon to the lively arts. For serious art forms, however, the benefits to date have been disappointing, although the arts have enjoyed an expanding audience through public television. Cable television will not create a revolutionary change in the arts, although it will have a positive effect on audience development.

In 1970 less than 10 percent of American homes received television programming through cable transmission as opposed to receiving it through the airwaves. In fact, most cable programs were merely broadcast signals that were relayed through a wire. By 1982 over 25 percent of American households had cable, and by 1990 that figure was over 60 percent. More significant, programming originated by or for cable has greatly increased.

When discussing the field it is helpful to distinguish between the transmission of the signal and the supply of the programming. A cable television system provides audio and video transmission to individual receivers via a cable. The cable is attached to a television set, replacing the need for an aerial. The cable television company supplies the transmission to a geographic area through a cable system. Cable systems were started by local entrepreneurs who recognized a need for quality television reception. These operators built the antennae, arranged for the cables to be strung or to be laid in the ground, and marketed the service to the community. The systems increased viewership, which made broadcasters happy, and subscribers happily paid a monthly fee to the system operators. But cable made it possible for the systems to deliver more channels than those that were allowed to receive transmissions through the airwaves; with this capability, operators soon began delivering additional programming for an additional charge—first-run movies, sporting events and so forth. The increased number of channels opened the market for increased programming and this led to the formation of cable television programming companies, which, in turn, led to an expansion of the market. Cable television systems became lucrative ventures and attracted the interest of other entertainment corporations. One of the first developments was the formation of cable television networks, called multisystem operators or MSOs. There are now hundreds of MSOs operating regionally and, in some cases, nationally. As with broadcast television, the more viewers, the more valuable the service. Because MSOs can attract more viewers than individual cable television systems, they are more attractive to advertisers.

MSOs are corporate entities that purchase, produce, and deliver programming to subscribers. Some large MSOs are subsidiaries of giant corporations, such as Time Warner, Cox, and Times-Mirror. An MSO is headed by a president, who is usually a director within the parent company as well. Under his or her supervision are departments of programming, finance and/or administration, advertising sales, marketing and franchising. Each of these is headed by a vice-president or director, who is reported to by regional or city representatives from the affiliated systems.

Much of the activity and growth of an MSO occurs when it is acquiring or renewing franchises. In order for a system operator to install cable, permission must be obtained from the city or local government. Because a cable television franchise is a potentially valuable asset, the competition to obtain franchises is very lively. MSOs form franchising teams to win these permits. Although activity in this area has slowed since most of the franchises were initially awarded, there should be renewed efforts as existing ten-to-fifteen-year franchise agreements expire and refranchising becomes necessary. A franchise team moves into a city that is accepting bids and develops a campaign designed to win the monopoly rights. The team, which reports back to the corporate headquarters of the MSO, includes the following personnel:

Franchise manager: supervises the staff, reports to corporate headquarters, and negotiates for the MSO with city representatives

Engineer: determines the feasibility and cost of constructing a cable television system and recommends needed equipment

Market analyst: prepares surveys to determine the potential size of the market and the programming it desires

Financial analyst: determines the cost of the system and helps to determine the franchise bids

Public relations manager: markets the concepts of the MSO proposal to the local press, community and government; works closely with public access interests

Each cable television company's franchise bid is evaluated, and a contract is awarded. Large cities may divide their areas geographically and award franchises to different operators. The systems then build studios, erect receiving stations, and wire the communities in anticipation of gaining subscribers. When a franchise agreement expires, a similar franchising process complete with teams is activated.

Eventually, a general manager is hired to run the cable television system and, having a function similar to the general manager of a network O & O, is responsible to the MSO or to cable network headquarters (See Chart 18). While supervising a staff of engineers, technicians, administrators, public-relations and marketing personnel, the general manager's primary responsibility is to maximize profits by increasing the number of subscribers to the system.

Subscribers pay a basic monthly charge to receive a package of programs, which include broadcast programs, some cablecast movies, sports, information programming, and some local programming. The cost of this service to subscribers and the cost of any additional pay services are determined by the franchise agreement, which may be further renegotiated by the general manager or at the corporate level. Subscribers may also purchase special programs like prize fights or first-run movies.

Many cable television system general managers have a background in television broadcasting. Important skills necessary for the position include a knowledge of programming, an ability to understand the technical aspects of television, and an ability to market the service. Also necessary is the ability to evaluate and supervise the required professional staff and to maintain budget and control functions for the system. The organization of a cable television system is similar to that of an affiliated or independent television station.

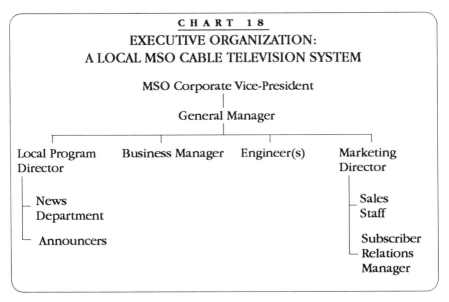

CHART 18
EXECUTIVE ORGANIZATION:
A LOCAL MSO CABLE TELEVISION SYSTEM

MSO Corporate Vice-President

General Manager

Local Program Director   Business Manager   Engineer(s)   Marketing Director

News Department

Announcers

Sales Staff

Subscriber Relations Manager

The easiest and surest entry into cable television is through sales. The system becomes more profitable as more subscribers are signed up. As is true throughout the arts and media industry, successful sales people quickly receive recognition and advancement. An initial door-to-door selling approach is followed by direct-mail and on-air pitches to maintain and increase subscribers and to sell additional pay services. Most systems pay commissions to their sales people and such jobs are plentiful for tirelessly aggressive candidates. There are also frequent openings for other cable television system jobs, most of which can utilize skills transferred from other types of arts and media organizations.

CABLE TELEVISION
PROGRAMMING COMPANIES

Many cable television systems have a capacity of over one hundred channels, which has greatly increased the programming market and the types of services available to subscribers. Fees paid by subscribers are divided between the system operator and the programming company that delivers the service; or the program is provided free and the programming company sells advertising time.

Programming corporations deliver their signals to cable television system operators via satellite, in effect becoming a national channel that is distributed through the cable television systems. Many programming companies are subsidiaries of larger communication or entertainment corporations: the Playboy Channel is owned by its publishing parent, the Disney Channel is owned by Disney, Inc., Arts & Entertainment and ESPN are owned by Capital Cities/ABC, Inc. The latter offers performances of classical music, plays, opera, and ballet together with interviews and features related to the arts. Some programming organizations produce original programs while others, such as Disney and Time Warner Communications, rely heavily on their large inventories of feature films. Other services are entering joint ventures with film and television companies to coproduce programs that are shown in movie theatres, on network television, and on cable television channels, and that are also sold as video cassettes.

The president of a programming corporation is usually an officer of the parent company and is the link with that corporation. The middle-management positions reporting to the president, usually with the title of vice-president, are responsible for finance, marketing, sales, company operations, and both the acquisition and production of programs.

LOCAL-ACCESS TELEVISION CHANNELS

Local-access television channels enable ordinary citizens in a community to originate or select their own programs, if not to participate in them as well. Many communities with cable television systems have designated local-access channels for the presentation of programs in such areas as health and social services, local sports, the performing arts, community events, and government affairs. Sometimes the cable television system operates these channels and sometimes they are operated by the local government, through the office of parks and recreation or through the mayor's office. Many communities have also chosen to form their own nonprofit local-access corporation to operate the channels independently.

A nonprofit local-access corporation is often funded through provisions made in the franchise agreement with the cable television system operator. Under such provisions, the operator supplies equipment, studio space, start-up funds, and ongoing annual support based on the number of paying subscribers within the system. A local-access corporation serves a number of functions: it operates the designated access channels and insures that these may be used by local residents for reasonable purposes; it educates and trains the community in the use of the equipment; it programs the channels that it controls. The executive director of a local-access corporation reports to the board of trustees, serves as the liaison to the cable television system operator, and functions as an advocate for the board and the community, insuring that the details of the franchise agreement are carried out. The executive director also controls the budget, supervises the staff, serves as chief spokesperson and fund-raiser, and sets up educational and training programs for the community.

Local-access corporations raise funds through grants, corporate underwriting, memberships, and individual contributions. Most have a small staff: executive director, secretary, and a studio manager and/or engineer. Those with annual budgets over $350,000 usually have a business manager, a local-access coordinator, a development director, a membership director, teachers, technicians, and camera people. Local-access channels are relatively new, so there is no established career path to the executive director position, although experience in fundraising, educational programming, and, importantly, a technical knowledge of television are prerequisites. Almost every cable television system has some form of local access. Communities that do not have separate local-access corporations have channels managed by the cable television system operator, and each operator usually has an access coordinator. Obviously, the job opportunities in this area are numerous and the experience gained provides an excellent stepping-stone to higher-paying positions with larger media corporations.

The major trade association for the cable television industry is the National Cable Television Association (NCTA), and the national service organization for local access, based in Washington, DC, is the National Federation of Local Cable Programmers (NFLCP).

FILM STUDIOS

Large film studios today, such as the MGM/UA Entertainment Company, are publicly owned corporations that are as active in the television, including cable system, markets as they are in producing for the traditional movie-theatre market. Because they are organized, staffed, and managed in a manner very similar to the television networks discussed above, our description of the film business will focus on its fundamental organization and the areas where it differs from the television business. (See Chart 19.)

Film studios are headed by a chief executive officer (CEO) who manages the daily activities of the corporation and its divisions and subdivisions, including relations with the banks and exhibitors. The title may be board chairman, vice-chairman, president, or, simply, chief executive officer; but, in any case, he or she is responsible to the board of directors and ultimately to the stockholders. Reporting to the CEO are a number of division presidents or vice-presidents who are responsible for the functioning of the following areas:

- *Acquisition and Creative Development:* The department that scouts for and assists the studio in acquiring film properties. These may be finished films that have been produced independently, or "treatments" of novels or story ideas that the studio acquires and then develops and produces itself, or that it has produced by an independent company in which it invests.

- *Production:* The department that assembles a scripted project and actually makes the film for the studio. An executive producer may be assigned to oversee details and to represent studio interests in the project—especially in matters of a monetary nature.

- *Business and Legal Affairs:* An area staffed by accountants, business managers, and lawyers who oversee studio finances, bookkeeping, licenses, and contracts. Executives in this department may work for the studio as a whole or may be assigned to specific film projects.

- *Marketing and Promotion:* This department attempts to determine the best method of selling a film by analyzing—often with the help of independent marketing researchers—the potential audience, by deciding where and when to release the film, and by coordinating efforts of the publicity and advertising executives.

- *Distribution and Sales:* Each film studio maintains its own distribution department, which leases films the studio has produced or acquired to movie-theatre operators around the nation, attempting to secure the most desirable theatres and showing times. The sales department negotiates the specific showing rights to such outlets as television networks, cable television companies, video-cassette distributors, and foreign distributors.

The president of a studio's film division, sometimes known as the production chief, reports to the CEO and is responsible for the acquisition, development, and production of film properties. In the old days, when the studios were less departmentalized and the production chief

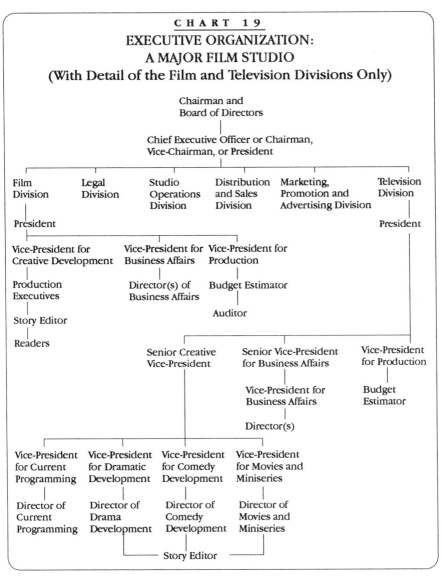

CHART 19
EXECUTIVE ORGANIZATION:
A MAJOR FILM STUDIO
(With Detail of the Film and Television Divisions Only)

Chairman and
Board of Directors

Chief Executive Officer or Chairman,
Vice-Chairman, or President

| Film Division | Legal Division | Studio Operations Division | Distribution and Sales Division | Marketing, Promotion and Advertising Division | Television Division |

President — Film Division

President — Television Division

Vice-President for Creative Development | Vice-President for Business Affairs | Vice-President for Production

Production Executives | Director(s) of Business Affairs | Budget Estimator

Story Editor | Auditor

Readers

Senior Creative Vice-President | Senior Vice-President for Business Affairs | Vice-President for Production

Vice-President for Business Affairs | Budget Estimator

Director(s)

| Vice-President for Current Programming | Vice-President for Dramatic Development | Vice-President for Comedy Development | Vice-President for Movies and Miniseries |

| Director of Current Programming | Director of Drama Development | Director of Comedy Development | Director of Movies and Miniseries |

Story Editor

was more autonomous, production chiefs included such luminaries as Louis B. Mayer, Jack Warner, Harry Cohn, and Darryl Zanuck. Today the film division president or chief is still the person who nurtures relationships with leading creative talents, such as Steven Spielberg, George Lucas, William Goldman, and Robert Redford.

Like most branches of the arts and media industry, the film business is a people business. Personal relationships and strong bonds are the basis upon which many projects are hatched and deals made; such business is conducted as often in restaurants and at cocktail parties as in the office.

A film division president oversees a staff in the creative development area and in the production department. In development there are executives at various levels who maintain daily contact with writers, directors, agents, and producers, developing ideas and concepts that are then fed to the executive for consideration. On a lower level there is a story department, where all material is also sent and evaluated. The story editor, who heads the department, usually assigns the material to a reader who provides written evaluation. If the material is recommended, the story editor will usually give it a second reading and offer a second opinion.

The production department is responsible for physically assembling a project from script to screen, as it were. Here the screenplay is broken down, put on a story-board, and budgeted. Story-boarding is the method used to determine a shooting schedule. Estimates are then prepared to establish the length of time needed for each set, character, location, and day's or night's filming. The budget, of course, determines the approximate cost of the entire production and is prepared by a budget estimator. Once a film goes into production, the business affairs department works very closely with the producer and the production manager with regard to the amount of hours the cast and crew work each day, the number of pages filmed in relation to the previously planned schedule, and whether or not the project is on budget for the day.

The business affairs department generally makes the deals with the above-the-line participants, such as the producer, writer, director, and cast. This department is largely comprised of lawyers. Upon completing a negotiation they set forth the terms of the deal in a deal memo, which is a temporary agreement that binds the two parties until the legal department prepares a more formal and extensive contract. It is not unusual for a contract to be completed and signed long after the services it defines have been performed.

Film distribution is the sales process by which a company sells a motion picture to exhibitors for screening. The distributor and the exhibitor split the box-office receipts. Profit-participants, such as the producer, the director, and the stars, get their shares from the distributor's net.

The television production division of a film studio works in a manner similar to the film division. The major distinction is that while the film division obtains its financing from the studio, the television division gets its primary funding from the buyer, which in most cases is one of the three television networks or a program network. In essence, the network commissions or licenses the studio to put together a specific production. In exchange, the network will pay for the rights to broadcast the presentation twice within an agreed-upon period of time, usually a couple of years. This payment by the network is called a license fee. Although the network provides most, if not all, of the production cost, it doesn't own the property. This gives the producer, in this case the studio, the right to generate additional income by distributing the property for syndication and in foreign and other ancillary markets.

The television division's president, whose role is similar to that of the film division president, oversees all development and production and answers to the studio CEO regarding all matters pertaining to the division—from shows coming in over budget to making a deal for the exclusive services of a particular writer. Answering to the president is a creative senior vice-president and a business affairs senior vice-president. The creative vice-president is responsible for the development of all new programs, as well as for overseeing current programs already in production. Like the president, the creative vice-president is also interested in bringing various properties and creative talent to the studio. The senior vice-president of business affairs oversees a staff that arranges all deals involved with the television division, from negotiating an actor's salary for a series episode to negotiating the license fee for a multi-million-dollar miniseries.

The business affairs department is usually brought in at the very beginning of a relationship between a development executive or producer and a writer. Even before the writer's concept is put on paper, the development executive will have business affairs make a deal with the writer's agent to cover every aspect of the concept's possible growth. In the event that the idea is successfully sold to the network and a script is subsequently ordered, all fees have already been negotiated.

Reporting to the senior creative vice-president are vice-presidents of drama development, comedy development, movies and miniseries, and current programming. Each area usually has a director of development and a story editor as support personnel. To illustrate how the system works, let's imagine that an independent producer contacts a studio executive and presents an idea or concept for a television series. If the studio executive shares the producer's enthusiasm, a number of studio meetings take place to work out the concept and to prepare a pitch for a television network. If the executive representing the network finds merit in the project, a pilot script is ordered. The producer and the studio then ask the business affairs department to negotiate a deal with a writer to write a story and screenplay based on the concept. If the network likes the script, it orders a pilot film to be made. The production department breaks down the script, prepares a budget, and employs a director, cast, and crew. When the pilot is completed, the network decides if it meets its current programming needs and, if so, the series is entered into the network's schedule.

The responsibility of the vice-president of movies and miniseries is to develop movies for television and limited-run series. These programs are geared for a one-time showing. Two to three hours is the standard length for television movies, while a miniseries may run anywhere from four to twelve hours.

The executive in charge of current programming is the liaison between the studio and the producer of a television series that is in production, and also between the studios and the network. This person will be involved with all stages of script development for each episode of a series or project; he or she must view the "dailies" or "rushes"of the film or tape shot the previous day, and must make certain that the production is conforming to the original plan.

INDEPENDENT FILM COMPANIES

A majority of films today are produced by independent film companies. These are usually headed by a president, who also serves as the producer or executive producer. Financing may be based on money earned from past productions, funds acquired from a studio in advance of production, or capital raised from private investors. If the independent film company has established a financial arrangement with a bank, it may underwrite the cost of producing a motion picture itself. Once the film is completed, a deal can be made with a studio for distribution. This is called a "negative pick-up," because the studio is buying a completed negative for distribution. Usually, however, the independent aligns itself with a studio for both financing and distribution purposes.

With the exceptions of a creative development executive, who solicits material for consideration, and a production and/or business affairs executive, most personnel who work for independent film companies are hired as needed for particular projects. These include the same types of specialists employed by studios, excluding those in the distribution and sales area.

Film studios and many independent film companies produce films for television, cablevision, and cassette distribution as well as for movie theatres. But this activity, as productive as it is, represents only one portion of the American film industry. There are literally thousands of other independent companies, many located outside Los Angeles and New York City, that specialize in educational, military, documentary, and industrial film production, not to mention those that produce television commercials. The majority of such companies are headed by an owner-producer, who conceives, develops, and produces films with the assistance of a small staff. But many entry-level and apprenticeship positions are available with such companies and provide good training for a career in the film business at large.

TALENT AGENTS

Talent agents represent creative artists, such as performers, writers, and stage directors, and must be licensed as businesses by the state in which they operate. Some must also be franchised by the labor union to which their clients belong, such as Actors' Equity Association or the Screen Actors Guild. Many agents work without any staff, while others establish a large office with numerous subagents and a support staff. Individual agents tend to specialize in one type of talent—literary, acting, musical, or whatever—while large agencies often handle a great diversity of talents. Not surprisingly, a majority of agents once were or aspired to be artists themselves, and this is very helpful in understanding their clients' abilities, problems, and needs. Nonetheless, agents serve a managerial function in the arts and media industry—a function that is central to the entire production process.

Agents work to accommodate the talent needs of producers, presenters, and publishers. Their payment, however, comes from their artist clients and is a flat 10 percent of whatever fee—including royalties and residuals—that their clients receive as a result of the agents' efforts. Some clients sign on with an agent for the purpose of obtaining a single employment or publishing opportunity, while others sign an agreement that permits the agent to be their exclusive representative for all opportunities over a specified time period. Even if a client finds work on his own or someone else secures work for him, the agent still receives 10 percent of all earnings. This 10-percent fee is standard throughout the industry and is not negotiable. What is highly negotiable, however, is the compensation that the artist will receive from the employer, and it is the agent's primary task to make that compensation figure as high as possible, thereby increasing the value of the 10-percent fee.

Successful talent agents possess business and negotiating skills together with a thorough knowledge of at least one artistic discipline, an understanding of the market for that discipline, and a very sharp eye for talent. It is common for people to enter this field in a secretarial or assistant position; then become a subagent; and then move up to a larger agency—often taking their clients with them—or establish their own agency.

Mention should also be made of casting agents, who are similar to talent agents except they are paid by producers to identify and deliver most if not all the performers needed for a particular project, be it a Broadway musical or a television commercial. The casting agent does not have agreements with a "stable" of clients but, rather, works with talent agents and individual artists. He or she must maintain a large file of resumes, photographs, and audition tapes, and must necessarily have something close to a photographic memory. Casting agents must also develop keen insight into the artistic tastes and visions of the producers, directors, and writers whose projects they are hired to populate. Needless to say, literary agents must be tireless readers, while agents for performing artists must spend much of their lives in an audience of one kind or another.

ARTIST MANAGEMENT

Artist managers provide the same services for their clients as talent agents, but they tend to serve them for longer periods of time, give more individualized attention to artistic and career development, and perform more services. In return for this they receive a fee ranging anywhere from 10 percent to 25 percent of their clients' contractual earnings. Most handle more than one client and specialize in a particular type of talent, such as classical pianists or film actors. The best managers are seriously concerned with developing and protecting their clients' careers, while also promoting them and negotiating their employment contracts. In the classical music and opera fields young artists often sign long-term contracts with artist managers, understanding that there will be few important engagements during the early years of their careers when they must continue to study, develop, and perform with lesser-known orchestras or opera companies. The manager "plots" the artist's career, sometimes foregoing large booking fees and intensive touring schedules for which the client is not artistically prepared. Then, when the artist has matured, the best and most lucrative venues are secured and both artist and manager benefit.

The best artist managers are very selective in choosing the talent they represent and have well-educated taste in their area of specialization. In addition, they must have extensive contacts and a reliable reputation among those people and organizations that hire or book artists: presenters, managers of concert halls, performing arts centers, theatre and opera companies, symphony orchestras, recording companies, not to mention casting agents, film companies, and others.

Artist managers, like agents, may function as a one-person business or within a large firm. In the larger companies—all but two or three of which are not-for-profit corporations or proprietorships—functions are decentralized and artists are handled through departments headed by vice-presidents (See Chart 20). Some divide talent by artistic discipline and some by the geographical regions of the nation and parts of the world in which their clients perform. Obviously, such positions require people who have specialized knowledge. Someone who has worked as a presenter in the Midwest would probably have good contacts among the presenters in that region and may, therefore, qualify for a position in an artist management firm, as may the former general manager of an orchestra who booked numerous soloists and guest conductors. Artist managers, among other things, are sales representatives and spend much of their time on the phone or in the field trying to garner employment for their clients. In a large firm other executives are responsible for marketing, publicity, touring, and contractual arrangements. The president and senior vice-presidents for talent are responsible for signing the talent and developing new talent. A few of the largest artist-management companies are Columbia Artists Management, Inc. (CAMI), and International Creative Management, Inc. (ICM).

It is not unusual for an artist-management company to work closely with a promoter, presenter, or producer in putting together a "package" of talent for a particular film, play, television series, opera season, music festival, or other project. The firm may sell a novel written by one of its clients to a film company, for instance, and then suggest one

---

C H A R T   2 0
EXECUTIVE ORGANIZATION:
MUSIC DIVISION OF A LARGE CORPORATE
ARTIST-MANAGEMENT AGENCY

Corporate Chairman

Legal Department

Vice-President of
Finance

Other Divisions

Division President

Vice-President for Sales   Director of Operations   Vice-President for Talent

Sales Representative   Travel Manager

Booking Assistant   Publicity Director

                              Office Manager

---

of its film directors, a few of its actors, and perhaps another of its writers to script the adaptation. It should be mentioned, however, that it is neither ethical nor legal for artist managers, talent agents, or casting agents to receive payment from both artist clients and management regarding the same set of contractual arrangements.

Some of the most successful artist managers began their careers in secretarial or clerical positions in the field, then moved into sales, and then up the ladder to talent development. This is a field with a tradition of promoting from within, so if it is of interest to you, plan to start at the bottom and keep your eyes open for advancement opportunities.

Highly successful artists may also employ a personal manager in addition to an agent or management firm. This person usually works full time for the artist and handles such personal matters as finances, investments, transportation, living and hotel accommodations, and maybe even the artist's legal affairs. It is possible, therefore, for an artist to be paying an agent 10 percent, a business manager or attorney 20 percent, and a personal manager 25 percent, leaving only 45 percent of earned income for personal use!

ARTS AND MEDIA SERVICE ORGANIZATIONS

Although service organizations that provide funding, technical assistance, and management and labor support for the arts and media industry are treated with detail in Chapter 8, they also deserve mention in a chapter that describes how that industry is organized. This is especially true because so many executive jobs with service and support organizations require knowledge and experience in the production areas that they serve. For example, an experienced fundraiser for an arts organization would be a good candidate for an executive position with a fund-giving organization; a finance director or legal counsel for an arts or media company would be qualified to work as a consultant for a management or legal assistance group; and one cannot imagine the executive head of a professional association, union, or guild who does not have direct experience in the profession or trade whose practitioners he or she represents.

Moving from arts and media management into arts and media service and support can be a gratifying career step, because, as in teaching, one is able to channel one's experiences, both good and bad, into helping others, benefiting the profession as a whole.

ARTS AND MEDIA SCHOOLS AND EDUCATIONAL PROGRAMS

As with positions in the service and support area, the field of education requires individuals, both teachers and administrators, with professional experience. There are thousands of different schools and training programs in the arts and media industry, and most require at least one professional administrator. Many have large, sophisticated management staffs, comparable to those in other arts organizations. Skills and qualifications are easily transferable. Educational programs that prepare students to work in the arts and media industry may be categorized as follows:

College and university schools or departments

Conservatories that grant degrees and/or diplomas

Professional schools and training programs

High schools and preparatory schools

Community schools

Summer training programs and workshops

Independent schools

Except for some of the independent schools, all of the above are operated as nonprofit organizations with a board of trustees, and all need to raise unearned income to supplement tuition and other types of earned income. In most secondary and higher education programs the chief administrator holds an academic title, or "line," and is also an instructor. This program chairperson reports to a principal, dean, vice-president, or president and is responsible for managing a budget, hiring and supervising teachers and staff fundraising, recruiting students, and, usually, producing or supervising live or electronic productions or exhibitions that are shown to the public. The demanding position of chairperson or program director in a major academic setting requires someone with leadership ability, strong professional and/or academic experience and reputation, and, usually, advanced degrees.

Colleges with sizable arts and media curricula also operate special television, theatre, and exhibition facilities—if not an arts center that incorporates all three. These are usually managed by a professional staff which is independent of the academic departments and programs, but which must work in a collegial manner to accommodate the needs of those programs. Campus arts and media facilities, as discussed earlier in this chapter under "Presenting Organizations, and Performing Arts Centers," provide countless administrative jobs that require qualifications comparable to those in other branches of the industry. Also, most do not require teaching or other academic credentials, even though many carry benefits similar to those enjoyed by faculty members.

During the past decade there has been a proliferation of academic courses and programs that concentrate in arts and media management on both the graduate and undergraduate levels and, what is more, academia has been eagerly seeking instructors and program heads who have a proven professional track record. Yet, the career option of working in academia seldom occurs to a working professional. The advantages of a faculty position in higher education often include the security of tenure or long-term contracts, liberal health and pension benefits, the comparatively calm campus atmosphere, and the psychic reward of sharing knowledge and experience with students who respect professional accomplishment.

There are also many opportunities for managers in independent schools and training programs. Many ongoing performing arts companies and visual arts institutions operate schools that hire executive directors, business managers, registrars, development directors, recruitment or marketing managers, not to mention instructors. Such schools can offer entry into arts and media management and can also provide valuable contacts within the profession.

Yet another option in career development is to move from an academic to a professional institution. As mentioned throughout this chapter, many types of arts and media companies and institutions fulfill some kind of educational function. This may entail art classes offered by a museum, technical training programs given for local-access users by a cable television system, appreciation discussions sponsored by an opera company, or the educational programming provided by a noncommercial radio or television station. Arts and media teachers or academic administrators have the knowledge and expertise to qualify for many of these jobs if they feel inclined to put their school days behind them.

CHAPTER SIX

JOBS IN FINANCIAL MANAGEMENT

While most American industries were quick to adapt modern technology to their business needs, arts companies lagged stubbornly behind. Only recently, for example, have many box offices accepted credit cards. And the use of computers by arts organizations is still a relatively new phenomenon. One strongly suspects that this was because of the dominance of old-school managers. Also, the performing and visual arts are "handcrafted" products, which make them economically anachronistic. Production-line manufacturing techniques don't work in the performing and visual arts, a factor that has created a long-standing economic dilemma. One cannot trim costs by eliminating the second movement from Beethoven's Fifth Symphony, for instance, or by reducing a string quintet to four players or by cutting two or three characters out of *Hamlet,* at least not without replacing musicians with synthesizers or replacing actors with robots. However, the presentation of the live arts on television and cablevision and the use of modern technology as a management and marketing tool have begun to assist the arts economically.

WHAT IS FINANCIAL MANAGEMENT?

The task of raising the capital necessary to start up an arts company or project is the responsibility of entrepreneurs, producers, or founding directors. After the initial funds have been raised, however, they must be prudently managed to insure that they are put to optimum use. And then revenues must be generated to cover operating costs, to sustain and expand production, and, in the commercial sector, to generate profits. Financial management is primarily the supervision of all funds and other assets for a company or organization.

The various jobs related to financial management play a vital role in facilitating the creative work of arts groups; these functions can also be creative in and of themselves. There is a story about an executive who interviewed three finalists for the job of accountant. He began by asking each candidate to add three plus three. The first two candidates immediately answered "six." But the third candidate paused for a moment, then asked the executive, "How much would you like it to add up to?" Guess which applicant got the job!

Sitting all day at a ledger or a computer dealing with numbers and balancing columns of figures requires an exacting mind as well as one that is able to come up with creative and honest solutions that may facilitate a particular project or even determine the existence of a project or of an entire organization. The financial or business managers for arts companies are often asked such questions as—

Where will the cash come from and when?

How can this grant proposal be presented so the funder will think we're solvent?

How can we avoid appearing to overfund this project?

Should we buy a new piano or rent one?

Which creditors can wait a little longer to be paid?

Will there be enough money to meet the next payroll?

Furthermore, the finance person is sometimes expected to answer these questions for artists who do not understand finance, for board members who do not understand art, for investors or funders who think they know more than the finance manager, and for hostile creditors who want fast payment instead of fast answers. Communication skills are essential to good financial management.

In a small organization there may be only one general manager or business manager to handle all pecuniary tasks and responsibilities. Large institutions and companies have a finance department in which responsibilities are divided among a vice-president or director of finance, controller, accountant, box-office or admissions manager, bookkeeper, and others. The main areas of concern for the finance person or department are—

1. Budgeting and budget control

2. Payroll and benefits

3. Insurance

4. Taxes

5. Banking, including loan procurement

6. Cash-flow projections and management

7. Periodic financial reporting, internal and external

8. Maintenance of daily ledgers and journals

9. Purchasing, renting, and inventory control and depreciation schedules

10. Supervision of the box office; accountability for ticket sales and other earned income

11. Management of grant and other contributory income

12. Investment of available funds

The head of finance reports directly to the executive director or president. If there are directors or trustees, the chief financial officer is also accountable to the board treasurer, who is probably also chairman of the board's finance committee. Although annual financial reports based on audits are prepared by an outside CPA with in-house assistance, with the results presented directly to the board, a busy organization will employ one or more accountants to handle the daily routine. Large organizations require a sizable staff to conduct the affairs of the business and financial department, which may include collecting, accounting for, and managing income from a wide variety of sources, as well as the management, control, and reporting of expenditures.

As illustrated by Chart 21, the finance department must work closely with other departments and, in fact, probably has more interdepartmental dealings than any other. For example, while the marketing department is responsible for generating ticket sales and other types of earned income, actual ticket orders, as well as mail orders for catalogue merchandise are usually processed by personnel who work under the finance officer. Similarly, the development director generates grants and other contributed income, but the money itself is received and managed by the finance department, which must also prepare financial reports for the grantors. Film and television companies depend upon sales and distribution departments, but once contracts and sales agreements have been made, they are turned over to a business affairs department for execution and income collection.

The most valuable business managers are those with the ability to offer their superiors clearly articulated sets of options regarding the possible use of money and other assets. This should be done objectively, without questioning the value of the policies and projects under discussion—that is for the board or top leadership to debate. On the other hand, if the organization cannot afford certain expenditures, the

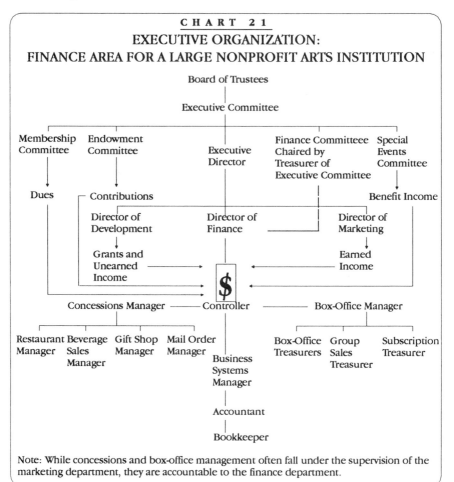

CHART 21
EXECUTIVE ORGANIZATION:
FINANCE AREA FOR A LARGE NONPROFIT ARTS INSTITUTION

Board of Trustees

Executive Committee

Membership Committee | Endowment Committee | Executive Director | Finance Committeee Chaired by Treasurer of Executive Committee | Special Events Committee

Dues | Contributions | Benefit Income

Director of Development | Director of Finance | Director of Marketing

Grants and Unearned Income | Earned Income

Concessions Manager — Controller — Box-Office Manager

Restaurant Manager | Beverage Sales Manager | Gift Shop Manager | Mail Order Manager | Business Systems Manager | Box-Office Treasurers | Group Sales Treasurer | Subscription Treasurer

Accountant

Bookkeeper

Note: While concessions and box-office management often fall under the supervision of the marketing department, they are accountable to the finance department.

president or board must be so informed. The more familiarity the finance manager has with the arts or media product and the more experience he or she has with the company or organization, the more valid the financial projections and recommendations are likely to be. Knowing the track record of a company and its relations with markets, vendors, and funding institutions is of tremendous help to a finance officer.

Many people who take finance jobs in the arts and media industry have no special background in the field and many soon leave those jobs for more lucrative positions in other industries. Entry-level salaries, especially in the not-for-profit sector, are usually lower than qualified candidates can command elsewhere, although finance jobs with large nonprofit and commercial arts organizations often pay very well. However,

financial directors can earn salary increases by saving money for their
organizations through skilled and creative management, just as a fund-
raiser can earn increased compensation by increasing the level of contributed income. Arts organizations are best advised to hire people
who have a special background and love for the arts, and managers of
small companies should acquire business skills to assist them until they
can afford to hire specialists.

DIRECTOR OF FINANCE

A director or vice-president of finance is the manager of the department and supervisor of a staff of specialists that may also include assistants and secretaries. The director usually has hire-fire authority and is
involved in the long- and short-range planning for the organization; he
or she also has responsibility for anticipating cash needs, securing
loans, reinvesting cash, managing an endowment or investment portfolio, and personally representing the company or organization to the
business and financial community, and to the board through a finance
committee.

The finance director must obviously have a strong business background, perhaps an M.B.A. in finance or equivalent training. Because
most arts and media organizations large enough to hire finance directors have their businesses computerized, these directors usually are required to have knowledge of data processing and computerized business systems. Their value to their employers, as mentioned, would be
enhanced by a knowledge of the particular art form, since many judgments are based on familiarity with arts-related materials, salaries, consultants' fees, royalties, equipment rentals, contracts, and other expenditures that directly affect the quality of the artistic product. This is obviously not an entry-level position. Responsibilities include designing
financial systems, participating in policy-making, filing of all governmental reports in a timely manner, and organizing the accounting function.

BUSINESS SYSTEMS MANAGER

Large arts and media corporations often require a specialist in computer technology who can assist with the purchase, operation, and
maintenance of computer hardware and software and also design computer programs. This is an operations position that may be included in
the finance department, although the job will obviously involve all departments that utilize computers—the systems manager may be hired

by the operations or marketing department. While a knowledge of the arts is not necessary, it would be helpful. This is especially true in regard to technological applications for stage, film, and television production. Specialists in these areas are often scene, lighting, or sound designers who have acquired additional skills in technology.

Small outfits that cannot afford a full-time systems manager must meet their needs by hiring consultants. Also, systems time-sharing is increasingly popular today. While there are numerous computer specialists available to handle such part-time work, comparatively few have a knowledge of the arts field, which makes it somewhat risky for small arts groups to hire them.

CONTROLLER

A controller—sometimes referred to in the archaic form, comptroller—has the main accounting responsibility in a business organization. The controller reports to the finance director or, in small companies, takes on many of the finance director's tasks and reports directly to the executive director or president. The controller must oversee production and other budgets, make realistic estimations of costs—revising these as required—and negotiate on behalf of the organization with suppliers, unions, renters, travel agents, and others. The job also calls for constant monitoring of expenses in relation to budgets.

The controller must be able to understand financial reports, budgets, and cash forecasts and must be creative in manipulating expenses and controlling costs. Although an advanced degree in finance may not be required, a facility with numbers is essential. The most qualified controller for a particular position will have hands-on experience in the arts field and will know, for example, how many work-hours it will take to build a set, restore a painting, rehearse a new symphony, rehearse a symphony already in the repertoire, or rehearse a replacement for an ailing tenor. The controller is also often asked to project expenses for extending an engagement, for example, or for videotaping a live performance, or for touring a production, or for renting the facilities to an outside group. For such reasons, controllers and, hence, finance directors, often begin their careers in some area of production management.

PRODUCTION ESTIMATOR

A production estimator's job is similar to that of a controller, except that this is the job title used in relation to film and television production. Here, for example, budgets are determined by story-boarding a screenplay, or breaking it down into scenes to determine the sets, characters, locations, and shooting time required to shoot each scene. Obviously, the person who estimates the exact costs for these elements must be very knowledgeable about media production; he or she probably has experience as a production, studio, traffic, or unit manager and, just as probably, is hoping eventually to move into a higher job in the business-affairs department of a media organization. Both controllers and production estimators are financial analysts of sorts and most combine a business background with a special interest in the arts and media field.

ACCOUNTANT

The accountant in an arts or media organization performs the same duties as an accountant in any other field and, therefore, requires little specialized knowledge of the arts—unless, of course, the person is required to assume additional responsibilities and become involved in the policy-making process, or unless the individual has aspirations to a higher position in the arts and media field. Excluding such possibilities, an accountant familiar with accounting in the nonprofit sector outside the arts world could make an easy transition to a nonprofit arts organization. Or one could easily move from most any accounting position in the commercial sector into a commercial arts or media company. Job duties usually include managing the payroll, keeping the ledgers and journals, compiling monthly statements, balancing the books, checking box-office and other sales statements, and providing the financial information necessary for grants applications or other special documents. The accountant should also have the technical knowledge needed to assist independent auditors in preparing for the audit at the end of the fiscal year.

An undergraduate degree in accounting would be a desirable qualification for this job, in addition to some knowledge of data processing. Some arts organizations operate on a cash-accounting basis, but there is a clear trend toward accrual accounting, and most large organizations already operate on this system. In fact many funding organizations require the accrual method as a condition for being considered for a grant.

BOOKKEEPER

A bookkeeper is responsible for recording all financial transactions in a daily journal and later transferring them to a ledger. The bookkeeper may also prepare the payroll, computing taxes and other withholdings as well as royalties, percentages, and commissions. When this position is supervised by an accountant or controller, it can be performed by someone with little rudimentary training who has a feel for numbers. It is a good entry-level position for someone interested in a career in financial management.

BUSINESS MANAGER

The generic term for all finance positions in an arts organization has always been *business manager.* This term could be expanded to include everyone from the director of finance to the bookkeeper and, in some cases, may even include the executive director. If you apply for a job with this title, we suggest that you look at the entire staff of the organization, and the specific responsibilities assigned to each person, in order to determine the business manager's functions. For example, if there is no executive director or general manager, the business manager will usually function as both director of finance and executive director. If the position requires that you report to the executive director *and* to the finance committee or board treasurer, the position will be similar to that of finance director. However, if the main duty of the position is to keep books—no matter what the title—it is basically a bookkeeper's position.

BOX-OFFICE MANAGER

Jobs related to the overall supervision and management of a box office in both the commercial and nonprofit sectors often involve an executive who works outside the box office itself. This may be the general manager, finance director, business manager, marketing director, house manager, or one of their assistants. In large theatres the job often requires an executive who can diplomatically impose management policy on unionized box-office personnel, called "treasurers." Such employees often have greater job security than their supervisors and are usually resistant to any changes in the way they handle tickets or customers, so the box-office manager's job may not be an easy one. Nonetheless, box-office operations must provide the accountability demanded by the finance office; must be consonant with the image that the marketing and promotion office is attempting to project to the public; must serve customer needs as efficiently and politely as possible; and must provide assurance that security of funds and accountability will be preserved.

BOX-OFFICE TREASURER

Box-office treasurers, sometimes unionized employees, are responsible for handling, allocating, distributing, and selling tickets, and probably have more direct contact with actual and potential ticket-buyers than anyone else in the organization. They may report to the business or finance director, to the general manager, to the marketing director, or to one of their staff members who serves as the box-office manager. Honesty and an ability to deal well with the public are desirable qualities, together with a disciplined accuracy in handling cash, tickets, telephone orders, and credit transactions. But there is no special training that cannot be learned on the job, so this may be considered an entry-level position and, unless one wishes to make a career as a unionized treasurer, a good beginning for a future in marketing or financial management.

CHAPTER SEVEN

JOBS IN MARKETING, PUBLIC RELATIONS, AND SALES

Executive directors and presidents of arts and media companies may be adept at managing computerized mailing lists, market surveys, and advertising, but the time involved makes it necessary, when the budget allows, to hire specialists in marketing, public relations, and sales who have the education and skills to devote themselves exclusively to these areas. These specialists possess expertise that may be applied to similar jobs outside the arts and media field. But, as with a finance or development officer, the marketing executive is valued according to his or her contacts and track record within a particular industry, discipline, and community. It takes a while to cultivate relationships with the press and media people who make decisions about which press releases and stories will get space or time and which will not; it takes time to research and understand the demographics of a community, thereby identifying the highest potential market for a product. And it takes time to develop profitable relations with the buyers of a product—presenting organizations, film studios or distribution companies, independent television or radio stations, art dealers, or whomever.

Jobs in marketing, public relations, and sales exist in all types of arts and media organizations excluding service and support groups such as unions, foundations, arts councils, and technical assistance organizations—although these organizations may have a public information officer, as described below.

WHAT IS MARKETING, PUBLIC RELATIONS, AND SALES?

If you can get someone's attention, pique their interest, plant the seeds of desire, and then make them take the action of buying the product or service, you are marketing. These four steps in the process of making a purchase—attention, interest, desire, and action—have been called the "Aida" marketing model.

Until recently, the marketing of arts and media products was overly bound by tired traditions. For example, Broadway shows only began to be advertised on television in 1973—which was only shortly after television ads for films and novels began appearing. Even the largest non-profit arts institutions didn't have a marketing department and didn't attempt to earn income through such devices as mail-order catalogues until recently. While press agents have long flourished on Broadway, very few marketing experts are employed there to this day. And, apparently, there is still only one way to design a circus poster. Diminishing subsidies in the not-for-profit sector, however, and rising costs industry-wide have necessitated an increase in earned income and, therefore, a need for imaginative third-century managers who can bring marketing theories and techniques from their graduate schools and apply them to the arts and media industry.

The out-of-date method of selling the arts is to rely exclusively on a press agent or public relations director. Such specialists remain important, but they are simply not marketers in the full sense of that term. Marketing encompasses all aspects of a product, including price and physical distribution, as well as promotion. Marketing relies heavily on research and analysis—studying past box-office records, for example—whereas promotion alone is usually concerned only with the media and printed publicity. The press agent gathers lists and makes contacts among editors, critics, feature writers, and media executives. The marketing expert studies not only those who communicate to consumers, but also the consumers themselves. Based upon the findings, he or she is then able to advise a company or organization as to what, when, and how much to produce or exhibit, as well as how to develop a plan to earn the income that is needed or desired. Viewed in this perspective, the work of a marketing department logically precedes most other activities. Until one can determine a need or desire for an artistic product, identify a large enough group of high-potential buyers, and map out a strategy for attracting those buyers, why purchase the grand piano, option the play, buy the building, acquire the art collection, or commission the composer? Yet, many arts and media managers still believe that a press agent alone will be able to fill the house.

Although some arts organizations maintain a marketing department that is separate from the press and/or public-relations departments, these areas are increasingly being combined under the direction of one executive—usually a marketing specialist. In most performing companies and visual arts organizations the marketing department also supervises all box-office and concession operations. Television, film, and cablevision companies usually have a sales and/or distribution executive, or such a department that functions independently from the marketing and public-relations areas. This is because most of their products or programming are sold or leased to exhibitors, networks, affiliates, or independent media outlets rather than directly to the consumer. After sales or rentals have been made, however, the marketing departments for such companies work with the buyers to promote products.

While marketing and public-relations specialists both work to generate sales, the job qualifications are somewhat different. The archetype of the modern public relations director is the sideshow barker of carnival tradition. Technology and the media have broadened the process of enticing the public, but the most successful promotion and public-relations people still have a bit of the barker in them, and successful entrepreneurs have always had a flair for selling tickets that is a show in itself. The names P. T. Barnum, Mike Todd, David Merrick, and Rudolf Bing immediately come to mind.

Press and public-relations executives may report to the marketing director or to the executive director or president. Titles in this area vary and the terms *press, promotion,* and *public relations* may be used interchangeably. Responsibilities also vary. Before accepting a public relations job, look carefully at the composition of the staff. There are few other areas in arts and media management in which there are so many go-fer chores that need to be done. Is the position you're being offered really an executive one, or does it require endless hours of running to the printer, delivering ad copy, distributing posters, and chauffeuring performers and VIPs around town? Small organizations require one employee to handle all press, public relations, and advertising duties, while large organizations divide these among various staff members.

While these days the top executives in marketing, press relations, and sales usually hold an undergraduate degree and, often, a graduate degree, most support positions in the area are at the entry level and do not require specialized training. However, most such positions require good writing, proofreading, typing, word-processing, and speaking skills. To advance in the field, a winning personality combined with quick thinking and lots of imagination will also be necessary.

DIRECTOR OF MARKETING

The director or vice-president of marketing is the manager responsible for conducting market research, for developing a marketing plan, and for organizing the staff to accomplish it. This executive usually reports directly to the executive director or president and to the marketing committee of the board, if such a body exists. It may be said that only fairly large arts and media organizations can afford to hire a marketing director, while small ones can't afford not to! (See Chart 22.)

The marketing director targets high-potential buyers for a product—an exhibition, concert series, television program, or whatever—and then advises those who have an interest in selling the product on how to develop promotion strategies that will reach those buyers. Hence, the marketing director may be responsible for a subscription campaign; the campaign for a single event; special offers, such as discounts, groups sales, multiple-event purchase; and all types of advertising. In addition, the marketing director may conduct or assist in the negotiation of tours, distribution deals, or sales. The latter would include the sale of any concessionary items, such as souvenir programs, food and beverages, and gifts. In the broadest sense, the position requires a person who, through a combination of data analysis skills and intuition, can perceive the public's attitudes regarding the company or institution and its products, and recommend specific methods for bringing the two together. Imagination and a sense of showmanship, combined with a graduate degree—preferably an M.B.A—are among the best qualifications for the job. A marketing specialist may move into the arts and media industry from other fields, given a willingness to absorb and understand the goals and nature of the artistic product at hand, and an individual style that is consonant with that of the hiring organization.

MARKETING MANAGER OR MARKET ANALYST

A marketing manager—the title could also be market analyst—reports to the director of marketing and is responsible for compiling and analyzing data for presentation to the director, much in the manner of a research assistant. Responsibilities also include compiling and refining mailing lists, supervising the preparation and dispatch of bulk mailings, and assisting with the details of special events, tours, and promotional campaigns. The job's emphasis is on the quantitative, the analytical, and the scientific as compared to the more creative, idea-generating responsibilities of the marketing director. The marketing

CHART 2 2

EXECUTIVE ORGANIZATION:
MARKETING, PROMOTION, AND SALES AREA OF A PERFORMING
ARTS CENTER

manager also tracks the expense budget for each project; determining, for example, how much it costs to attract each new subscriber compared to the cost for each renewal. Required skills are specialized, but may be learned through workshops and in vocational college courses. Knowledge of statistics and computers is necessary.

DIRECTOR OF MEMBERSHIP

Many nonprofit performing and visual arts institutions seek to attract members—also called friends or patrons—who pay a tax-deductible annual fee to the institution in exchange for special privileges, such as free parking, invitations to special receptions or lectures, and the like. This fee is over and above what they pay for admission tickets and can constitute an important source of revenue for the institution. While the volunteer work of board members, special guilds, and committees is very important to the success of membership drives, a salaried executive may be required to coordinate such activities and to provide the follow-up services that are promised to the members.

Nonprofit radio and television stations also invite membership, usually by means of periodic on-air appeals combined with newspaper and direct-mail advertising, and, here again, a salaried membership director or coordinator is usually required. The position usually falls within the marketing department, although it may be supervised by the special events director or by the development director.

DIRECTOR OF AUDIENCE DEVELOPMENT

In many performing arts organizations the director of audience development is head of the marketing area and is, in fact, a marketing specialist. Otherwise, he or she reports to the director of marketing and is responsible for increasing the sale of subscription, series, group, special events, and individual tickets. The audience development director works closely with volunteer committees and attempts to increase patrons' involvement with the organization and to attract new patrons. The audience development director must be an outgoing, articulate, and personable individual who can mix comfortably with VIPs and socially prominent members of the community, many of whom provide the core of volunteer work that attracts and maintains the nucleus of a loyal audience. A college education is helpful, though not necessary. This is often a good entry-level position for a mature, energetic, and intelligent person who is also an enthusiast of the particular arts organization.

SYSTEMS SPECIALIST

As more sophisticated computers and business machines are acquired by arts and media organizations, it becomes necessary to hire in-house specialists who can design programming as well as advise the organization about the purchase, rental, and maintenance of such equipment. This often proves more cost-effective than hiring consultants or merely taking the advice of computer sales people who, of course, often put their own interests above that of the organization. A systems specialist may have various job titles and may serve a number of departments. In large organizations a number of specialists maybe employed to manage specific operations such as a computerized ticket system, computerized stage lighting and sound systems, or computerized office systems. The position does not require specialized knowledge of an organization's artistic product or creative operations, unless the job is involved in the production area; but special training in computer sciences is necessary in both cases.

DIRECTOR OF PUBLIC RELATIONS OR DIRECTOR OF PRESS RELATIONS

A director of public relations, sometimes called a promotion director, is the head of a department, usually with authority to hire and fire. He or she may report to the marketing director or directly to the executive director or president. This executive is responsible for placing information about the organization with the media and for helping to create and protect the public image of the organization. The most common means used to accomplish this include the following:

1. Press releases
2. Speeches and public pronouncements from various participants in the organization
3. Press interviews and press conferences
4. Placement of feature stories and articles
5. Critics' reviews
6. Free listings and announcements in the media
7. Program and playbill notes, articles, biographies
8. Press kits and special information packets
9. Special appearances, events, and other "happenings"
10. Letters, announcements, invitations

Perhaps the most important requirement for a career in publicity and public relations is the ability to communicate well, especially in writing. Few public relations people can succeed without the ability to write succinctly, creatively, and correctly. Typical challenges facing the public relations professional may include how to reduce volumes of information about a composer or production into a one-page release; how to create excitement about a replacement performer whom nobody has ever heard about; how to soft-pedal the personal problems of the executive director; and how to explain why, after just receiving a $5-million endowment from a wealthy patron, the organization still needs another $5 million. An in-depth knowledge of the art form is not always required, although it is certainly desirable. Also desirable is the ability to work quickly and accurately under tremendous deadline pressures. A large number of professional contacts in the press, media, advertising, and publishing fields is also a big plus, as is a college education that combines journalism, advertising, and the arts.

The director of public relations, or of press and media relations, is the liaison between his or her company and the print and media outlets that communicate to the public. Responsibilities common to this position involve—

1. Keeping up-to-date lists of newspaper, magazine, radio, and television editors, reviewers, and feature writers and using them to greatest benefit

2. Maintaining a list of deadlines that show when copy, ad placements, listing placements, and mailings are due—and meeting due dates

3. Arranging press conferences, interviews, and photo sessions and supervising them

4. Inviting press members to performances and exhibitions and maintaining good relations with them

5. Acting as host for visitors, artists, press, VIPs, board members, volunteers, and others

6. Supervising the distribution of posters, leaflets and giveaways

Although a college education is required for most high-paying jobs in this category, it is certainly possible to begin with a small organization and then, perhaps, acquire additional training as you continue to gain experience. Because personal contacts play such an important role in successful press relations, it is easier to climb the job ladder in the same city or area than to move around geographically.

PRESS AGENT

The title of press agent is generally used by self-employed individuals who work for artists and organizations on a specific project as consultants or as independent contractors—as opposed to working on salary for nonprofit organizations (See Chapter 9).

DIRECTOR OF PUBLIC INFORMATION

The title of public information officer or director of public information is usually associated with an arts council, service organization, foundation, museum, or corporate broadcasting company—in other words, organizations that do not usually promote or sell tickets to events. A public information officer usually holds the highest public relations position within such an organization. He or she is responsible for the public's perception of the organization and serves as the chief spokesperson for it. This requires full knowledge of its operations and personnel, together with an ability to communicate its goals and policies to the public. Typical duties for this job include—

1. Writing press releases

2. Preparing position-papers, reports, speeches, and articles

3. Supervising the production and printing of annual reports, pamphlets, and brochures

4. Acting as a liaison to other arts, media, foundation, service, and government groups

5. Lobbying on behalf of the organization

This is obviously a highly visible position. One must be diplomatic, persuasive, and accurate, and be able to think on one's feet. For these reasons a person who has worked in a government post that requires interaction with the public, or for a large corporation or lobbying group, can often easily transfer his or her skills to the arts and media industry. Experience in customer relations, counseling, and even box-office management would be immediately transferable to public information positions with small organizations.

DIRECTOR OF COMMUNITY RELATIONS

Large performing companies and visual arts organizations often sponsor tours and other outreach programs. For example, the Charlotte Opera has a touring program that presents over 200 performances annually to schools, libraries, and community centers throughout North Carolina. These performances provide extra work for company members, as well as income and statewide exposure for the organization, which, in fact, is dependent upon smaller surrounding communities for its survival. In cases like this, the director of community relations plays a critical role in forming a partnership with civic groups, school boards, social and service clubs, unions, churches, and chambers of commerce. The responsibilities of the position include—

1. Addressing civic groups and clubs as a representative of the organization

2. Providing promotional material and publicity to the sponsoring groups

3. Enlisting the support of local groups for the purpose of fundraising and audience development

Likely candidates for this position come from the ranks of the local community. It is necessary to know the customs, interrelationships between organizations, and the leaders of the various interest groups, as well as to fit comfortably into the community. This may be an entry-level position for someone with prior experience as a volunteer or for someone familiar with local school boards and civic groups.

DIRECTOR OF ADVERTISING

Most arts and media organizations use the services of outside advertising or graphic design agencies. Some meet their advertising needs exclusively in this way, others employ in-house specialists and only occasionally hire independent agencies. Advertising must reflect the policies and decisions of the marketing, promotion, and sales departments; the executive in charge of advertising reports to the head of those areas. Whether advertising is part of the job of a marketing, promotion, or sales executive, or is the responsibility of a full-time position, the functions are the same:

1. Purchasing advertising space in the print media

2. Buying advertising time on radio and television

3. Supervising the production of display ads

4. Creating, designing, and/or supervising all advertising copy

5. Negotiating with or supervising all copywriters, graphic designers, and printers

6. Controlling the advertising budget and deciding how this budget will be spent

A natural path to the position of advertising director would be from the commercial advertising world. An account executive who also understands and has a sensitivity to an art form could draw on his or her experience to meet the advertising needs of a theatre, dance, or cable television company. Other skills and experience in the illustration, graphics, and printing fields are also transferable to organizations in the arts and media industry.

Courses and seminars on marketing often include information on advertising, as would a graduate program with a concentration in marketing and promotion. Such an education may not be necessary to get a career started in the advertising area, but would become so if you wished to work into higher positions.

CONTINUITY MANAGER

The continuity manager in a television or radio station works with the sales department and the advertising agency, or directly with the advertiser. The continuity manager is assigned to write copy for the station—introducing programs, for example—and also rewrites agency or client copy. The continuity person also edits copy before it is aired to insure that it conforms to station and FCC standards. This is a good position from which to move up in the advertising and marketing field.

DIRECTOR OF SALES OR SALES MANAGER

In large film studios and film companies a sales director may be a vice president who reports directly to the president or production chief. Sales responsibilities are divided between domestic and foreign markets and, perhaps, between movie theatre exhibitors and the major television networks, cable system operators, and/or video-cassette retailers. The word *sales* is somewhat misleading here because, except for the cassette market, virtually all major films are leased rather than sold. In any case, once a deal has been made, the business department collects and processes the payments, and the legal department devises and monitors all sales or leasing contracts and agreements.

Commercial broadcasting networks and companies earn their money by selling advertising time around their programming. The director of sales is the person responsible for selling that time and, on the network level, heads a staff of regional and local sales managers who work with advertising agencies and local businesses to sell commercial time. The director works closely with the network's research departments—which is a marketing function—and with station management to determine the advertising rates that will be charged, and to develop sales strategies. This executive must combine excellent managerial, planning, and selling skills and usually has at least a few years experience as a salesperson. Director or vice-president of sales is a high-paying, high-leverage, and very mobile position within the broadcasting field.

In the cable television business the director of sales, or sales manager, supervises the door-to-door sales people who are attempting to attract subscribers to the cable television system.

In the live arts, sales directors are the box-office, admission, or ticket-service managers described below.

TICKET SERVICE MANAGER

The ticket service manager is a key position with many opera companies, symphony orchestras, and other organizations that rely on subscription sales to gain their audiences. This manager supervises the processing of subscription orders: assigning seat locations, handling all subscription requests and complaints, and providing statistics to the marketing department regarding the sales progress during subscription campaigns. The ticket service manager either supervises the box-office staff or works closely with it and, in some cases, with outside ticket agencies, such as Ticketron. Because this executive may be the only management representative with whom a subscriber or ticketbuyer speaks, it is important that he or she conveys a positive image of the organization—return or repeat business is crucial to future sales. Conversely, reporting to the marketing director about customer reaction to publicity and advertising is an important function. The ticket service manager also works with the development department to assure that important donors and key corporate sponsors are given special attention and, when possible, to identify potential new donors. Other duties of the job include making recommendations about pricing tickets, supervising group sales, maintaining subscriber and ticket customer lists for mailing purposes, keeping records of all ticket income, and overseeing a staff and the necessary paper work.

GROUP SALES MANAGER

A fundamental principle of economics holds that it is cheaper to sell a hundred units of a product once rather than to sell one hundred units individually. Hence the importance of group sales. While series or subscription sales aim to sell each customer a number of different events, group sales aims to sell one event or performance to a large group of people, often offering a discount as enticement. When the volume of group sales is high, a director or manager is hired to process such sales and, more important, to increase them. This requires direct contact with numerous ticket and travel agents, theatre-party organizers, educational institutions, social and professional organizations, and former group buyers. Group sales is supervised by the marketing department, or by the ticket service manager in large organizations.

SUBSCRIPTION SALES MANAGER

When the volume of subscription sales is high and is not handled by a ticket service manager or by the box-office staff, a subscription sales manager is hired to process the considerable paper work involved and, perhaps more important, to keep the subscribers happy. Thus, this is really a public relations job, though it also requires an eye for exacting detail.

MERCHANDISE MARKETING MANAGER

When special merchandise is sold that is tailored to an organization or to its primary product—plays, operas, films, or the corporate logo, for example—a merchandise manager is hired within the marketing department to supervise the design, manufacture, and sale of such items. Museums, galleries, and performing arts companies often reproduce and sell their posters. And countless other items are designed around a particular company or production: T-shirts, ash trays, buttons, tote bags, umbrellas, post cards, souvenir booklets. These, combined with other merchandise that reflect or relate to the image of the organization, are often sold in lobby gift shops and through mail-order catalogues, providing much-needed sources of earned income. Obviously, jobs in this area require a background in business, marketing, and sales, with no special arts knowledge.

When film studios and networks generate special merchandise to capitalize on their most popular performers, shows, or characters, the manufacturing rights are sold to specific designers or companies, and while the studio or network is not involved in distribution and sales, they may be entitled to a percentage of any profit that is made. Numerous lawsuits, incidentally, have centered around the question of who has the legal right to sell certain subsidiary rights to whom.

CONCESSIONS MANAGER

Arts organizations that operate in large facilities may have the space and the inclination to house beverage stands or bars, restaurants, gift shops, parking facilities, coat-checking services, and a variety of vending machines. When these are leased to independent concessionaires, the organization is placed in the role of a landlord, and the rental agreements are handled by the business or financial department. These agreements may call for flat rental fees or a percentage of concession sales, or both. In other cases, the organization operates the concessions itself, assuming all the business and personnel obligations. A concessions manager may be hired to oversee the management and operation of each enterprise. This job is obviously far removed from the artistic concerns of the organization, yet customers will hold the organization accountable for whatever happens to them while they are on the premises. Good public relations, then, is an important element in concession management.

When concessions involve merchandise generated by the organization, they are supervised by the marketing department. Otherwise they come under the control of the building operations department and may be supervised by a house manager. Running a concession may not seem like a very promising beginning for a career in arts management, yet we hasten to mention the fact that the Shubert brothers started out by selling orange drinks in the lobby of a theatre in Syracuse, New York!

SALES PEOPLE

As we have seen throughout this chapter, sales people are in demand in almost all branches of the arts and media industry. Indeed, salesmanship is at the core of virtually all of American industry. While sales jobs may first be offered on a commission basis, with no salary guarantees, successful sales people can quickly move up to important executive positions. Virtually all arts and media organizations that have something to sell always have the need for a good new salesperson. This is why sales is such an easily accessible entry-level area, and why you should consider starting in sales if you are thinking about building a career with an arts and media organization. It is a proven method for getting to know the territory and for moving up, perhaps all the way to the top.

Looking across the industry, entry-level sales positions can be summarized as follows:

The performing arts: box-office treasurers and staff people who process subscription and group-ticket orders; also sales clerks for special merchandise and concessions

The visual arts: museum admissions clerks, gift shop and merchandise sales people, and gallery sales agents

Broadcasting: Sales representatives who sell air time to advertisers and also those who sell programming to affiliate and independent broadcasting companies

Cablecasting: Sales people who interest customers in buying the basic cable service and then in buying additional pay services; also sales representatives who sell time to advertisers

Film: Studio and film company sales people who lease films to both domestic and foreign film exhibitors, to television and cablevision companies, and to other organizations; also sales representatives for film distribution and video-cassette companies

CHAPTER EIGHT

JOBS IN FUNDRAISING, FUND GIVING AND IN SERVICE ORGANIZATIONS

J obs related to the business of fundraising and philanthropy are found exclusively within the not-for-profit sector. While commercial enterprises often seek outside money to fuel their projects, such money is loaned or invested by those who usually expect to share in profits earned from their enterprise. Raising investments is the job of a financier or chief finance officer, who, for example, may also be the producer, the gallery owner, or the company president. On the other hand, money given to nonprofit organizations is donated, and a donor's only return may be a tax deduction and the pleasure of assisting a cause, project, or institution that is dear to his or her heart. Arts service and support organizations, including unions and professional associations, are often active in both the nonprofit and commercial sectors.

WHAT IS FUNDRAISING?

The word *development* has become a euphemism for *fundraising* and is now the most frequently used term when describing activities and job titles in this area. A development director whose main responsibility is fundraising should not be confused with an audience development director, whose main responsibility is to increase ticket sales, or earned income, and who works within the marketing and promotion area. In the film and television fields the word *development* is most commonly applied to the creative process of developing screen properties, or scripts, from novels, plays, or original scenarios.

The days when a symphony orchestra or a dance company was supported by a single philanthropist or when a new production at the Metropolitan Opera was underwritten by a single check from a Mrs. Rockefeller or a Mrs. Belmont are over. One does occasionally hear of a multi-million-dollar gift to finance a new museum wing or to construct a new concert hall, but, for the most part, the task of funding the arts in the not-for-profit sector is much more difficult and complex than it used to be. Even if the artistic director or general manager is qualified to serve as a fundraiser—and most do devote some time to this chore—he or she seldom has the time to accomplish all that's required. Hence, the position of director of development or, in large institutions, a department of development headed by a vice-president and supported by a sizable number of employees and volunteers.

DIRECTOR OF DEVELOPMENT OR DEVELOPMENT OFFICER

All development officers must have exceptional verbal and writing skills, as well as the personality to interact successfully—the buzz word is *interface*—with corporate and foundation leaders, government funding officers, and philanthropists. Warm, outgoing, effervescent people tend to function well in this field, provided that they are also clearheaded and doggedly persistent in the pursuit of their goal, which is money. In short, the job requires a sophisticated and charming beggar! This is not an easy role for most people to play, and even those who do it well tend to weary of the job after their initial years of success.

Recent cuts in government funding for the arts, and the resulting increase in competition for foundation and corporate support, have shifted the need away from development officers who are merely good proposal writers and increased the demand for a new breed. Development officers today must have the ability to research, identify, and secure funding from a wide and often unusual array of sources. Nine out of ten requests are likely to elicit negative responses. And the one positive response is likely to require five meetings, twenty phone calls, and a small mountain of research data, correspondence, and grant proposal drafts. Again, the operative word for this professional is *persistence.*

Development officers can and often do transfer their skills to the arts and media industry from other fields, such as education or healthcare. But a fundraiser in the arts must learn the specific sources that fund the arts and must cultivate potential donors, board members, and others who are especially supportive of a given institution or project. Such contacts, together with a knowledge of the community, comprise the most valuable assets in a fundraiser's portfolio. Because they deal mainly with prominent and cultured people, most development officers have at least one college degree and a broad knowledge of the arts.

The basic function of development is to raise the unearned income necessary to make up the difference between revenues and operating

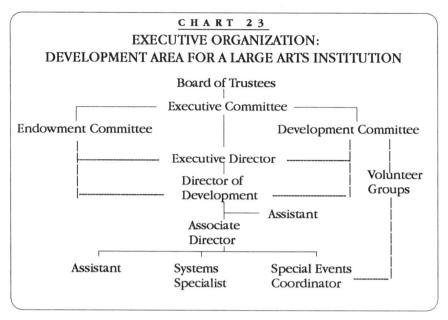

CHART 23
EXECUTIVE ORGANIZATION:
DEVELOPMENT AREA FOR A LARGE ARTS INSTITUTION

expenses. The director reports to the executive director and works closely with members of the board of trustees, whose members should be ready and willing to provide contacts and lend meaningful support. If board members are not supportive, the development person's job is difficult, if not impossible. In large institutions the development director supervises a support staff and has access to word processors and computers that assist in conducting research, gathering and storing information, and soliciting funds. (See Chart 23.) While small sums from individuals are often solicited by mail, larger contributions almost always require personal contacts. A development director must have the ability and presence to make personal appeals to foundation and corporate contributors, arts council executives, and potential individual donors. Often accompanied by a board member or someone from the artistic staff, the fund-raiser must present a strong, well-documented, and informed case on behalf of his or her organization. In summary, the director will be responsible for—

1. Identifying and contacting potential donors through research and board contacts

2. Supervising the preparation of written proposals and grant applications

3. Designing direct-mail, telephone, and other fundraising campaigns

4. Preparing reports on how funds were allocated for the funding agencies, board development committee, and the executive director

5. Personally soliciting funds through visits to prospective donors and thanking those who actually donate

6. Conceiving and supervising special events, galas, sweepstakes, and other approaches to raising funds

As discussed in Chapter 3 and documented in the Career Kit, there are many opportunities to learn the mechanics of fundraising for the arts through seminars and workshops. These should be attended periodically by professionals working in the field, as well as by neophytes, so that they may keep abreast of the ever-changing tax laws, government agencies, and economic trends that influence the field of philanthropy.

ASSOCIATE OR ASSISTANT DIRECTOR OF DEVELOPMENT

A development associate or assistant complements the efforts of the director of development by executing the extensive research and paper work required in this area. Typical duties are—

1. Researching the funding histories and requirements of corporations, foundations, and other funding sources

2. Maintaining files on the histories of individuals, including board members, who are donors: their professions, memberships, dates and amounts of their contributions, services volunteered, and other pertinent information

3. Keeping mailing lists up to date

4. Keeping a calendar of deadlines for grant applications and status reports

5. Acknowledging in writing all contributions received, however small

6. Preparing text and statistics for proposals

7. Assisting with special events

The associate must be an excellent writer and very organized. A missed deadline can mean losing a grant, and not thanking an individual for a contribution can mean losing that contributor for the future. Many development offices now depend heavily on data processing so that typing, word processing, and computer skills are usually required. This is a good entry-level position, except when direct experience is required. It may also be a good step up for someone with experience as a copy editor, researcher, or secretary who is seeking to develop a higher-paying specialization.

SPECIAL EVENTS COORDINATOR

Most boards of trustees for nonprofit arts and media organizations have a number of auxiliary committees made up of volunteers who raise money for the organization: Friends of the Theatre, the Opera Guild, the Women's Club, Friends of Channel Thirteen, and so forth. These groups organize events such as dinner parties, receptions, and tours, and also assist in running galas, benefits, and telethons. They not only raise money by selling tickets, souvenirs, and other items, they also provide valuable community-relations services and build grassroots credibility for the organization.

The special events coordinator is a salaried staff person—a kind of in-house Pearl Mesta or Elsa Maxwell—who usually reports to the development director and who coordinates and acts as host of special events. The special events coordinator must be able to organize, recruit, and supervise volunteers. Many such coordinators are women in the upper social strata of the community who possess the social grace and position necessary to direct volunteers who have interests and backgrounds similar to their own. It is not unusual for women who are reentering the job market after some years absence to be considered for this position.

ARTS COUNCILS

The National Endowment for the Arts (NEA) and the National Endowment for the Humanities (NEH) are the two federal agencies that are most frequently mentioned in connection with federal subsidy for nonprofit projects in the arts and media industry. Additional federal funding is provided by the Corporation for Public Broadcasting (CPB) and by various cabinet-level agencies. NEA and NEH also provide funding for the fifty-six state arts agencies, including American Samoa, Guam, the Northern Marianas, Puerto Rico, the Virgin Islands, and the District of Columbia, all of which are members of the National Assembly of State Arts Agencies. In addition there are over fifteen hundred local and community arts councils that are funded by state arts agencies, local governments, and private and corporate contributions.

Most arts council policies are determined by an independent council, panel, or advisory board. These bodies, composed of appointed citi-

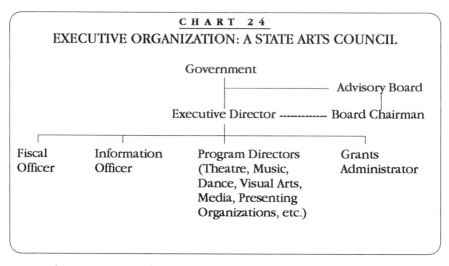

CHART 24
EXECUTIVE ORGANIZATION: A STATE ARTS COUNCIL

Government

——————————————— Advisory Board

Executive Director ———————— Board Chairman

| Fiscal Officer | Information Officer | Program Directors (Theatre, Music, Dance, Visual Arts, Media, Presenting Organizations, etc.) | Grants Administrator |

zens who serve on a volunteer basis, have no legal authority but function in much the same way as a board of trustees for nonprofit organizations. The major function of an arts council is to—

1. Provide financial support to arts and media organizations and to individual artists through the awarding of grants or "contracts"

2. Provide technical assistance

3. Present arts programs, workshops, and performances in public facilities and schools

4. Disseminate information about the arts and the media

Some councils operate facilities and produce programs; others "buy" services for the public through direct contracts or grants. Chart 24 illustrates an organizational model of an arts council.

Because chairpersons for arts councils are appointed by elected officials, a number of very unlikely and seemingly unsuitable appointees have been named at federal as well as state and local levels. Celebrities from the arts world, the socially prominent, political campaign staff managers, and wealthy contributors to political coffers have been appointed to such posts, without having had any prior experience in arts administration. Some have proven themselves to be highly effective leaders, others have not. The career professionals who work for arts councils, however, are usually proven administrators, who possess college degrees and experience in the field.

UNITED ARTS FUNDS

United arts funds are service organizations that raise money for the arts through federated or joint appeals. Funds are raised from the community—including business, the general public, government, and/or foundation sources—and are distributed to arts and media groups that are members of the fund. The function of a united arts fund or council is to—

1. Determine the goals of a campaign

2. Solicit the funds on behalf of its constituents

3. Determine the distribution of the funds, thereby guiding the arts policy of the city

4. Provide arts and media groups technical assistance, as well as informational and nonfinancial services

5. Engage in programming activities

The board of a united arts fund is composed of prominent business leaders and philanthropists, as well as board members and managers from major arts institutions in the area. The staff, which works under the supervision of an executive director or president, is divided into four categories: administration, fundraising, programs and services, and facility management and technical assistance. Volunteers are also utilized in all areas. Notably, the executive director of a united arts fund is among the highest paid professionals in the nonprofit arts field.

PRIVATE FOUNDATIONS

A foundation is an incorporated nonprofit organization whose function is to distribute funds, or grants, to eligible individuals and organizations. It is similar to an arts council, except that its assets are not derived from tax-levied money, but from private estates or corporate earnings. The policy of a foundation is determined by a board of trustees—foundations are nonprofit organizations, even though associated with the private sector and with commercial corporations and the board is empowered to grant funds according to the stated guidelines of the foundation's by-laws. Most small foundations are administered by a lawyer, estate executive, or part-time director. Large foundations have a president, chairperson, or director, who is supported by a professional staff.

Jobs within foundations are among the most sought after in the nonprofit arts and media field, and for good reason. Foundations are

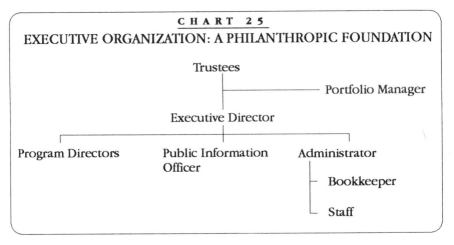

CHART 25

EXECUTIVE ORGANIZATION: A PHILANTHROPIC FOUNDATION

Trustees — Portfolio Manager

Executive Director

Program Directors | Public Information Officer | Administrator
— Bookkeeper
— Staff

well funded and do not have to raise operating funds; they are usually concerned with broad issues that have long-range ramifications; they usually pay the professional staff very well. There are, however, a few realities that the arts administrator should consider when seeking a position with a foundation:

1. Foundations are not only concerned with the arts; most philanthropic grants in America are made to medicine, education, and the sciences—few foundation giving officers, therefore, are concerned with the arts exclusively.

2. Foundations seldom advertise for staff positions, but rely upon recommendations, word-of-mouth contacts, and in-house promotions.

3. Foundations receive many solicitations and inquiries from groups seeking funds and job-seekers. They may be less responsive to cold calls and standard networking techniques.

Large foundations with multiple departments, such as the Ford and Rockefeller foundations, are set up much as arts councils are. An executive director or president reports to the trustees; and program directors evaluate proposals and prepare reports with the assistance of an administrative staff.

CORPORATE GIVING OFFICERS

Since the 1986 Tax reform act, the federal government has lessened tax incentives for corporate giving. While such incentives still exist, comparatively few corporations utilize them.

Beyond the financial benefits, corporations are increasingly using their contributions for public relations purposes. By sponsoring national tours of ballet companies or art exhibitions, for example, Philip Morris Incorporated has been able to associate its name with culture and the arts, which, in turn, adds to its national visibility. The oil companies have found that public television is an effective medium for reaching up-scale viewers, so they underwrite numerous cultural and scientific programs. In fact, PBS is sometimes referred to as the "Petroleum Broadcasting System"!

Corporate-giving positions are on the most-popular list among administrators working in the development area. Yet, such jobs seem out of reach or difficult to obtain because—

1. A corporation's giving-policy is usually based on the return on investment that may come from enhancing public image and strengthening a community where there is a plant or office—or by directly benefiting employees of the company.

2. Corporations like to promote from within and, therefore, will recruit business-types for most junior positions.

3. Giving-policies are an extension of the overall corporate policy—and frequently an expression of the personal interests of the corporate board president or chairperson—and those best suited to interpret those policies, it is felt, are veterans of the firm.

Not all corporations involved in philanthropy maintain a special giving office. Often this function is performed by the public-relations or community affairs department. Whatever department or individual executive title is used, a corporate giving officer is charged with—

1. Interpreting corporate policy as it relates to the arts, social services, health, and education

2. Representing the corporation in the community

3. Supplying information and making recommendations on grant applicants to the corporate-giving advisory board

The position also includes other public-information and public-relations functions.

It is interesting that while jobs in a corporate-giving office are often offered first to executives within the firm, many avoid moving into this area for fear of stalling their business careers. This fact provides at least a small hope to outside applicants.

PROFESSIONAL ASSOCIATIONS

A professional association either represents people working for a particular type of arts organization, such as the American Association of Museums, or people working in a particular job category, such as the National Society of Fundraising Executives. An association is organized as a nonprofit corporation, with a board of trustees that is appointed or elected. These organizations are supported by fees or annual dues from members—who may be individuals or organizations—and in many cases by grants and contributions. The functions of a professional association are—

1. To act as a clearinghouse for information, statistical data, and materials about the profession
2. To lobby for members within industry, government, and before the public
3. To provide technical, managerial, and educational assistance and special programs
4. To set up and run national and regional conferences that bring together members of the profession

An association's staff members usually have prior experience in the field and a deep interest in it. Most associations depend greatly upon the participation of their volunteer boards and members, who are called upon to serve on panels at conferences, to accept unsalaried consultancies, and the like. The typical organizational chart for the staff of a national membership association is shown below. (See Chart 26.)

UNIONS AND GUILDS

Performers, creative artists, directors, many types of managers, and most craft technicians working in the commercial or nonprofit sectors of the arts and media industry belong to trade unions that are chartered by the AFL-CIO, or to professional membership organizations, commonly called guilds. Unions and guilds are nonprofit organizations that draw members from the trade or profession they represent: Actors' Equity Association, the Screen Actors Guild, the Dramatists Guild, the International Association of Theatrical Stagehands and Employees, the Association of Theatrical Press Agents and Managers, to name a few. The chartered unions undoubtedly have more clout with top management than do the unchartered guilds, as illustrated by the 1982 antitrust suit that was initiated against the Dramatists Guild by the League

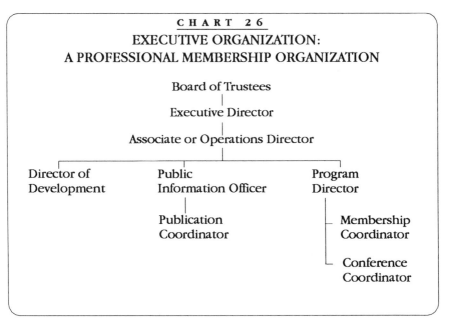

CHART 26
EXECUTIVE ORGANIZATION:
A PROFESSIONAL MEMBERSHIP ORGANIZATION

Board of Trustees

Executive Director

Associate or Operations Director

Director of Development · Public Information Officer · Program Director

Publication Coordinator · Membership Coordinator · Conference Coordinator

of American Theatres and Producers, which protested that playwrights should not be protected by minimum-payment and royalty standards but should negotiate individually with each producer for each production. Such action against card-carrying members of the performers', stagehands', or camerapersons' unions, of course, would threaten industry-wide walkouts.

Unions and guilds are formed to represent their members to management regarding such matters as contracts, salaries, working conditions, benefits, and pensions. They are financed by membership fees, annual dues, and, in some cases, by a percentage of their members' earnings from union- or guild-related jobs.

The management of a union or guild is similar to that of arts-service and technical-assistance organizations. There is a board, nominated and elected by the membership, that hires the chief operating officer, who holds the title of executive secretary or executive director. This individual, along with a staff is responsible for—

1. Executing the policies of the union

2. Representing the union and its membership to the industry and to management

3. Assuring legal and proper compliance with the basic minimum contracts of its members

4. Protecting the finances of the union or guild

5. Disseminating information to union or guild members

6. Providing information to the press and the public

7. Overseeing union pension funds, benefit programs, and the like

The chief executive officer is usually a member of the union or someone closely connected to it, such as a former legal counsel or working member of the profession. The other staff members do not necessarily come from the rank and file. It is common for staff members to be specialists in particular aspects of management or to be generalists in the field. The chief executive officer must be an accomplished advocate for the membership and must also be sensitive to the internal policies of the organization in order to represent and satisfy the many different factions that inevitably exist within the organization. Leadership and administrative abilities are also an obvious requirement.

There is no typical organizational structure for a union or guild office. Depending upon the size of the membership and the complexity of the organization—some have a national office with regional affiliates called "locals"—the duties outlined above are handled by one or more staff persons.

During rehearsal and production periods for filmed, taped, or live projects, a union member may take on certain administrative duties by serving as a deputy and representing fellow members to management. These positions are in some ways managerial, although they are not part of management per se. In a symphony orchestra the position is called personnel manager; other positions of this type are shop steward or deputy. Experience in such positions would, of course, be a good primer for jobs either in the union office or with management.

TECHNICAL ASSISTANCE GROUP

Technical assistance groups are established to provide management assistance, advice, and services to nonprofit arts organizations. They are formed according to the type of arts group they represent—Museums Collaborative, for example—and by areas of expertise, such as Volunteer Lawyers for the Arts, the Arts and Business Council, or Business Volunteers for the Arts. Technical assistance groups are usually nonprofit organizations subsidized by contributions and grant monies and perhaps by small fees charged to their clients. Their boards are composed of leaders from the profession as well as experts from the commercial business world who wish to contribute their time and expertise. Some corporations "loan" certain executives to technical assistance groups or to specific arts organizations for limited periods of time, during which the corporation continues to pay the executive's salary.

Consulting services and advice are provided by specially trained program directors who have worked in the field and by outside consultants hired to supplement the regular staff. Some of the better-known organizations in this category are the National Federation of Local Cable Programmers and Theatre Communications Group.

CHAPTER NINE

JOBS IN PRODUCTION AND OPERATIONS MANAGEMENT

If there is one area of the arts and media industry in which job titles vary greatly in relation to job functions, it is the area of production and operations management. Titles are not consistent even within the same type of arts organization. For example, the operations person for a symphony orchestra may be called the orchestra manager when there is also a general manager; or a general manager when there is an executive director. In dance the position may be called director of operations, company manager, or production manager. It is possible to find a production manager who is actually a go-fer, and another who runs the whole operation. An office manager may be a mere receptionist; a research director may be doing the job of a curator. In film and television, floor manager and traffic manager are operations positions with responsibilities that vary greatly. So when you are interviewing for a job in this area, listen very closely to the job requirements and, if possible, check them out with current or former employees of the organization.

WHAT IS PRODUCTION AND OPERATIONS MANAGEMENT?

Operations is a catchall term for any job involved with the daily functioning of a facility or with the production aspects of a business. An operations manager, although responsible to senior management, is not directly involved in policy decisions or planning on the corporate or board level; the job is restricted to internal management duties. It is meant to complement senior management by freeing top executives from the bulk of internal chores. The operations manager is concerned with directing the flow of communications between departments, supervising staff and administrative functions, and maintaining the good morale of the staff. Operations in the arts and media industry could be divided into three categories or departments with the following overall functions:

1. *Production Management:* controls productions costs; coordinates schedules of technical, creative, and management personnel before and during productions; conducts contract reviews and contract administration; supervises special events and touring productions

2. *Building Management:* oversees maintenance, security, house management, space allocation, rentals, box office, concessions, insurance, medical and safety problems, repairs, and renovations

3. *Office Management:* supervises employee relations, including benefits, compensation and salary reviews, grievances, and contract compliance; orders supplies and equipment and maintains an inventory; organizes internal communications and office systems

Each of these areas may have a manager who is supervised by a department head or by the general manager or executive director. More so than other positions, production management jobs relate most directly to the artistic product itself and may therefore fall under the supervision of the artistic director or one of the creative artists, such as the conductor or the scenic designer. For example, the personnel manager works with the conductor to organize rehearsals; the stage manager works under the director of a production to help supervise the actors; and the technical director works under a scenic designer to help supervise carpenters and other craft employees. In small organizations, operations jobs usually combine management responsibilities with craft functions, so that the technical director may also serve as the stage electrician or carpenter, for instance.

PRODUCTION MANAGER

(See above. Also see Production Manager for film and television.)

FACILITIES OR BUILDING MANAGER

(See above.)

OFFICE MANAGER

(See above.)

COMPANY MANAGER

A company manager for a Broadway production or for a first-class national tour is a member of the Association of Theatrical Press Agents and Managers (ATPAM). For most other performing arts, film, and television productions the job title is usually production manager or production assistant. This person is accountable to the general manager or executive producer and is responsible for solving routine personnel problems related to the cast, the musicians, stagehands, and the technicians; for providing payroll information; and for distributing checks to those people paid by the producer. He or she also serves in lieu of a tour manager when a theatrical production is on the road, securing housing for the company, making travel arrangements, and the like.

HOUSE MANAGER

The house manager is also a member of ATPAM in Broadway and other large unionized performing arts facilities. He or she is employed by the landlord to oversee the smooth operation of the facility, to verify box-office statements, and to supervise the security personnel, ushers and ticket-takers, and the maintenance staff. The house manager is to the landlord what the company manager is to the producer. In non-unionized facilities, the house manager reports to the general manager and may not have any responsibilities related to the box office other than accountability for the ticket stubs. In large museums, galleries, and media facilities this job may come under the title of buildings and grounds supervisor and include tremendous security responsibilities.

STAGE MANAGER

In all theatres that employ Actors' Equity Association (AEA) members, the stage manager must also belong to AEA. Opera, dance, and musical theatre companies that work under American Guild of Musical Artists (AGMA) contracts must sign their stage managers to AGMA contracts. The title of stage manager is sometimes used in film and television credits to indicate people who do little more than relay cues to actors and camera operators. AEA membership for stage managers is somewhat illogical since they fulfill an operational function that is managerial as opposed to creative or purely technical. Even the job title defines it as managerial.

Large commercial productions and institutional performing arts companies employ production stage managers who supervise rehearsal scheduling, monitor compliance with union rules, and supervise stage managers and assistant stage managers, who are in charge of the stage, the performers, and the crew only during performances. This job entails coordinating various activities with the company and house managers and requires a person who can think quickly and pay exacting attention to detail. Because stage managers work closely with artistic and stage directors, many often become directors themselves; others move into the management area.

TECHNICAL DIRECTOR

In the performing arts a technical director is a person who supervises all the craft elements and staff workers who are involved in assembling the physical production: carpenters, electricians, audio and visual engineers, and technical crew members. In film and television this function may be handled by a chief engineer or a production supervisor. The job requires a thorough knowledge of all the craft and technical aspects of production together with organizational and leadership ability. This is a good stepping-stone toward a stage manager position or a higher production management position.

TOUR MANAGER

Large modern dance and large ballet companies, opera companies, symphony orchestras, rock groups, dance bands, and even cabaret stars employ tour managers—when this job is not filled by a company manager—as do small regional companies that maintain busy touring schedules. A tour manager travels with the company and often precedes it into the next performance city. He or she is a representative of both management and performers and usually deals with presenters. The presenters are under contract to the producing or packaging organization to provide specific stage, dressing room, auditorium, and technical facilities, and the tour manager sees that such commitments are upheld or that alternate plans are made so that performances may take place. The tour manager must have a thorough knowledge of both union contracts and booking contracts; he or she must prepare and distribute the payroll, arrange transportation and living accommodations, oversee local publicity and promotion efforts, and generally serve as a loving parent to keep spirits and, therefore, performances at a high level. Some of these duties may be handled by the home producing office or by the presenting organization, or by a personal manager when a major star is involved. But usually there must also be an advance manager or coordinator of some kind who checks to make certain that what has been contracted and requested is actually going to be provided.

MUSIC ADMINISTRATOR

Music administrators are employed by large symphony orchestras and by some opera companies. This is an operations position that requires someone with a professional understanding of music. The music administrator reports to management but has a dotted-line relationship with the artistic or music director. He or she is responsible for—

1. Setting rehearsal schedules for the company and the soloists

2. Arranging "covers," or substitutes, for the important performers

3. Arranging accommodations, travel, hospitality, and amenities for visiting artists

4. Preparing lists of substitute programs, performers, and pieces so that the music director can make informed decisions

5. Working with the general manager to negotiate artists' contracts and to control the budget

6. Keeping a record of past programs and making suggestions for future programming

The music administrator must know approximately how long it will take the orchestra to rehearse a Bruckner symphony or a Mozart concerto, as well as which singers have sung which parts and sung them well, which pianist can play a Beethoven concerto on two days notice, and the like. In some organizations the music administrator supervises a librarian and library staff and works closely with the personnel manager of the orchestra.

PERSONNEL MANAGER

In the performing arts the personnel manager is unique to symphony orchestras and is usually filled from the ranks of the musicians; in some cases the job is a stepping-stone to a general-management position. The personnel manager supervises the musicians—not telling them how to play or interpret the music, but telling them when to appear for rehearsals, when a break is due, and so forth. He or she represents the players both to management and to the conductor on all matters concerning contracts, conduct, discipline, and work performance.

The personnel manager also assists in setting up auditions and in hiring extra players and substitutes. As with stage managers, personnel managers often belong to a performers' union.

CONTRACTOR

Small music organizations, especially those without a full-time orchestra, usually use a contractor to assume the functions otherwise performed by a personnel manager. A contractor may also supply union musicians to orchestral groups, Broadway shows, road shows, cabarets, nightclubs, recording studios, and other enterprises that require union musicians. Depending upon his or her abilities, the contractor supervises musicians' careers, negotiates contracts, and satisfies management demands. A skillful contractor can exert tremendous control over the musical activity in a particular area, deciding who plays where, when, how often, and for how much. Some are also working musicians themselves.

LIBRARIAN

In a small orchestra the music librarian is one of the musicians, while in a large orchestra the librarian is a full-time administrator whose responsibilities include renting and purchasing music parts and scores, controlling the costs for such expenditures, organizing and maintaining the music library, and supervising assistant librarians.

Film studios and television networks with a large collection of films or teletapes may also employ people to keep track of and supervise such inventories. Museums employ archivists, conservators, and collection managers to fulfill a similar function, as described below.

CURATOR

The title of curator in a visual arts organization may be given to any person who is in charge of overseeing a collection. In small museums and galleries the chief curator is also the executive director or general manager. Where large collections are involved, the curatorial staff is departmentalized, and each curator may supervise assistants and specialists who work exclusively in a particular wing of a museum, or in a particular area or on a particular aspect of a collection.

CONSERVATOR

A conservator for a museum is a curator who is responsible for the care, preservation, and repair of objects in the collection.

EXHIBITION DESIGNER OR DIRECTOR

Exhibitions for commercial galleries are usually designed by the gallery director or manager, in consultation, when possible, with the artist. Museum exhibitions may be conceived and mounted by an exhibition director or by a member of the curatorial staff. Major exhibitions usually require that art works be loaned from a variety of far-flung sources. This necessitates negotiations for the loans, travel and insurance arrangements, security, and other factors that may require many months if not years to consummate. In such cases the exhibition designer works closely with the senior management of the museum and its legal counsel, and may also have to negotiate with foreign governments, religious institutions, tribal chieftains, crowned heads, corporate presidents, individual art collectors, and a broad assortment of other personages.

REGISTRAR

Registrar is the title given in large museums to a staff person who organizes, documents, and keeps track of art objects in the museum's collection.

COLLECTIONS MANAGER

A collections manager works with the conservator in a museum to maintain a catalogue of the collection and to oversee the moving and storing of items in the museum's collection.

DIRECTOR OF ACQUISITION, RESEARCH, AND/OR PUBLICATIONS

Large museums often hire a research director to oversee in-house and field research that is sponsored by the museum, special educational research programs, and visiting researchers who use the collection. Museums may also employ a director of acquisition, who works under the museum director and is responsible for buying or otherwise acquiring new items. Independent consultants, agents, and art dealers may also be retained to search out, recommend, and acquire objects either on a permanent or loan basis. If the museum publishes catalogues, exhibition programs, magazines, research papers, art books and other materials, there may also be a position for a full-time publications director.

Research and acquisition, as discussed in Chapter 5, are also important to film, television, and cablevision companies, although mainly in the contexts of market research and product or property development.

GALLERY MANAGER

When an art gallery is not managed by the owner, a gallery manager or director is hired to supervise the day-to-day operations. This includes hiring and supervising the staff tending to all business and sales matters, and coordinating the art displays and exhibitions. It also entails press and public relations work, together with the management of exhibit openings and special events.

PRODUCTIONS MANAGER (FILM AND TELEVISION)

Although this chapter opens with a general definition of production management, the job of production manager deserves special attention because of its importance in the film and television branches of the industry. The production manager reports directly to the executive producer for a project or to whatever senior executive is responsible for seeing that the project meets artistic and budgetary goals. This often gives the production manager even more power than the film director, because if this manager reports that the project is running over budget—which could result from any number of factors for which the director is supposedly responsible—it could and sometimes does result in the director being fired. Perhaps appropriately, production managers are members of the Directors Guild of America (DGA). Specifically, they are responsible for allocating and controlling budgeted funds; scheduling rehearsals, locations, and shootings; hiring union employees; arranging for necessary transportation; and securing permits and rentals for location or studio production purposes. Obviously, this job offers ideal training for becoming a film or television producer.

LINE PRODUCER

A line producer is the person who coordinates the day-to-day activities of a film production, including all the creative and business personnel. Not to be confused with the executive producer, who sets the film in motion either with the idea and concept or with the packaging elements, the line producer works closely with the director in determining the elements for the production.

UNIT MANAGER

The unit manager works under the production manager in overseeing all business aspects of the film's production relating to the hiring of crew, scheduling the shooting, and coordinating the various departments so they function as one unit. While this job may be filled by the production manager on small film projects, large projects that are shot at different locations concurrently may require unit managers or a number of assistant unit managers.

PRODUCTION AUDITOR

The production auditor assists the production and unit managers in preparing the production budget, disbursing funds, accounting for expenses incurred, and forecasting the estimated final cost of production on a daily basis. These figures are the basis on which both major and minor decisions are made regarding the project at hand and the personnel involved with it. A background in business and accounting would obviously be an asset in this position, but curiosity and the willingness to persist in validating the propriety of costs are the hallmarks of a successful auditor.

PRODUCTION OFFICE COORDINATOR

The job of production office coordinator is comparable to any office manager's position. In the film and television areas it involves overseeing the administrative details and personnel management of a production company or unit; acting as the representative of the producers on certain matters; and in the absence of a large staff, fulfilling numerous clerical and bookkeeping functions.

PROGRAM DIRECTOR

This important job requires a person who can coordinate the entire programming schedule for a broadcasting or cablecasting station. This may include the scheduling of syndicated programs, as well as those produced by the network and by individual stations. It also involves developing original concepts, buying the rights to existing properties, hiring employees, negotiating for studio or location sites, and scheduling production time as well as air-time. The job of program director is at the middle of the executive ladder and is a good spot from which to move up.

TRAFFIC MANAGER

The traffic manager for radio, television, and cablecasting stations schedules all air-time, both programming and advertising; schedules announcers; and coordinates the work of the program directors and the advertising sales people. In small companies this job is usually combined with another, such as announcer or news editor. It requires precise thinking together with a knowledge of the station's market and audience profile.

STUDIO OR STATION
OPERATIONS ASSISTANT

Small film, cablecasting, or broadcasting companies have a need for an all-around person who can handle numerous details in various aspects of the business—everything from inventing sound effects to scouting locations and doing the payroll. This producer's assistant, or guy or gal Friday, is likely to be the first staff person whom the producer hires. While it is an excellent first job in the media branch of the industry, it does require some specialized training or background, together with organizational ability and a willingness to perform both menial and higher-level tasks. The job title may be anything from intern to assistant to the producer, depending upon the size and budget of the company.

FRANCHISE MANAGER

When a cable television company is in the process of seeking new markets, it assembles a team of employees to win from the authorities of a given community or municipality the franchise agreement that will enable the company to operate a cable system in that area. The team is usually comprised of an engineer, a market analyst, a financial analyst, and a public relations specialist; it's headed by a franchise manager who must supervise the team, negotiate the agreement with city representatives, and report all dealings to the corporate headquarters. While this job ends when the franchise process is completed, it provides a broad range of experience in managing a cable television company or a television station.

DIRECTOR OF EDUCATION
OR DIRECTOR OF OUTREACH

Colleges, schools, conservatories, and special programs train future artists, technicians, and managers; in turn, performance and media organizations sponsor activities that are designed to educate the public-at-large. While the management of schools and educational programs is discussed in Chapter 5, it is appropriate here to examine arts and media organizations that engage in educational activities. Many opportunities exist for a person with experience on one side of the coin to flip that knowledge to the other.

Museums and performing arts organizations have realized the potential value of educational programs as marketing devices to build future audiences, particularly among the young, and to create an appreciation and understanding of an art form, which, in theory, creates a larger demand for it. Indeed, outreach efforts are essential for the survival and growth of arts organizations because they rely on a continuing influx of new patronage to supplement current support and to replace lost patrons.

One of the earliest and best-received examples of educational programming was the nationally televised "Young Peoples Concerts" of the sixties, which featured Leonard Bernstein and the New York Philharmonic. These programs featured accessible music with appealing narration designed to entertain the young. Like all educational programming, these special concerts were designed to attract new audiences by presenting works in an entertaining and easily understandable manner. Another purpose is to bring the arts to new audiences. This is most efficiently achieved through the broadcast media. And most such programming is carried by public radio and television stations, which, after all, were originally licensed for the purpose of educating the communities they serve.

Educational programming by arts and media companies is generally designed to fulfill one or more of the following goals:

1. To increase the performing opportunities for a company and also to provide more exposure and income

2. To increase an audience base and prepare future audiences

3. To enrich and inform an audience

4. To market an organization to new constituencies

5. To enhance the public image of an organization as well as its patrons and/or sponsors

The person responsible for these important functions may be called director of education, director of outreach, or community affairs director. Specific duties of the job may include—

1. Conceiving and developing programs

2. Developing curriculum and course content

3. Hiring, training, and supervising teachers or program directors

4. Developing materials such as study guides, brochures, and press releases

5. Coordinating educational outreach programs with artistic directors and performers

6. Representing the organization to the outside community and to special interest groups

The director of education is a senior-management position that usually requires skills in marketing, fundraising, public relations, and audience development, as well as a knowledge of pedagogy. This executive usually reports directly to the general manager or executive director and works in close partnership with other department heads. Because outreach programs frequently involve extensive touring, the education director may also function as a tour manager—selling performance dates, arranging transportation, working with sponsors on publicity, and organizing guest lectures, demonstrations, and workshops—or he or she may supervise a tour, or a company manager and a technical crew.

A director of education in a museum is usually involved in designing, supervising, and marketing education programs within the museum—these may include special weekend or evening art classes, group tours, and membership events. The position may involve hiring and training administrative staff, guides, and instructors as well as producing brochures and special materials. Obviously the museum's education director must work closely with the membership director, the public information officer and, especially, with the curators to develop specific programs around the permanent and visiting collections and exhibitions. Such jobs are often filled by people who have teaching backgrounds in the arts as well as managerial expertise.

DIRECTOR OF PUBLIC ACCESS

A new position in the field of education for the arts and media industry, as mentioned in Chapter 5, is the coordinator or director of public access for local cable television systems. Public access, sometimes required by local franchise agreements, sets aside a certain amount of air-time or a number of independently controlled channels for the exclusive use of the community in presenting locally produced programming. In other words, the cable television company has no control over the content of such programming and offers the air-time on a noncompetitive, first-come basis. A director of public access is responsible for—

1. Contacting local groups and providing them with information regarding the opportunities for using public-access airtime

2. Setting up classes in the technical aspects of producing public-access programming

3. Offering technical advice on production, but not on program content

4. Monitoring the programs

5. Setting up and controlling program schedules

Although public-access channels are operated for the benefit of the community, cable television systems use them as marketing tools to increase the number of local viewers and to create goodwill for the system within the community.

INTERNSHIP DIRECTOR

Although apprenticeships, or internships, probably date back to the beginning of organized society, they are a fairly recent phenomenon in the field of arts and media management. Happily, however, there are now countless opportunities to work as an intern and thereby begin a career in this industry—both in the nonprofit and commercial sectors. Television networks, film studios, repertory theatre companies, museums, performing arts centers—all have internship programs and the larger ones have full-time internship directors or coordinators. Most such positions carry a salary, but some are filled by volunteers.

An internship director often has a background in teaching as well as a special dedication to the organization with which he or she is working. The job entails recruiting qualified interns, who usually work for little or no salary, placing them within the organization, and monitoring their work to be certain that both the interns and the organization derive the greatest possible benefit from this relationship.

CHAPTER TEN

BECOMING INDEPENDENT

It seems appropriate to begin the last chapter of this book by re-peating a theme from the first chapter: The arts and media indus-try today is replete with opportunity for the introduction and devel-opment of new products, companies, and services. While much of this opportunity will be explored by established corporations and in-stitutions, there will certainly be enough left over to challenge the minds and energies of individual entrepreneurs and independent-minded specialists. Chapter 5 describes how the various branches and disciplines within the industry are organized, but it does not claim that present practice is perfect or that it cannot be improved. Indeed, many critics and practitioners feel that improvements, indus-try-wide, are an urgent necessity. If you agree and if you believe that you have a contribution to make, then you must decide whether to work within an existing organization or to strike out on your own.

EVALUATING YOUR READINESS

Almost everyone dreams of becoming his or her own boss at some time. Most of us would like to set our own working hours, make a lot of money, and be fully in charge of our professional careers. But if you are thinking of going independent, you'd better take a hard look at the realities. First of all, self-employed people—especially when they first establish businesses—must work much more than the standard eight-hour day, five days a week. Are you ready to virtually marry your work and have it move in with you? Second, it costs money to establish a new business, and it takes even more money to support yourself until the business shows a profit—if it ever does. Are you financially ready to make a necessary investment and even to sustain a loss, if that should be the result? Third, there is a lot of well-established, highly successful competition in almost any specialization you may select. Are you ready to compete for potential clients or properties given your present knowl-edge, experience, reputation, and contacts?

Many people with a lot of money and a little interest in the arts and media industry have become producers, gallery owners, or landlords even though they possess a minimum of experience. This is fine as long as they have the intelligence to hire good general managers or other business agents. Many of the most successful entrepreneurs have learned their businesses from the bottom up—as have other types of independent managers and business people in the field. It must be said, however, that striking out on your own requires a mixture of—

1. Self-confidence that borders on arrogance

2. Courage that is nearly blind

3. Self-motivation that is endless

4. Ambition that is almost crazed

5. Optimism that is a little naive

People who are their own bosses often say that they never would have gotten into the business if they had known when they started what they know now. And, indeed, if someone presented you with a list of all the pitfalls, liabilities, and trouble that could befall you, chances are—if you're sane—you'd go on collecting a paycheck.

Psychologically, the optimum time to go independent is after you have acquired a good amount of experience and before you've become too secure or comfortable in your life-style. Comfort and routine tend to reduce one's ability to take risks. Of course, the situation is different if you are financially independent—for example, retired from your first career and seeking to transfer your knowledge to a second. Or, you may be a practicing attorney, accountant, or other professional who decides to give up a corporate position and take on clients in the arts and media field.

If you feel that you have a reasonable chance for success in your own business and you have the start-up resources at hand, you should probably go ahead when your desire to do so is hot. After all, if you fail you can always go back on someone else's payroll. But if you don't make the attempt, you may pay heavily with a lifetime of regrets.

FORMING A PRIVATE CORPORATION

The reasons why a self-employed professional should form a corporation instead of operating as an unincorporated business are discussed in Chapter 6, which also covers the most common types of corporate structures. But it is prudent to reiterate the importance of this formality here.

To become incorporated you will need to hire an attorney—not just any attorney, but one who is familiar with the type of business you are incorporating. The attorney will assist you in drawing up the papers of incorporation, conducting a corporate name search—no two corporations may have the same name—and filing with the appropriate city, state, and federal authorities. This process usually takes from two to six weeks and, except in very complicated cases, should not cost a great deal of money. The time and the money are worth it to protect your personal estate from your business liabilities.

Many people who earn good livings in the arts and media industry are self-employed. It would be impossible to describe all the different ways such professionals work, but the following list shows the most common independent pursuits. Sometimes a professional offers services in more than one activity—such as a landlord who also serves as producer or an attorney who handles general manager responsibilities—or a unique combination of special skills and interests.

ACCOUNTANT

There are only a handful of large accounting firms that specialize in theatrical and media clients: Lutz and Carr and Coopers and Lybrand in New York City and Price-Waterhouse in Los Angeles are some examples. This is a competitive field open to CPAs with a knowledge and love for the arts. Aside from providing the usual tax, accounting, bookkeeping, and payroll services, accountants may also serve as business managers, financial consultants, and money managers for individual and corporate clients who are successful enough to need these services. In the media world there are openings for general accountants as well as for production accountants and auditors. For ambitious CPAs with a good work-record such positions can lead all the way to the top of the corporate career ladder, or to the establishment of their own accounting firms.

ADVERTISING AGENT

No very large advertising agency can afford to specialize in arts and media accounts exclusively. However, because performing arts producers, film studios, and television networks usually farm out their advertising campaigns, some agencies retain an executive who concentrates on such clients. There are also about a dozen small advertising agencies that do specialize in arts and media accounts, and most that do are located in New York City and Los Angeles. If you are a person with marketing experience, are acquainted with a number of potential clients, have access to one or more imaginative graphic artists, and wish to go independent, setting up your own advertising agency to service this industry could be a viable way to earn a living; although the field is highly competitive.

ART DEALER

(See under "Art Galleries" in Chapter 5.)

ARTIST MANAGER

(See under "Artist Management" in Chapter 5.)

ARTISTS' REPRESENTATIVE OR AGENT

(See under "Talent Agents" in Chapter 5.)

ATTORNEY

A number of law firms and many individual attorneys specialize in one or more aspects of what is generally called entertainment law. The television networks and large film studios, of course, maintain legal departments with attorneys on staff to devise and approve contracts and agreements, oversee corporate legalities, represent the corporations in any litigations brought against them, and to initiate legal actions against others. Many of the busier theatrical producers, unions, guilds, and cable television companies also retain full-time attorneys. Because the arts and media industry depends so heavily upon literary, dramatic, musical, choreographic, and photographic properties, matters pertaining to copyright law are often of central concern, and a number of lawyers concentrate on this complex subject. Some attorneys have grown rich by providing their services to theatre and film producers in exchange for a percentage of the profits. Working closely as legal counsel to a producer from the beginning of a project provides a good way to become involved in entertainment law. Most legal professionals in this field have a genuine love for the arts, and many have made meaningful contributions to the artistic process by nurturing and protecting their artist clients, and by working with arts companies and organizations. It is also true that many top leadership jobs in the industry are held by people who have earned a law degree. This is not coincidence, but is due to the fact that sound legal training is a major asset in dealing with the growing complexities not only in the arts and media industry but in most others as well.

CASTING AGENT

(See under "Talent Agents" in Chapter 5.)

CONSULTANT

Anyone with specialized knowledge and skills may offer his or her services as an independent consultant—and thousands do! Fund raising, marketing, promotion, and finance are four specializations in high demand, especially by arts and media organizations in the nonprofit sector. If you have been an executive with several well-known arts organizations and have established a wide and well-respected reputation, becoming an independent consultant may be an attractive option. It also helps if you have spoken and continue to speak at arts and media conferences, gotten a book or two published, written articles for trade publications, and otherwise established yourself as an expert. Don't worry that such exposure will amount to giving away your hard-learned secrets for free. That kind of small-minded thinking has probably defeated more consultants than it has helped. Clients are impressed by credentials earned in the work place and also by a reputation that is known in the open forum.

Consultants have the option of working out of their own homes, although a lot of local travel and air travel are often necessary. Consultants must also enjoy selling their services, an activity that takes up at least half a consultant's time. It is a good idea to check out the competition before devising a fee schedule. Begin by taking a close look at your personal and business expenses—what is the minimum hourly, daily, and monthly income you must earn to cover these? This is the yardstick that will measure your profit or loss, your success or failure.

CONTRACTOR

(See Chapter 9.)

DISTRIBUTOR

Many film, television, and cable television corporations have distribution departments with staffs that lease their properties to a variety of outlets. But there are also numerous independent distributors; these are people who have cultivated business contacts with local, national, and foreign movie exhibitors, television stations, and cable system operators, to which the independent distributors lease the screening rights for films for which they are licensed to do so. Other distributors work in the video-cassette market and sell their products to cassette retailers. Most filmmakers prefer to have their products financed and distributed through a preproduction deal with a major studio. Their second choice is usually a preproduction deal with an independent distributor. But in many cases, a filmmaker must first form a production company and shoot the film, and only then hope to find a distributor who will market it. Distributors must be good sales people with a wide range of contacts in the industry and a keen sense of the media marketplace. It should be mentioned that film distribution is further removed from the artistic process than any other line of work discussed in this book.

GALLERY OWNER

(See also "Art Galleries" in Chapter 5.)

A gallery owner is most often an art enthusiast and collector who believes sufficiently in his or her own taste and perception of the art market to operate a gallery. Many are financially well off and, at least initially, do not have to depend upon their gallery profits to earn their living—which is wise. Of the thousands of galleries in the United States and Canada, many fold each year, and many more operate at a loss. Like producing plays or films, operating an art gallery is a highly speculative venture. A person entering this field for the first time should hire an experienced director or manager and also rely upon the services of marketing and promotion consultants with proven track records. If one buys an existing gallery, it may be wise to retain the director or original owner long enough to observe how the business functions.

Most galleries specialize in the works of particular artists or in a particular style or period of art, and develop a clientele of collectors and buyers for the works they exhibit. No gallery can be all things for all people; most owners feel lucky if they attract a few faithful buyers.

GENERAL MANAGER

(See Chapter 5.)

IMPRESARIO OR ENTREPRENEUR OR FINANCIER

Impresario is a rather archaic term that refers to a person with great entrepreneurial ability who produces or presents and promotes artistic ventures, usually on a large or spectacular scale. Florenz Ziegfeld,

Sol Hurok, Billy Rose, and Mike Todd were all well-known impresarios—but, unfortunately, they are all dead. The services that they once provided are now supplied by corporate executives or by independent producers, who usually gamble with other people's money rather than with their own. Whatever the source of the capital, however, an impresario or an entrepreneur is responsible for providing it and is therefore the financier.

LANDLORD

Film studios, Broadway theatre owners, and movie-theatre chains are landlords, as are the trustees for museums, public parks, zoos, libraries, film archives, nonprofit theatre facilities, and performing arts centers. Most such landlords have an artistic as well as financial interest in their real estate, which is fortunate for the industry when the market goes through a slump. But a considerable portion of business in the arts and media industry is conducted in space that is rented from landlords who have no special interest in its well-being, and this can be unfortunate.

The private ownership of an arts facility is a special kind of trusteeship, because such facilities are comparatively rare and often highly valued by the communities they serve. Few people mourn the demolition or conversion of a local restaurant, gas station, or abandoned factory. But when the wrecking ball threatens the local theatre—even a movie theatre—a public outcry is likely. Of course the landlords of such facilities hope to make profits and are entitled to do so. The trouble is that many are inexperienced or uninterested in the arts and unwilling or incapable of hiring managers or finding tenants who can successfully operate the facility.

People with the capital and ambition to become involved in the commercial theatre sometimes buy a stock theatre, a dinner theatre, or even a few Broadway theatres. This provides instant entry into the industry, and with the right management is a sensible beginning. Capital is all that it takes to become a landlord of a commercial arts facility. The owner may then personally operate the facility or do so in absentia.

PACKAGER

Anyone who chooses performance material and brings performers together with a director is a packager. The difference between a packager and a producer is that the former does not supply the capital for the project at least not beyond his or her basic office expenses and operating costs. Rather, the packager is paid by the buyer(s), who must absorb all rehearsal and preproduction expenses, royalties, salaries, travel, and other costs. The exception to this is when a production is sold as a unit package, in which case the packager meets all expenses and the buyer writes a single check to cover these, and also to pay the packager's fee or commission. But this payment is made up front, or prior to the first performance of the production, so the packager's financial outlay is again minimized.

The most common types of packaged shows in the performing arts disciplines include bus-and-truck tours of popular plays and musicals that the packager sells to presenting organizations a few performances to each; and shows that are sold for one- and two-week engagements at winter and summer stock theatres and dinner theatres. Or the packager may put together a Vegas-style nightclub show, an industrial show, a television movie or miniseries, or a commercial. In any case, the packager must have all the qualities of a producer as well as contacts with potential buyers in the appropriate industry markets.

PERSONAL MANAGER

Highly successful artists may employ a full-time personal manager instead of or in addition to an agent or an artists' management firm. A personal manager usually attends to the artist's finances, investments, travel, appointments, living accommodations, and in some cases legal affairs. Payment may be in the form of a salary or a percentage of the artist's earnings, or a combination of both. It is not unusual for a personal manager also to be the artist's spouse or close friend, although such a dual relationship requires extraordinary qualities in both parties if it is to endure.

PRESENTER OR BOOKING AGENT

An independent presenter or booking agent is a person who engages attractions—be they theatrical productions, concerts, nightclub acts, or films—on behalf of some type of presenting organization. This is usually done in exchange for a percentage of the box-office net or gross, though there may also be the guarantee of a fee or commission to cover the agent's operating costs. Booking agents may be used by absentee landlords of performance facilities, or they may work in conjunction with community groups and arts societies whose purpose is to sponsor visits by performing artists or companies, or to run a lecture series, or to offer a film series. Booking agents must have experience and contacts with packagers, artists' representatives, producers, distributors, and others who are responsible for supplying the appropriate product. Some presenters—not to be confused with presenting organizations with an in-house manager who performs this function—have made significant contributions to the cultural health of the communities they serve. Most work alone or with a single secretary or assistant and have low overhead.

PRESS AGENT OR PUBLIC RELATIONS CONSULTANT

While the larger arts and media organizations have their own marketing, press, and promotion departments, as discussed in Chapter 7, there are thousands of small companies and one-time projects in the arts and media industry that require independent press agents and/or other promotion specialists. Some utilize large advertising agencies while others turn to one of the hundreds of independent press or public-relations agents. Most such agents specialize in a certain type of arts or media account: Broadway theatres, Off-Broadway theatres, nonprofit performing companies, nightclubs, film companies, or cable television companies. A good press agent or public relations person must have a working relationship with many members of the media, as well as with printers and graphic designers. He or she must have well-honed writing abilities and a knowledge of marketing, as well as imagination, inventiveness, and flair.

A public relations agency may merely write and distribute press releases and feature stories, or it may design and execute a whole marketing campaign, which also includes newspaper and media advertisements, direct-mail promotions, press parties and interviews, and special happenings.

PRODUCER

In the arts and media industry a producer is any person or organization that provides the capital to finance a given project or product. In the not-for-profit sector the producer is really the institution or organization itself, because *it* provides the financing. In the commercial sector, an individual may personally put up the needed money or, more often, may raise it from private and corporate investors, with whom the producer enters into a partnership and agrees to share any profits. An individual who produces in the commercial theatre is likely to have worked in the industry for a number of years; he or she perhaps belonged to the Association of Theatrical Press Agents and Managers, and has also worked as a general manager. The only essential requirement for being a producer is to have a property—meaning a script or something upon which a script could be based—and to own the option to produce it if it is not in the public domain. But experience in this profession is of prime importance, as is the ability to attract investors and the best artists for the project at hand. Only a small number of shows presented live or electronically ever show a profit, so producing is a highly speculative venture.

A majority of films now produced are the results of the efforts of independent producers, who function much like Broadway producers. Instead of leasing a theatre, however, film producers must sooner or later—preferably before the film is shot—enter into a contract with a distributor who will lease the showing-rights to exhibitors.

All producers must spend a great deal of time hunting for properties or ideas that they wish to produce, and for which they believe there is a sufficient audience to make the project worthwhile. The process entails seeing as many plays, films, and television shows as possible; reading countless original manuscripts, scenarios, and story treatments, even unpublished works in galley form; and keeping in contact with literary agents and publishers. Selecting what to produce is the most vital decision a producer makes, after which comes choosing the necessary artistic talent for the project. This process requires an in-depth familiarity with the professional work of hundreds of artists and other people in the industry, which means that producers must spend a lot of time as entertainment consumers. (See also Chapter 5.)

THEATRE ARCHITECT OR ARCHITECTURAL CONSULTANT

All professional architects, including those who design or redesign performance facilities, must be licensed by the American Institute of Architects. Theatre architecture is a small field and also an interesting and highly specialized one, because a theatre architect must have a general understanding of the needs of artists and audiences in terms of using a facility. The architect usually works closely with a variety of consultants, including specialists in acoustics, stage systems and equipment. The most satisfactory performance facilities are usually built according to the needs of an existing performing arts company. Specifications are developed through consultations involving the architect, management, and the artistic directors. Unfortunately, however, many theatres and performing arts centers are commissioned by civic organizations, universities, or other groups before a performing company is established. In this event, there may be no notion of how the facility is going to be used. The result can be a building that tries to satisfy a variety of potential users but ends up satisfying none.

Some degree-holding licensed architects have become scenic designers and vice versa; these two fields are complementary and, when the requisite skills are combined, offer a wide range of possible design projects and consulting opportunities.

CONCLUSION

JOBS IN THE NINETIES

In the preceding chapters we have described the arts and media industry and the wide variety of managerial and administrative positions that are necessary to guide and support it. We also suggested various ways to plan your career and get the specialized training you need, and we discussed how to conduct a successful job search. But planning a career requires not only that you look at your strengths and weaknesses; you also must understand how the industry is changing.

While nobody has yet discovered a foolproof method for predicting the future, it is possible to derive some reliable long-range projections from a careful examination of current trends and key developments. We would like to conclude by looking back at the arts and media in the 1980s and speculating on how the management of this field and its job market are likely to evolve in the nineties.

TREND-SETTING INDICATORS

The latter part of the eighties was a time of tremendous economic, social, governmental and technological change. Through a series of major corporate takeovers, in a climate of growing government debt and deregulation, the American business environment was completely restructured. Social patterns were transformed by the rise of the two-income household and the one-parent family; by the growing dominance of new classes of the population, as the baby boomers aged and certain minority groups became the majority in many U.S. cities; by widespread computerization; and by increasingly diverse and intense competition among alternate leisure-time activities. In the years ahead, those managers and entrepreneurs best able to adapt to these changes, or at least to keep pace with them, will be the most likely to succeed.

Government

The 1980s were the Reagan years and, oddly enough, since both the President and his wife had been film actors, the Reagan administration was not supportive of the arts. It began with an attempt to dismantle the National Endowment for the Arts; fortunately, it succeeded only in trimming the Arts Endowment's budget and in holding increases at or below the rate of inflation. The administration also diminished the funding role of the Corporation for Public Broadcasting (CPB) and other government funding agencies, including the Institute for Museum Services (IMS). Finally, it reduced the pass-through funds to states and community arts agencies and cut many other social service programs, such as the CETA (Comprehensive Employment Training Act) and HUD (Housing and Urban Development) grants, that had been used to support the arts throughout the seventies.

"Reaganomics" sought to reduce government spending and to encourage the private sector to make up the difference. This policy of privatization also included deregulation and, among similar actions in other fields, the federal government relaxed many of its restrictions on the broadcast media, which had the effect of loosening the oligarchic hold of the three major networks. During the late eighties, NBC and ABC became part of larger, non-media corporations, thus joining the three major film studios controlled by larger corporations: Warner Brothers, owned by Warner Communications, and now Time Warner; Paramount Pictures, a division of Gulf and Western, recently renamed Paramount, and Columbia Pictures, bought during the seventies by the Coca-Cola Company. Weakened regulations also radically changed the ownership of independent television stations and allowed the formation of gigantic communications conglomerates that owned cable and broadcast stations, newspapers, magazines, publishers and movie chains. And by no longer regulating the amount of advertising allowed on commercial television, the government encouraged an increase in the proportion of commercial to programming time. Even public broadcasting experimented with forms of commercials in order to cultivate new sources of revenue, and subtle plugs for consumer goods were incorporated into theatrical movies. Thus, in the eighties, privatization was accompanied by increased commercialization; this trend will continue in the nineties.

Ironically, at the same time that nonprofit organizations were hustling for new and expanded sources of income, the tax reform bill of 1986 reduced the incentives for individual and corporate giving to the arts. The bill had a particularly negative impact on the donation of art works to museums, by eliminating the significant tax benefits previously enjoyed by donors. In addition, the government began to question the income-generating activities of arts organizations, such as gift shop sales, parking, and rental fees; some of these activities were made taxable. Most chilling of all, perhaps, was a letter sent by the Internal Revenue Service in the summer of 1988 warning nonprofit organizations of the service's plans to enforce an old, previously ignored tax ruling stipulating that only the gift portion of a contribution is deductible and excluding costs incurred by the nonprofits for food, liquor, gifts, theatrical production and the like.

Arts councils at all levels of government, in reaction to tighter budgets and the federal policy of privatization, began to rely more heavily on matching grants and to demand more quantitative evidence—such as audience statistics and figures showing the generation of local revenues—that their grants were having a positive impact on other income sources. Increasingly, arts councils chose to fund proven, noncontroversial projects, and several state council and Endowment grants were rescinded or denied on the basis of artistic content—themes or depictions deemed indecent, pornographic or un-American.

As arts council budgets continue to shrink, fund-seekers for nonprofit organizations necessarily will become more aggressive. In fact, the more powerfully connected organizations will deal directly with local, state and federal legislators to secure funding. This could further weaken the role of arts councils.

The Economy, Business and the Arts

The late eighties were a time of unparalleled growth and dynamic change for American corporations. Fueled by low inflation and higher productivity, the Dow Jones averages reached historic highs, and corporate America began a spree of takeovers, borrowing, spending and production that had a major and direct impact on the arts and media industry.

The dominance of the television industry by the three major commercial networks, a given for decades, was diffused by mergers, takeovers and the proliferation of new delivery systems. Capital Cities bought ABC; General Electric bought NBC and its parent company, RCA (which GE proceeded to dismantle); and CBS was taken over from within by an executive with a financial rather than a broadcast background. New networks—both programming, like Arts and Entertainment, Bravo and ESPN, and broadcast, like Fox and TNT—were formed, and the overly optimistic initial promises of cable were mitigated by the failures of cable arts programming. If nothing else, the media became a more complicated, more competitive marketplace with room for entrepreneurs and risk takers, although with considerably higher stakes than in the past.

The accelerated economic growth of the eighties also had an impact on museums and art galleries. One need only look at the auctions of impressionist and modern art masterpieces to understand the magnitude of change. With paintings by Van Gogh selling at over $50 million, the ability of museums to acquire the best works became severely limited. It appears that corporate and super-rich collectors—mostly from outside the United States—will continue to capture some of the most important acquisitions.

Escalating labor costs put tremendous financial strains on many nonprofit performing arts institutions, and a series of bankruptcies and failures resulted. The Kansas City Orchestra, the Oakland Symphony Orchestra, the Nashville Symphony and the Oklahoma Symphony— each an established part of its city's cultural fabric—filed for protection from creditors and folded during the latter part of the eighties, as did the Alaska Rep and numerous off-Broadway theaters, dance troupes and regional ballet companies. Many others suspended their seasons, cut back on the number of performances or steered clear of the experimental and controversial. While no one reason can be cited for this trend, mounting labor costs and increased tensions between labor (the artists) and board/management teams were leading factors.

The economics of commercial films escalated to unheard-of levels. By 1988, the average Hollywood film cost $20.1 million to produce and $6.6 million to promote. This encouraged the consolidation of the industry into a small group of high rollers able to take chances on big-budget, potentially big-box-office projects. It also brought to prominence a type of bottom-line producer who held tight reins on all the nonartistic aspects of filmmaking.

"Blockbuster" multimillion-dollar international touring exhibitions and Broadway musicals made the news and the profits during the eighties, and major institutions and commercial producers will continue to exert control over these venues in the nineties. They also will provide the most lucrative career opportunities.

Entertainment-as-product (everything from films and rock stars to ballet companies and jazz ensembles) is now one of America's leading exports and growing imports. This has not escaped the notice of the corporate community, which will continue to exploit the arts and entertainment field in a variety of ways. The arts management professional who is open to such possibilities, adept at negotiating, able to grapple with the complexities of labor issues, and sophisticated in finance will be rewarded during the nineties.

Philanthropy

Corporations in the late eighties began to develop a new rationale for *funding*, as opposed to *giving*. This resulted partly from the changing tax laws, partly from an increasingly faceless and rapidly shifting corporate ownership and management, and partly from the profit goals of marketing strategies toward profit-making. A major corporate foundation, for instance, began to require arts groups to negotiate with local or regional managers, who were given the power to determine whether a project was worthy of funding before the proposal could be advanced to the foundation. Such policies, of course, are based on the marketing potential of a project, not solely on its artistic merit. Corporate marketing has also led to some interesting partnerships. For example, a major ballet company funded by AT&T was scheduled to perform in a series sponsored locally by a presenter whose underwriting came from Northern Telecom, a direct competitor of AT&T.

Philip Morris and R.J.R. Nabisco bought credibility and sought to counterbalance their negative public images as tobacco sellers by conspicuously underwriting classical and popular arts activities, such as the Kool Jazz Festival and the Next Wave Festival at the Brooklyn Academy of Music. In this way, corporate giving offices were superseded by corporate marketing/advertising offices. Funds provided through these channels have fewer tax restrictions and can have a more direct impact on corporate profits and yet, do not come under the scrutiny of shareholders.

Private foundations found it more and more difficult to justify their arts contributions in the late eighties as greater demands were placed on them by decreases in government funding for education, health and social service programs. Until major progress is made in solving such monumental problems as AIDS, drug abuse, homelessness and the failure of public education, foundations will be hard-pressed to justify giving their limited resources to the arts.

Contributions by individuals constitute the greatest proportion of unearned income for nonprofit arts and media groups, but the revenue potential from this source does not look promising for the nineties. Tax reform legislation has eroded the tax advantages of private giving along with the write-off privileges previously enjoyed by wealthy backers of Broadway shows and other commercial entertainment ventures. Long gone are the days when an independent producer could bankroll an entire Broadway musical or a wealthy patron of a major opera company could hand the general manager a check to underwrite a whole production. During the nineties, only major corporations will be able to afford such checks, and these will not be forthcoming unless the arts company performs in communities where the corporate sponsor conducts business.

Society

The United States is becoming increasingly pluralistic. With changing demographics, the nineties will bring a noticeable shift in the traditional power structure of American society and politics. For example, in the state of California the largest population group will be Hispanic, and the typical resident of Los Angeles will be a twenty-six-year-old male.

It can be expected that the market for such established "mainstream" art forms as opera, theater and classical music will continue to decline. But this should be counterbalanced by a growth in the artistic ferment and achievements of black, Hispanic and Asian artists, companies and institutions, as segments of the population once regarded as "emerging" or "minority" move closer to the political, economic and cultural mainstream. This clearly points to a need for well-trained arts managers from our major ethnic groups. But such training is not being provided. Indeed, the failure of our educational system at the primary and secondary levels denies the vast majority of American blacks and Hispanics the possibility of higher education. Yet, minority artists and entrepreneurs are finding their own doorways to the successful financing, production and marketing of their projects, and this trend will accelerate in the nineties.

Technology

Technological innovations will continue to revolutionize every aspect of our lives, including the way we produce, manage and consume arts and leisure-time products. In the media, the major new development will be the introduction of high definition television (HDTV), which will create a booming market for new hardware and new programming, although much of the production in both areas will take place outside the United States. Advancing video cassette and related technologies will continue to cause labor problems, with actors and other creative personnel in the electronic media pressing for a redefinition of royalty rights, a share in the control of distribution and use, and the protection of film products from such practices as piracy and colorization.

By the early nineties, high-resolution image data bases will begin to transform the visual arts. Just as the printing press effected the transition from the oral to the written preservation and transference of knowledge, so image processing will usher in a new era of visual communication that will go considerably beyond the word processing capability of today's computers. Even now, the Guggenheim Museum, among others, is busy putting its entire collection into computer memories. In the foreseeable future all museums of all types will be on line with at least part of their collections. The potential that this offers for cataloguing, publishing, collecting, presenting and understanding visual information is staggering. It soon will change the manner in which museums are used, and eventually will have an incalculable impact on the entire visual arts world.

Advances such as those mentioned above will fuel the ongoing debate over the nature of art, not to mention how the arts should be managed: Are the sounds created by a synthesizer or emulator as valid artistically as those created by live musicians? Is the art created by an image processor really art? Do high-resolution reproductions of an art work offer the same visual experience as the original? Does society have a moral obligation not to tamper with original art works, such as paintings and films? What kind of compensation should artists receive for the computer storage and use of their works, and how can this be administered? What are the implications for the distribution and use of art works in outer space?

ARTS AND MEDIA MANAGEMENT IN THE NINETIES: A FORMULA FOR SUCCESS

Given all the changes that will occur in the arts and media industry during the nineties—in both the commercial and nonprofit sectors—its managers must possess a variety of special skills, qualifications and commitments. While earlier chapters describe the personal assets and training likely to lead to successful management careers, our focus now shifts to the three concerns we believe will be most dominant in the arts management field itself: professionalization, commercialization and internationalization. To a great extent, the survival if not the profitability of every arts and media company in the next decade will depend on the manager's understanding of and ability to manipulate these forces.

Professionalization

As the older generation of self-taught managers and executive directors is replaced by recent recipients of graduate degrees and by executives with established track records in the corporate world, the field of arts management will become more widely recognized as a respected profession, and this in turn will bring the arts and artists greater acceptance in mainstream American life. Even now, to enter and advance in the arts management profession, an undergraduate college degree and specialized training are necessary credentials. As the profession becomes more complex—and this is happening with incredible speed—the credentials required to sustain a career in this field will continue to multiply. In fact, the limited pool of qualified—one might even say talented—executives for top positions in the arts and media industry virtually guarantees an abundance of job openings for the foreseeable future. At the end of the eighties, numerous senior-level positions remained unfilled for long periods because appropriate candidates could not be found. Eight major ballet companies simultaneously were looking for executive directors; ten major art museums were without directors for substantial periods; and during the same period, ten symphony orchestras were searching for managers.

The need for highly qualified managers at leading arts and media companies will continue, and this will contribute to the professionalization of arts management. Wages and other types of compensation in both commercial and nonprofit companies will increase, making these positions more attractive and, eventually, more competitive. By the late eighties, many nonprofits already were paying in six figures for their top executive and from $70,000 to $90,000 for senior managers; bonus and commission payments are now part of the compensation package for nonprofit arts managers—a custom brought over from the private sector. Such payments are based on dollar amounts related to the number of subscriptions or memberships, group sales, and grants or contributions brought in. This practice is not without inherent dangers. Nonprofit managers could be tempted, indeed motivated, to endorse programming decisions merely on the basis of grant availability or audience surveys, in much the same way that media programming decisions too often are based on ratings points.

The wave of bankruptcies among nonprofit performing and visual arts organizations, as well as cable and broadcast companies, that occurred in the eighties points to a need for managers who have the knowledge and skills to avoid financial catastrophe. It also underscores the need for more sophisticated human resource management, including labor and employee relations and contract negotiations.

Lay boards often attempt to professionalize arts companies by recruiting corporate executives from the business world to serve as salaried presidents or general managers. Although this practice may diminish the artists' control over the artistic product, it is likely that the business school will continue to exert a powerful influence on the arts and media industry, especially within the larger institutions. One of the central tenets of the business school approach is that management is a science and that managers should not be guided only by the product they are managing—business is business, and the arts business is no exception. In the eighties, a small invasion of corporate executives from the for-profit sector have taken the reigns of several major nonprofit arts companies, including the Metropolitan Opera, Pennsylvania Ballet, Lincoln Center, the Hudson River Museum, the Columbus Symphony Orchestra, the Alabama Symphony and the Kennedy Center. During the same period, a number of ballet companies hired retiring corporate executives as salaried presidents, with almost no long-term success.

It is reasonable to speculate that in the nineties more and more arts managers will attain full board membership, higher salaries and greater respect in the business community. They also will share or dominate leadership in relation to artistic or curatorial directors, although the division of authority will continue to be debated. Trustees frequently will become salaried executive directors of nonprofit cultural institutions, blurring the distinction between management and board. Career crossovers between commercial and nonprofit arts and media companies will become commonplace. Communication skills will be valued even more than they are today. And the demands placed on arts and media management professionals will intensify, as will managers' responsibilities to staff, creative personnel, the community and, most important, the art.

Commercialization

By the end of the eighties, declines in unearned revenue for nonprofits and increases in costs and competition for commercial ventures already were promoting greater commercialization in both sectors, a trend that shows no signs of abating. This means that, in managers at all levels, entrepreneurial instincts and skills will be highly valued, along with abilities in marketing, finance, promotion and sales. There will be a growing emphasis on direct and telemarketing and on marketplace studies and focus groups. Classic marketing techniques will supplant the "Danny Newman" approach to selling tickets, and serious arts groups more and more often will turn to merchandising. Consider the following evidence of this trend in the eighties:

- The Joffrey Ballet offered a line of dance and leisure wear.
- Placido Domingo and John Denver recorded an album together.
- The Metropolitan Museum opened a gift shop outlet in a suburban mall.
- A Saturday-morning action cartoon was in reality a thirty-minute commercial for the characters in an animated feature distributed in theaters.
- Countless dolls, coloring books, board and video games, breakfast cereals and clothing lines based on characters in movies and TV shows went on sale in retail outlets nationwide.

And consider some of the ways in which serious arts organizations, as well as municipal governments, were capitalizing on their fixed assets and goodwill:

- New York's Museum of Modern Art permitted a luxury condominium to be built on top of its facility so that income earned from the project could fund museum expansion.
- It became commonplace for museums, arts centers, theaters and orchestras to rent out their facilities for such income-producing events as corporate parties, private functions, film locations, TV commercial production, graduations and performances by outside groups.
- A number of city governments opened film and television offices to encourage production in their municipalities and thus to increase local tax revenues.
- An increasing number of privately and governmentally sponsored building projects included mixed-use facilities in large developments aimed at revitalizing downtown communities, such as Toronto's HarborFront, Baltimore's Inner Harbor and New York's South Street Seaport.

- KUSC, a public radio station, produced music recordings for the listening services of commercial airlines, and WNYC in New York leased part of its television broadcast band to commercial companies.
- Caramoor Center for the Arts in Katonah, New York, created a managing director position responsible for generating income from such projects as tours, weddings and the licensing of objects and designs owned by the not-for-profit corporation.

In the 1990s the risks of financial failure on Broadway will continue to mount, thereby prolonging the era of mega-buck musicals; yet, it will be less expensive for foreign producers to test new shows in this country than in some foreign capitals. Commercial producers and theater landlords will continue to forge alliances with nonprofit companies for the purpose of developing new work with commercial potential. Such projects will further blur the perceived differences between nonprofit and commercial theater. Blockbuster exhibitions will continue to attract the greatest museum attendance. Classical music management and presentation will be dominated more and more by commercial agencies, by private agents and by artists' managers who control solo and ensemble fees and availability. And movie deals will become more complicated, involving theatrical releases, pay cable, video cassette rentals and sales, and the merchandising of product tie-ins.

Obviously, the trend toward commercialization does not favor the interests of experimental art; on the contrary, it encourages popularism. By the end of the century, changing times and values likely will result in a reaction against commercialization. But whatever the standards of excellence may be, it is certain that art and artistic by-products will be more widely and inexpensively available than ever before.

Internationalization: The Global Manager

Accessible air travel combined with extraordinary ground and satellite communications systems are fast turning the world into a global village. Information of all types—scientific, sociological, political and aesthetic—is so widely available that international transactions and projects are as easily accomplished as local arrangements. The 1990s will serve as a transitional decade in the humanity's evolution toward a largely interdependent world community that, combined with major shifts in national economies, will present this country with unaccustomed opportunities and frustrations.

During the early nineties, the European Community will become a powerful economic competitor, Hong Kong will revert to the People's Republic of China and that nation, together with the Soviet Union and Eastern Europe, will open enormous potential markets for the export of Western arts and entertainment. U.S. participation in foreign markets, however, will continue to be influenced by our trade imbalance, the national debt and the weakness of the dollar against the yen and the deutsche mark. Just as Sony purchased CBS Records and Bertsmaller AG bought RCA Records, foreign corporations will continue to take advantage of opportunities to buy American entertainment corporations at a discount. The weakened dollar will make it more difficult for this country to attract world-class artists and ensembles to our shores, but conversely, international touring for U.S. artists and ensembles will become more profitable. As a case in point, in 1984 it cost a Tokyo promoter $750,000 to bring an American dance company to Japan. In 1989 the same company was paid $1,250,000 for the same tour—but this was $125,000 less in yen because the dollar had fallen.

The growing internationalization of the arts and media industry will be manifest in a number of trends throughout the next decade, including the following:

- Multinational corporations will continue to use the arts to promote their images and products. A recent example is United Technologies' sponsorship of international tours by French museum exhibitions to enhance the company's reputation with the French socialist government.

- Arts organizations in the United States will continue to compete with foreign arts groups for corporate and individual support. Already, by the end of the eighties, London's Tate Gallery and Royal Academy of Art, along with the Louvre in Paris, had fundraising operations in this country.

- American cities will continue developing arts exchange programs to enhance their images internationally. The Atlanta Symphony, for example, has toured 350 performers to six cities in Europe, with funding from Atlanta-based corporations and local government.

- Foreign film productions will make major inroads into American markets, and many U.S. stars will work under foreign contractors and management.

These new realities call for arts management professionals who are prepared not only for local and national markets, economies, governments and communications networks but for international ones as well. Clearly, the nineties will usher in the age of the global arts manager: multi-lingual, well traveled, open-minded, sensitive to the arts and tuned into the possibilities of cross-cultural projects and exchanges.

TOWARD THE MILLENNIUM

Society is measured by its art—a truism that patrons of the arts have always recognized. Supporting artists is the best insurance against mortality. Among the patrons immortalized by the artists they supported are pharaohs, emperors, kings, queens and a long list of other royals who took their noble obligations seriously; popes, prelates, priests and sects that took their spiritual obligations seriously; industrialists, tycoons, heiresses and other wealthy capitalists who took their debt to humanity seriously; and, more recently, corporations that took their investors and consumers seriously and governments that took their voters seriously. The arts will survive without patronage, but they may not flourish. Humanity will survive without the arts, but it may not flourish. If humanity is to survive *and* flourish, the arts too must flourish, and this is possible only with patronage. Yet, as we approach the millennium, neither corporations nor governments—the leading arts patrons in the second half of the twentieth century—seem willing or able to support the arts fully, wealthy individuals are no longer capable of absorbing the rising costs, and even the largest and most solidly established religious and educational institutions are hard-pressed for funding. Given this situation, how will the arts be able to help humanity flourish in the next millennium?

As we have discussed, the managers of all types of companies and institutions in the arts and media industry are rapidly gaining respect, responsibility and power. Increasingly arts managers are dictating the terms: which artist will be contracted, what art will be created, how the art will be produced and distributed, who will consume it, how much it will cost and how long it will last. Increasingly, arts managers are controlling both the financial and the artistic resources. At this level of decision making, arts and media managers are fast becoming the primary impresarios and patrons of the future. They are the de Medicis, the Diaghilevs and the Huroks of the next century. Like the other patrons before them, the new manager-patrons did not ask for guardianship of the arts. This responsibility has been thrust upon them simply because there was nobody else around. Their success in managing it will depend upon the quality of their leadership, the degree of their enlightenment and the goals of their trusteeship.

At the same time that the dynamics of arts production and patronage are changing, technology has completely refashioned the dynamics of communications, opening limitless channels and creating sophisticated networks that are helping to shape political ideologies, national economies and cultural developments. In fact, so global and pervasive is its influence that technology itself might be called the new superpower.

While science and art are sometimes viewed as opposite disciplines, they share a common goal: to reveal the truth. It should not be surprising, then, if scientific technology opens the floodgates of artistic creativity in the next millennium. Because both art and science require freedom for investigation and expression, because both are blind to differences of race, creed and nationality, and because both dedicate their efforts to a belief in tomorrow, there is every reason to believe that universally available communication technologies will engender democratization, uncensored access to information and improved understanding among nations. Given the potential of its partnership with the arts, this technology also could foster humanitarianism, by accessing the dreams and aspirations of people everywhere as inspiration for new visions of a better world.

There is every reason for the arts and media management industry to approach the millennium with optimism.

THE ARTS AND MEDIA MANAGEMENT CAREER KIT

THE ARTS AND MEDIA MANAGEMENT CAREER KIT

GRADUATE PROGRAMS IN ARTS ADMINISTRATION

While the following list is up to date as of publication, college programs in this field are still evolving in terms of their curricula requirements. While many programs exercise flexibility in regard to application deadlines, such dates are often inflexible when it comes to financial assistance deadlines. For further guidance in selecting the right program for you, see Chapter 2.

Some of the programs in this listing cover the arts management field as a whole, though most concentrate on the performing arts or have a particular emphasis on arts administration. We have not listed graduate programs in museum management because virtually all of these offer degrees in art history with a concentration or special option in management. Perhaps the best and most comprehensive guide for both graduate and undergraduate programs in museum studies is *Museum Studies International 1988,* which includes programs in the United States and abroad. Published jointly by the Office of Museum Programs of the Smithsonian Institution and the International Council of Museums, it is available from the Office of Museum Programs, Building of Arts and Industries, Room 2235, Smithsonian Institution, Washington, DC 20560. (Send $8.00 by check payable to Smithsonian Institution.)

Courses and degree programs related to broadcast management, film production, and media studies are too numerous to list here, but Chapter 2 provides the titles of the best references, which you can find in most libraries.

THE AMERICAN UNIVERSITY
Kreeger 201
Washington, DC 20016
202/885-3420

The Arts Management Program is part of the Department of Performing Arts, and focuses on specific problems affecting all the arts; such as public relations, fundraising, marketing, and audience development.

Degree Requirements: Forty-five (45) credits to earn the M.A. degree, including a thesis, internship (may be waived), and comprehensive examination. The program takes about two and one-half years to complete. Also, Master of Public Administration degree candidates may select Arts Management as their area of specialization.

Admission Requirements: Bachelor's degree from an accredited college or university, with a grade point average of 3.0 or better, calculated on the last 60 semester hours credit of course work completed, and two letters of recommendation. A personal interview is strongly recommended.

Application deadline: April 15 for the fall term; November 1 for the spring.

BROOKLYN COLLEGE OF THE CITY UNIVERSITY OF NEW YORK
Department of Theatre
Brooklyn, NY 11210
718/780-5989

The program is designed for persons with a background in dance, music, or theatre who wish to become professional managers or artistic directors in one of these areas. There is a strong emphasis on practical experience, requiring very many hours of fieldwork.

Degree Requirements: Forty-five (45) credits for the M.F.A. degree in Performing Arts Management, three practicum assignments (totalling 600 hours of field work), and a four-month professional residency with a performing arts organization, including a related thesis report. The program is four semesters long (two years).

Admission Requirements: Applicants must have an undergraduate degree with a grade point average of at least 3.0. Two letters of reference must accompany the application, and an interview is strongly recommended. No entrance examinations are required.

Application deadline: June 1.

CALIFORNIA STATE UNIVERSITY, DOMINGUEZ HILLS
1000 East Victoria Street
Carson, CA 90747
213/516-3636

The program in Arts Administration aims to develop a wide range of business capabilities and leadership skills and to address issues affecting arts organizations in contemporary society. Emerging cultural majorities and development and education of new arts audiences are a major focus of the program. Cultural pluralism is a dominant characteristic of the school.

Degree Requirements: Thirty-two (32) units plus 12 hours of undergraduate study in business and the arts for the M.A. degree in Arts Administration. A major research paper and residency also are required. Those students who are full-time administrators with arts organizations must write a thesis in lieu of a semester-long residency. All arts administration courses carry with them either a community service project or an internship.

Admission Requirements: Undergraduate degree with a 3.0 grade point average, and undergraduate study or employment in the arts. Two letters of recommendation are required, addressing the applicant's listening, speaking, and writing skills as well as leadership potential. Knowledge of more than one art form and work experience in management are highly desirable. Applicants submit essays addressing their career history and goals, and a paper or essay demonstrating critical thinking skills and writing strengths. An interview with the director, in person or by telephone, is also required.

Application deadline: Open.

CARNEGIE MELLON UNIVERSITY

The School of Urban and Public Affairs and College of Fine Arts
5000 Forbes Avenue
Pittsburgh, PA 15213-3890

The Arts Management program is designed for students interested in managerial positions at performing and visual arts organizations, and for managers and policy makers in local, state, and federal government agencies who deal with the performing and visual arts.

Degree Requirements: Two-year, full-time program leading to the Master of Arts Management degree. An internship is required during the summer between the first and second years of the program. A thesis or major paper is not required.

Admission Requirements: Undergraduate degree and a comprehensive knowledge of an art form. Three letters of recommendation, the GRE or GMAT test, and a 250-word essay are required along with the application.

Application deadline: March 15, to be considered for need or merit based financial aid awards. Applications submitted after March 15 are considered for financial aid as available.

CASE WESTERN RESERVE UNIVERSITY

Mandel Center for Nonprofit Organizations
Weatherhead School of Management, 450 Enterprise Hall
10900 Euclid Avenue
Cleveland, OH 44106-7235

The Graduate Program in Nonprofit Management is designed for managers and leaders in fine and performing arts, cultural, educational, human service, and other nonprofit organizations. The curriculum includes study in ethics, organizations and management, economics, nonprofit law, quantitative methods, finance, marketing, public relations, human resource management, group dynamics, strategic planning, systems and operations. The program is multi-disciplinary and utilizes faculty from the schools of management, applied social sciences, law, and the university at large. Classes are offered evenings, weekends, and in intensive formats. Substantial financial assistance is available to qualified students. Approximately 38 percent of the students are from arts and cultural organizations.

Degree Requirements: The Master of Nonprofit Organizations (MNO) degree requires forty-five (45) credits of graduate study. No thesis or internship is required.

Admission Requirements: An undergraduate degree from an accredited institution, official transcripts, a personal essay, two reference letters, GMAT scores, $25 application fee. Experience and/or familiarity with nonprofit or arts and cultural organizations and potential for executive-level leadership are considered. No previous academic work in business, management, or nonprofit sector studies is required for MNO admission.

Application deadline: MNO applications are reviewed monthly through June 30 for admission the following fall. However, initial admission and scholarship decisions are made in March and April so early application is encouraged. There are no mid-year admissions.

COLUMBIA COLLEGE
600 South Michigan Avenue
Chicago, IL 60605
312/663-1600 (Ext. 652)

The Arts, Entertainment, and Media Management program specializes in media management, the music business, performing arts and visual arts management, and computer management in the arts. Faculty and advisors are working artists, performers, and managers at leading arts, entertainment, or media organizations.

Degree Requirements: A two-year, 42 credit program leading to the M.A. degree. Both an internship and a thesis are required.

Admission Requirements: An undergraduate degree with a 30 grade point average. Applicants should have undergraduate course work in accounting and computer programming, or competence in these areas, prior to entering the program.

Application deadline: August 15 for the fall term; December 15 for the spring.

COLUMBIA UNIVERSITY/TEACHERS COLLEGE
Program in Arts Administration
Box 78
New York, NY 10027
212/678-3271, 3268

Columbia's Master of Arts degree in Teachers College provides the basic theoretical and practical preparation for careers in arts administration, arts education, or a composite of these two areas. The program represents an alliance of Teachers College, the Graduate School of Business, and the School of Law.

Degree Requirements: The MA degree requires the equivalent of two years of full-time study. Course requirements are sixty (60) points of credit, including a core curriculum in arts administration, arts law, business, and education.

Admission Requirements: A bachelor's degree from an accredited institution, at least three years of relevant experience, and a strong foundation in at least one aspect of the arts are required. A resume, description of career objectives, three recommendations, and the GRE exam must be submitted in addition to the application. An interview is required for all finalists.

Application deadline: March 15 for Preferred Decision; May 15 for late applicants.

DREXEL UNIVERSITY
Arts Administration Program
Department of Performing Arts
Philadelphia, PA 19104
215/895-2452 or 215/895-2453

The program prepares students for management positions in a wide range of arts organizations, including performing, visual, community, government, and service organizations; as well as arts divisions in foundations and corporations, and artists' representative organizations. It seeks to incorporate management skills, political and social policy, and technical writing and technologies in the arts.

Degree Requirements: Forty-five (45) credits, one and one-quarter years of full-time study, for the Master of Science degree. Both a thesis and an internship are required. The internship is done after completing all course work.

Admission Requirements: Bachelor's degree with a 3.0 grade point average for the last two years of undergraduate work, and a 3.0 grade point average for any graduate work. Applicants with lower than a 3.0 average, but not lower than 2.75, must have high scores on the GRE examination and very strong letters of recommendation. Applicants must have taken one course in financial accounting, one course in marketing, two courses in the history or literature of an art field, and two courses in practical or creative aspects of an art field.

Application deadline: September 23 for the fall term; December 6 for the winter; March 6 for the spring; and May 29 for the summer.

THE FLORIDA STATE UNIVERSITY
Institute of Science and Public Affairs
School of Visual Arts
126 MCH Carothers Building, B-171
Tallahassee, FL 32306-3014
904/644-5473

Arts Administration study at Florida State University is multi-disciplinary, incorporating the unique aspects of various arts disciplines with training in administration and management. Students enroll through the Departments of Art Education, Music Education, or the School of Theatre.

Degree Requirements: Thirty-six (36) semester hours of course work are required for the master's degree, either the M.S. in Art Education/Arts Administration, M.M.E. in Music Education/Arts Administration, or M.F.A. in Theatre Management. The master's degree can be completed in one year of full-time study. Nine hours in arts administration courses, nine hours of an internship, nine to eighteen hours course work in the base discipline, and three hours of electives in a second art discipline are required for each of the master's degrees. The school also offers the Ph.D. in Art Education/Arts Administration.

Admission Requirements: A baccalaureate degree with at least a B grade average as an upper level student. Individuals with a background in one of the arts may apply for the master's degree in any one of the arts disciplines. Students without an arts-related undergraduate degree may request evaluation for entrance into the program. Evaluation for admission to the program is available through the various departments offering the degree.

Application deadline: At least one month before the start of the term.

GOLDEN GATE UNIVERSITY
536 Mission Street
San Francisco, CA 94105
415/442-7851

The Graduate Program in Arts Administration takes a pragmatic approach, focusing on the arts organization manager's functions and responsibilities in the areas of finance, budgeting, fundraising, marketing, public relations, production management, personnel administration and law. The program is designed to accommodate working students, with most classes held during the evening.

Degree Requirements: The school offers three degrees in Arts Administration, the Master of Business Administration, Master of Arts, and the Certificate in Arts Administration. Course work requirements are 57 units for the M.B.A.; 48 units for the M.A., and 24 units for the Certificate. All students must write a final thesis. Internships are available through the program, but are not required.

Admission Requirements: A bachelor's degree from an accredited college or university with a grade point average of at least 2.5 is required for applicants to the M.B.A. or M.A. programs, as well as two years experience in an arts-related position. Also, applicants must be interviewed by the Program Director. Applicants to the Certificate program must submit a resume to the Program Director, detailing their educational background, business experience, and experience in the performing or visual arts.

Application deadline: None.

INDIANA UNIVERSITY
Graduate School
Business Building, Room 660F
Bloomington, IN 47405
812/885-0282

The Arts Administration program is designed to train managers for arts commissions and councils, arts centers, museums and galleries, and the performing arts. The program is directed by an interdepartmental committee drawn from the School of Business, School of Music, Department of Theatre and Drama, Department of Fine Arts, William Hammond Mathers Museum and the Indiana University Art Museum.

Degree Requirements: A minimum of 39 hours of course work (43 with prerequisites) in Music, Theatre and Drama, Fine Arts, Business, and Arts Administration for the Master of Arts degree. A full-time internship for four to twelve months in length is required, along with an extensive evaluation report.

Admission Requirements: Undergraduate degree in music, visual arts, theatre and drama, dance, economics, or business administration. Candidates admitted to the program have an average of 3.5 grade point and 600-675 scores on each section of the GRE, verbal and quantitative.

Application deadline: February 15.

LESLEY COLLEGE GRADUATE SCHOOL
Management Division
29 Everett Street
Cambridge, MA 02138
617/349-8355

The Arts Administration Program emphasizes the role of the administrator as manager and creative problem solver whose objective is to increase broad public and private participation in the arts. Most students have strong backgrounds in studio or performing arts, art history, and other arts-related fields.

Degree Requirements: Thirty-eight (38) credits to earn the Master of Science in Management degree, including an internship. Average time to complete the program is about two and one-half years.

Admission Requirements: A bachelor's degree from a regionally accredited college. (In some cases the bachelor's degree can be waived.) In addition to academic credentials, significant consideration is given to the applicant's evidence of leadership, organizational experience, background in the area of specialization, and career objectives. A personal interview with a faculty member of the Management Division is required following submission of the application. Students are admitted in both the fall and spring semesters.

Application deadline: Applications are accepted on a rolling basis, and applicants are encouraged to apply as early as possible.

NEW YORK UNIVERSITY

School of Education, Health, Nursing, and Arts Professions
Department of Organizational and Administrative Studies
300 East Building, Washington Square
New York, NY 10003
212/998-5505

The Performing Arts Administration program aims to train managers of the highest caliber to direct performing arts institutions in the areas of general management, marketing, development, programming, planning, board and volunteer development, and organizational goal formation. Program advisors counsel students in their academic and internship experiences in order to make a smooth transition from school to active service in the arts.

Degree Requirements: Fifty-four (54) credits are required for the M.A. in Arts Administration, including 12 credits of internship. A major paper is required as part of the cultural policy seminar.

Admission Requirements: A bachelor's degree from an accredited college or university with a minimum 2.5 grade point average. In addition, applicants must have a background in one or more areas of the arts and prior experience with a cultural organization. The program demands significant individual initiative and judgment, so therefore a degree of maturity is expected in those accepted to the program.

Application deadline: Rolling admissions: applicants are encouraged to apply as early as possible.

NEW YORK UNIVERSITY

School of Education, Health, Nursing, and Arts Professions
Department of Art and Arts Professions
34 Stuyvesant Street, Barney Building, 3rd Floor
New York, NY 10003
212/998-5700

The Visual Arts Administration Program focuses on museums, other nonprofit visual arts organizations, galleries, and other entrepreneurial profit-making activities. Its goal is to train managers who are responsive to the contemporary art world but understand the ethical responsibilities of caring for and interpreting material culture.

Degree Requirements: Fifty-four (54) points are required to earn the M.A. degree in Arts Administration. Courses are offered on a rotating basis so part-time students can easily finish the program in three years. A thesis is expected in the form of the program's "culminating experience." Four internships are required, each equaling 3 credits or 135 hours of work.

Admission Requirements: Admission is limited to no more than fifteen students each semester. Applicants often have three years of experience in the visual arts as an employee or a volunteer. A background in art history is desirable. The minimum grade point average is 2.5, as established by the university. Students must be highly motivated and self-directed in shaping their curriculum and participating in school and outside activities.

Application deadline: January for fall admission; August for spring admission.

SANGAMON STATE UNIVERSITY
Springfield, IL 62794-9243
217/786-6535

The Community Arts Management (CAM) Program imparts not only knowledge of general management and planning skills, but also skills and knowledge that pertain specifically to the arts. The program focuses on the management of multi-arts organizations, such as community and state arts agencies, arts centers and service organizations. However, many graduates have entered careers in orchestra, theatre, museum and dance company management.

Degree Requirements: Fifty (50) hours to earn the M.A. degree. Every graduate degree candidate must complete a Master's project demonstrating mastery of some area within the major field of study. An internship is required, working eight hours per week. Field experience, working full-time at an arts organization, or additional part-time internships are required in the final semester.

Admission Requirements: Sangamon State University has an open admissions policy at the graduate level and will accept applicants who document completion of an undergraduate degree. Admission to the CAM program is based upon experience in the field, academic achievement, leadership qualities and communication ability. Applicants must submit transcripts, an autobiography, statement of career intent, a resume and three letters of recommendation. Graduate entrance examinations are not required, and there is no established minimum grade point average.

Application deadline: None, but application by March 1 for the fall semester assures best consideration.

SOUTHERN METHODIST UNIVERSITY
Meadows School of the Arts
Dallas, TX 75275-0356
214/692-3425

The primary objective of the program in arts administration is to provide formal educational experiences which will include the necessary depth and breadth in the arts and in business to produce persons highly qualified for entry into the field of arts administration. The 24-month program offers a dual degree in a Master of Arts in Arts Administration and a Master of Business Administration.

Degree Requirements: Seventy-five (75) credits are required for the M.A./M.B.A. degree. Part-time practicums place students in a variety of arts settings and responsibilities during the first five semesters. During the final semester, interns are placed with major arts organizations in Dallas and nationally for 12 weeks of full-time work.

Admission Requirements: A maximum of ten students are accepted into the program each year. Candidates must have a baccalaureate degree in an arts field with a minimum cumulative grade point average of 3.0. Applicants must have a satisfactory score on the GMAT, submit a resume of experience, and have an interview with the program director.

Application deadline: February 1.

STATE UNIVERSITY OF NEW YORK AT BINGHAMTON
School of Management
Binghamton, NY 13902-6000
607/777-2630

The primary goal of the M.B.A. in the Arts Program is to graduate students who are fully prepared for managerial and administrative challenges within the arts, and who also have the vision, sensitivity, and humor to be effective in influencing future policy regarding the appropriate role of the arts in society.

Degree Requirements: The program requires completion of 64 credit hours with a 3.0 grade point average for the M.B.A. degree in Arts Administration. All students must complete a supervised internship lasting approximately sixteen weeks. Following the internship, an analysis of the experience must be written.

Admission Requirements: Prospective students are urged to communicate their interest in the program to the Director's office before submitting a formal application. An undergraduate degree is required, including courses in calculus and computer programming. All students must take the GMAT examination; foreign students must also take the TOEFL. A personal interview is required except in cases of extreme hardship.

Application deadline: March 15.

TEXAS TECH UNIVERSITY
The Graduate School
P.O. Box 4460
Lubbock, TX 79409
806/742-2781

The Fine Arts program takes an interdisciplinary approach to the arts. Its aim is to produce graduates who are able to provide leadership in the arts, well trained in their specific field and knowledgeable in the arts in general. Not all students specialize in arts administration but the emphasis is available in each of the Fine Arts majors. The program encourages work in business administration or public administration. Individual programs are tailored to meet the specific interests and strengths of each student.

Degree Requirements: Forty-nine (49) semester hours work beyond the master's degree, excluding the dissertation, for the Ph.D. degree in Fine Arts (Arts Administration Specialty). Nineteen (19) hours are required in the interdisciplinary core and thirty (30) hours in the major. Carefully selected and supervised internships are arranged for students pursuing the administration emphasis. Internships are at least six months long. A doctoral dissertation is required.

Admission Requirements: Applicants must have a master's degree in an arts field, a good academic record, and scores for the GRE. They also must be recommended by the major department, and approved by the Fine Arts Doctoral Committee and the graduate dean.

Application deadline: Six months before proposed entry to the program.

THE UNIVERSITY OF AKRON
Department of Theatre Arts
The College of Fine and Applied Arts
Akron, OH 44325-1005
216/972-6470

The Arts Management Program is an interdisciplinary offering in the College of Fine and Applied Arts. It emphasizes preparing the student to deal with the complexities of policy, as well as with the intricacies of working in the field. The program's primary concern is the changing dimensions of the professional nonprofit arts field.

Degree Requirements: A minimum of forty-two (42) hours, including a thesis of original research, is required for the M.A. degree. All students serve a professional arts internship, usually between the first and second years of study, which is a critical component of the student's professional development. After the internship, remaining course work and practical applications are selected to strengthen the potential for success in the student's chosen professional area.

Admission Requirements: A baccalaureate degree, preferably with a concentration in the arts. Most successful students have worked for some arts organization after earning an undergraduate degree. Practical work experience is considered to enhance the student's commitment to graduate training, which is critical to academic and professional success. The minimum grade point average for admission is 2.75, and the GRE examination is not required.

Application deadline: None, but applicants seeking graduate assistantships must apply no later than April 1.

UNIVERSITY OF ALABAMA
Department of Theatre and Dance
P.O. Box 870239
Tuscaloosa, AL 35487-0239
(205) 348-5283

The University of Alabama and the Alabama Shakespeare Festival offer a two calendar year program in Theatre Management/Administration. The first year is spent on campus taking academic courses, followed by fifteen months of an intensive academic and practicum-oriented learning experience on location in Montgomery at the Alabama Shakespeare Festival.

Degree Requirements: Sixty (60) semester hours are required for the Master of

Fine Arts degree. A residence session at the Alabama Shakespeare Festival is required, giving students experience in marketing, development, business and general management, and facility operations. A thesis is not required.

Admission Requirements: Applicants must meet the admissions criteria established by the University of Alabama Graduate School. Candidates must have successfully completed a baccalaureate degree in an arts field, scored a combination of 1500 on the 3-part GRE or a 50 on the GMAT, and submit three letters of recommendation along with the application. A maximum of four students are admitted each fall.

Application deadline: March 15 for fall admission.

UNIVERSITY OF CALIFORNIA, LOS ANGELES
Anderson Graduate School of Management
405 Hilgard Avenue, Room 5356
Los Angeles, CA 90024-1481
213/206-4052

The Arts Management Program prepares individuals for major managerial roles in private and public nonprofit arts organizations, including arts councils, dance companies, museums, opera companies, public radio and television stations, symphony orchestras and theatres. The UCLA program is one of the few offering the rigorous training of the MBA program, complemented by courses specific to arts management interests.

Degree Requirements: Twenty (20) courses are required for the M.B.A., Management in the Arts degree. A six-month residency in an arts organization is required following the first year of course work. A project which examines a strategic issue for the student's residency organization satisfies the comprehensive exam requirement for the MBA.

Admission Requirements: Admission is based on the applicant's undergraduate academic record, GMAT score, and evidence of a strong commitment to the arts, usually demonstrated by full-time work experience in the arts. Ten to fifteen students are admitted each year, only for the fall semester. Prior courses in business are not required, but students must have a working knowledge of algebra and differential calculus before starting MBA course work. Applicants are encouraged to visit the campus and to talk to people involved with the program.

Application deadline: March 15.

UNIVERSITY OF CINCINNATI
Arts Administration Program
College-Conservatory of Music, M.L. 003
Cincinnati, OH 45221-0003
513/556-4383

The program is designed to meet multipurpose needs in the management of the performing and visual arts. The school is located in one of the top performing arts schools in the country, and has strong ties to a superior visual arts school and to a solid MBA program in the University of Cincinnati's School of Business.

A joint program leading to the degrees of Master of Business Administration (MBA) and Master of Arts in Arts Administraton was recently developed. Students admitted to the joint program may earn both degrees in 3 years of full-time study. Candidates must meet the admissions criteria and be separately accepted by each.

Degree Requirements: A two-year, full-time program combining academic training with practical experience. Two internships, for a total of three academic quarters, and a research project and paper are required. The school is committed to developing the full management potential of the individual student through directed studies (tutorials), where the student's progress in the program, problems, and planning for internship and future career are addressed.

Admission Requirements: An undergraduate degree with a grade point average of at least 3.0, although probationary acceptance at somewhat lower levels is possible in special cases. The GMAT is mandatory for the joint program; the GMAT is required for the Arts Administration program, but if the GRE has already been taken, it may be used as a substitute. An essay explaining the applicant's reasons for seeking admission and professional goals, three letters of recommendation, and a personal interview with the program director also are required.

Application deadline: The last day in February.

UNIVERSITY OF MARYLAND
Department of Theatre
College Park, MD 20742-1215
301/405-6676

The Master in Fine Arts in Theatre is a multi-disciplinary degree requiring both formal course work and practical experience in the management of academic, nonprofit, and commercial theatres.

Degree Requirements: The program is 60 credit hours of study for the M.F.A. Degree in Theatre, normally requiring three years to complete. The student's undergraduate and graduate course work, and professional experience taken together will provide for competencies in the three areas of business, journalism, and theatre. Internships are required, usually earning 12 academic credits. Each student also must complete a thesis providing documentation and analysis of all tutorial and internship projects.

Admission Requirements: Applications are evaluated based on the quality of the student's previous academic work (must have an undergraduate degree), letters of recommendation, scores on the GRE or similar test, statement of career objectives, and a portfolio including a resume and samples of previous work.

Application deadline: March 1.

UNIVERSITY OF NEW ORLEANS
College of Liberal Arts
Lakefront
New Orleans, LA 70148
504/286-6574

The degree prepares students to serve as administrators and managers in all types of arts institutions, including galleries, theatres, performing arts centers, community arts centers and comparable institutions for public education. The program is interdisciplinary, involving the departments of Drama and Communications, Economics and Finance, Fine Arts, Management and Marketing, and Music. It is built on graduate courses offered by these departments and on specialized courses in Arts Administration.

Degree Requirements: A minimum of 36 credits (18 credits of foundation courses are required before or after beginning the program) for the M.A. degree in Arts Administration. Successful performance on a comprehensive examination is required before the student enrolls in the required Internship in Arts Administration. Each student writes a report on the internship based on management concepts or on the resolution of a management problem posed during the internship.

Admission Requirements: Students must apply to both the Graduate School of the University of New Orleans and the Master of Arts in Arts Administration program. An applicant must have a bachelor's degree from an accredited college or university, a combined score of 1000 on the GRE or minimum of 400 on the GMAT, and a grade point average of 2.5 for undergraduate work and 3.0 for post-graduate work.

Application deadline: One week before registration. Deadlines for graduate assistantships are April 1 and November 1 for the fall and spring semesters.

UNIVERSITY OF WISCONSIN-MADISON
Graduate School of Business
1155 Observatory Drive
Madison, WI 53706
608/263-4161

The Center for Arts Administration was established at the Graduate School of Business to meet the need for trained administrators in visual arts, performing arts, arts service, philanthropic, and public broadcasting organizations. A special feature of the program is that the School of Business offers other programs and curricula in the not-for-profit sector, giving students in the Arts Administration program exposure to both disciplines of profit and not-for-profit management. The Center also conducts and distributes research, in which students have the opportunity to participate. They examine issues and problems in arts administration and publish the results of their work.

Degree Requirements: A minimum of 24 credits is required for the M.A. degree in Arts Administration, in addition to a core of business courses that can be taken before or during the program. A Master's paper of practical substance and merit is required of each student. Also, an internship with an arts organization is required, its form and duration depending on the organization and the student. *Admission Requirements:* A bachelor's degree from an approved institution with a grade point average of 3.0 or higher and a satisfactory score on GMAT examination. In addition to acceptance by the Graduate School of the University, applicants to the Arts Administration Program are reviewed by a special admissions committee. Ten applicants are accepted each year. Candidates are evaluated on the basis of grade point average, test scores, three letters of recommendation and a statement describing work experience, career objectives, skills, and education. *Application deadline:* February 15.

UTRECHT SCHOOL OF THE ARTS
Interfaculty
P.O. Box 1520
3500 BM Utrecht
THE NETHERLANDS
(31) 30 33 25 01

The Art Management, Art Mediation, and Art Policy program offered by the Interfaculty of the Utrecht School of the Arts is a full-time, three-year graduate program. Compiled by the school's Centre for Arts Management, the program consists of post-graduate courses in the field of arts management as well as practical training in arts institutions. Students are taught art theory and history as well as management, and there is an emphasis on individual development.

Degree Requirements: The educational program consists of six parts: management courses and training; art theory and history; various on-the-job programs in art institutions; international orientation; participation in organizing projects for other students in the School of the Arts; current developments in the arts and art policy.

Admission Requirements: Applicants must have successfully completed a B.A. program in the arts or have been awarded a B.A. in a different field but have also been active in the arts sector. Students must also possess an affinity for art and culture, demostrable organizational talent, and interest to develop in an international sense. A research project and paper are required.

Application deadline: May 1. The admission procedure consists of a written and oral section held in early spring.

VIRGINIA TECH
Division of Performing Arts
Blacksburg, VA 24061
703/231-5335 (Department Head)
703/231-4670 (Program Director)

The Program in Arts Administration/Stage Management is a personalized course of study aimed to meet the student's individual background, needs, and goals.

There is no formal curriculum, based on the realization that everyone comes to the program with different interests and experiences and does not need the same training or experience as others. There is a strong emphasis on production involvement and practical application through work in the school's production activities and other arts organizations.

Degree Requirements: Fifty-four (54) semester hours, including an internship and thesis or final project, are required for the M.F.A. degree in Arts Administration or Stage Management. To complete the degree, each student must demonstrate knowledge of and practice in the following: 1) creating the environment in which the artist can reach his or her full potential; 2) guiding, directing, and motivating individuals in an organization; 3) securing the organization's foundation for it to grow and develop; and 4) possessing the essential skills for managing a complex arts organization.

Admission Requirements: Applicants must have an undergraduate degree and achieved a cumulative grade point average of 2.75 on all college work. Students may be admitted on a special or provisional basis with a lower average. Three letters of recommendation, a current resume, and interviews are required along with the application. GRE scores are unnecessary.

Application deadline: February 1. Acceptances by April 1.

YALE UNIVERSITY
Yale School of Drama
222 York Street
New Haven, CT 06520
203/432-1515

The Theatre Administration program focuses on nonprofit theatre, but accepts students interested in the commercial theatre, film, electronic media, and management of other performing arts institutions. The program involves a combination of classroom work and practical experience on the administrative staff of the Yale Repertory Theatre. Students pursue individualized programs of work and study after completing the basic requirements. The philosophy of the program is that the professional work experience constitutes the heart of the educational process and, accordingly, such work assignments are the students' top priority.

Degree Requirements: Three years of courses and work assignments at the Yale Repertory Theatre to earn the M.F.A. degree. Also, students are required to attend a weekly Management Issues Forum. Theatre Administration students are encouraged to take courses in other departments of the School of Drama and in other schools, such as the Law School and the School of Organization and Management. A thesis and internship are not required. However, third year students may be permitted to write a thesis or conduct a special project in lieu of working at the Repertory Theatre. Also, virtually all students spend one semester of their second year on an internship at another institution.

Admission Requirements: Applicants must have an undergraduate degree, and most have significant professional work experience in theatre or other fields before entering the program. Applications must be accompanied by a statement of purpose, a transcript, GRE scores, three letters of recommendation, and a resume. Applicants are invited for personal interviews.

Application deadline: February 15.

YORK UNIVERSITY
Faculty of Administrative Studies
4700 Keele Street
North York (Toronto), Ontario M3J 1P3
CANADA
416/736-5082

The Program in Arts and Media Administration is Canada's only graduate program combining the Master of Business Administration course work with arts management. The Program's major objectives are to train potential arts and media administrators in management skills; provide them with meaningful practicum experiences in arts and media organizations; to undertake research into arts and media management issues, and cultural and communications policy; and to provide training to practicing professionals in arts and media management.

Degree Requirements: Twenty (20) courses, normally requiring two years to complete, to earn the M.B.A. degree in Arts and Media Management. Students are required to undertake an internship during the summer term between the first and second years of their studies, unless they have sufficient prior professional experience in arts or media management. Students also are expected to do practicum work with campus arts organizations during the first year of their studies. All M.B.A. students must complete a major group exercise, equivalent to a thesis, encompassing a strategic analysis of a corporate structure. Arts administration students focus on arts or cultural institutions.

Admission Requirements: Applicants must have an undergraduate degree from a recognized university with at least a B average over the last two years of study. Scores on the GMAT examination and two letters of recommendation must be submitted along with the application. Candidates for admission must demonstrate a commitment to the arts or cultural industries, possess a formal awareness of the history of at least one art form or of basic theories of communication; and have experience in creating art or a background in a communications medium.

Application deadline: June 1 for September admission; October 15 for January admission; and February 15 for April Admission.

ARTS AND MEDIA
MANAGEMENT INTERNSHIPS

Internship positions in the arts and media field combine working with learning and are intended to provide hands-on experience for those interested in pursuing a career. A worthwhile internship will offer the participant a broad overview of the organization's management and allow that person to take part in specific projects under the supervision of the management staff and to observe a variety of meetings and events related to the organization's work.

Because many internships are nonsalaried or provide only a small stipend, the intern should look upon the arrangement as a quid-pro-quo-situation: the intern's wages are experience and contacts rather than salary. You are advised to examine the position carefully before accepting. Avoid the danger of becoming a go-fer or file clerk and make certain that the people for whom you will be working have good reputations and management practices.

Many service organizations, management assistance groups, and unions offer internships—sometimes called apprenticeships or fellowships—as seen in the list that follows, and more information may be obtained by contacting them directly. In addition, the majority of nonprofit performing arts companies offer internships in the management areas, as do an increasing number of commercial arts and media corporations. For example, the three major broadcasting networks accept interns, who are really nonsalaried trainees, and often hire them for regular positions. In fact, this is one of the best ways to break into a network job. For a listing of internships in film and television see the Guide to College Courses in Film and Television (Peterson's Guides Inc., Box 2123, Princeton, NJ 08540) and consult Factfile #2, "Careers in Film and Television" (National Educational Service of the American Film Institute, John F. Kennedy Center for the Performing Arts, Washington, DC 20566).

Current listings in internships with performing arts companies can be found in *Internships* (Writer's Digest Books, 9933 Alliance Road, Cincinnati, OH 45242), and in *STOPOUT! Working Ways to Learn* (Garrett Park Press, Garrett Park, MD 20896). *ArtSearch* and *The National Arts JobBank*, as detailed under the Job Referral section of the Career Kit, also list current internships as they become available.

The list that follows is only a sampling of several dozen interesting and well-established internship programs. There are countless other possibilities for this type of training in the arts and media industry. Certainly, you should not discount making direct personal contact with an organization or individual from whom you wish to learn. Offer your services gratis, or for very little, and you may soon find yourself climbing a sturdy career ladder!

ALLIANCE OF RESIDENT THEATRES/NEW YORK (ART/NY)
131 Varick Street, Room 904 (Theatre: all management areas)
New York, NY 10013-1410
212/989-5257

ART/NY's internship program provides practical, hands-on training to aspiring professionals at any stage of their careers. This national program operates year-round and is widely regarded by New York City theatre managers as a valuable resource for recruitment of new talent. Since 1984, over 500 interns have been placed in member theatres including New York Shakespeare Festival, Circle Repertory Company, Manhattan Theatre Club, Musical Theatre Works and Mabou Mines among others.

Full- and part-time internships are available in all aspects of theatre management and production (excluding acting). Positions vary in length from several weeks to 12 months and may be tailored to each individual's needs.

AMERICAN DANCE FESTIVAL (ADF)
P.O. Box 6097, College Station (Dance management)
Durham, NC 27708-6097
919/684-6402

ADF offers eight-week internships in administration and production during its annual season in Durham, North Carolina. Internships generally begin the last week of May and continue through the last week of July. Areas in which internships are offered include: marketing, media relations, community development and fundraising, production management, special projects administration, box office management, school administration, food and housing coordination, transportation management, concessions operations, and front of house management. In addition to a stipend, interns attend over 35 performances, observe panel discussions, seminars, and lectures. A weekly seminar is offered to discuss the internships, hear from visitors, and address relevant issues in arts administration.

AMERICAN MUSIC CENTER
30 West 26th Street, Suite 1001 (Music: performance of
New York, NY 10010 contemporary American music)
212/366-5260

Internships for undergraduate and graduate students interested in music are arranged on an individual, informal basis. Although internships are non-paying, college credit may be granted with the approval of the student's school.

THE AMERICAN MUSIC SCHOLARSHIP ASSOCIATION

1826 Carew Tower   (Music: public relations and general administration)
Cincinnati, OH 45202
513/421-5342

Internships are offered each year, the length and beginning times for which are flexible. A public relations intern handles local and national press and media; an administrative intern handles office management, membership information, and correspondence. There are no specific criteria for acceptance.

AMERICAN SYMPHONY ORCHESTRA LEAGUE

777 Fourteenth Street, NW   (Symphony orchestra management)
Suite 500
Washington, DC 20005
202/628-0099

The Orchestra Management Fellowship Program is a one-year internship administered by the League in cooperation with member orchestras. Up to eight Fellows are chosen each year. They receive a stipend of $14,600 plus travel expenses. Fellows spend approximately four months with two major orchestras and one regional or metropolitan orchestra; in addition, they spend two weeks at the League's offices, one week at an orchestra management seminar, two weeks in New York City, and one week with an urban or community orchestra.

ARTS AND BUSINESS COUNCIL, INC. (ABC)

25 West 45th Street, Suite 707   (Arts administration: minorities)
New York, NY 10036
212/819-9287

The Sybil C. Simon Multicultural Arts Administration Internship was created to encourage minority participation in arts administration. Minority undergraduates from colleges in the New York City area work during the summer with arts organizations in New York City. Interns are paid a stipend.

ARTS MIDWEST

528 Hennepin Avenue, Suite 310
Minneapolis, MN 55403
612/341-0755

Arts Midwest's "Leadership Development Program" offers three paid twelve-week residencies each year for individuals pursuing careers in arts administration. Residents work Monday through Friday from 8:30 a.m. to 5:00 p.m. and spend approximately three quarters of their time assisting Arts Midwest's professional staff in daily operations and one-quarter of their time in staff, panel, and board meetings, and learning Arts Midwest's general operations. Each resident receives a $4000.00 stipend for the twelve weeks. Applicants must have a B.A. or a minimum of three years experience working with an arts or community service organization. All candidates must be current residents of

Illinois, Indiana, Iowa, Michigan, Minnesota, North Dakota, Ohio, South Dakota, or Wisconsin. For complete deadline, eligibility, and application information, contact Arts Midwest.

BOX OFFICE MANAGEMENT INTERNATIONAL (BOMI)
333 East 46th Street, #1B
New York, NY 10017
212/949-7350

Internships are available at BOMI for students interested in association management, public relations and marketing.

BUSINESS COMMITTEE FOR THE ARTS
1775 Broadway, Suite 510
New York, NY 10019
212/664-0600

Internships are available in a variety of areas of the organization to work on a project basis. Most interns are undergraduates with a background in the arts and art history who perform mostly research-oriented duties. There is no stipend, but college credit can be arranged through the student's school.

INTERNATIONAL SOCIETY OF PERFORMING ARTS ADMINISTRATORS (ISPAA)
P.O. Box 200328
Austin, TX 78720
(Location: 11307 Toledo Drive
Austin, TX 78759)
512/346-1328 or 512/338-0606

The ISPAA Internship Program places an intern in a non-profit organization or school which presents arts performances or is concerned with arts activities. Candidates must be upper-level undergraduate or graduate students at (or graduates of) an accredited college or university and interested in arts administration careers. A stipend of up to $1,500 is granted for a period of 90 days to one semester.

KENNEDY CENTER EDUCATION PROGRAM
Internship Coordinator   (Arts education and theatre)
The John F. Kennedy Center for the Performing Arts
Washington, DC 20566
202/416-8800

Three- to four-month internships are offered during fall, winter/spring, and summer terms with Advertising, Alliance for Arts Education, the American College Theater Festival, Cultural Diversity Affairs, Department of Productions and Theatre, Development, Educational Services, Friends of the Kennedy Center, Group Sales/Subscriptions, Government Relations, Marketing, Media Relations, the National Symphony Orchestra Education Program, Public Affairs, Theatre for Young People, and Very Special Arts (an educational affiliate for people with disabilities). Applicants must be upper-level college students, graduate students, or teachers of the arts. Interns can receive a stipend of $500 per month, and may earn college credit from their respective universities.

LINCOLN CENTER FOR THE PERFORMING ARTS
Internship Coordinator   (Performing arts: operations)
70 Lincoln Center Plaza
New York, NY 10023-6583
212/875-5423

While the constituent companies that perform at Lincoln center may offer internships, so does the general operating office for Lincoln Center as a whole. Two interns are hired each year on a highly competitive basis. Both three-month positions begin in June and pay approximately $375-$400 per week. Applicants must have completed at least one year of graduate study in any master's degree program.

MID-ATLANTIC ARTS FOUNDATION
11 East Chase Street, Suite 2A
Baltimore, MD 21202
301/539-6656

The Foundation offers twenty paid internships for visual artists in the mid-Atlantic region. Interns process applications and implement peer review panel meetings for the Regional Fellowships for Visual Artists. The internship provides contact with artists and arts professionals and an opportunity to participate in the operations of a regional funding and service agency. Internships are for 12-16 weeks between January and May, the work schedule is flexible, and the stipend for 1991 was $1000. For complete application and deadline information, contact the Director of Visual Arts at the Foundation.

THE NATIONAL ASSEMBLY OF LOCAL ARTS AGENCIES (NALAA)
927 15th Street, NW
12th Floor
Washington, DC 20005
202/371-2830

The NALAA Internship Program provides people interested in gaining knowledge of local arts development with a comprehensive overview of community arts administration or specific areas affecting arts administration today. It also provides opportunities for individuals with skills in research, marketing, development, advocacy, or graphic design to apply their skills to the nonprofit sector.

NALAA internships provide training to individuals to prepare them for careers in arts administration or in nonprofit organizations. Interns usually help develop, implement, and evaluate one of the organization's programs. Positions are either part-time or full-time and vary in length. Academic credit may be earned, and stipends are sometimes available.

NATIONAL ASSEMBLY OF STATE ARTS AGENCIES (NASAA)
1010 Vermont Avenue, NW
Suite 920
Washington, DC 20005
202/347-6352

Internships are available to college and graduate students to work in one of the Assembly's program areas. Generally interns work during the summer, but alternative schedules may be arranged. Interns are paid varying amounts according to their individual situations.

NATIONAL ENDOWMENT FOR THE ARTS (NEA)
Arts Administration Fellows Program Administrator   (Arts councils: operations)
Nancy Hanks Center
1100 Pennsylvania Avenue, NW, Room 219
Washington, DC 20506
202/682-5786

The NEA Arts Administration Fellows Program offers in-house fellowships for arts managers who have demonstrated a strong commitment to their field. Fellows work with the NEA staff and attend seminars, lectures, and panel meetings. Approximately twelve fellows are selected for each of the eleven-week fall, spring, and summer fellowship periods. Grants for this highly competitive program include a stipend of $5,500 plus round-trip coach fare to Washington, DC. Non-paid internship programs are also offered for undergraduate students.

NATIONAL TRUST FOR HISTORIC PRESERVATION
Office of Human Resources   (Museums and architecture)
1785 Massachusetts Avenue, NW
Washington, DC 20036
202/673-4120

A summer internship program for students interested in architecture, art history, history, and the humanities.

NEW YORK CITY URBAN CORPS
32 Worth Street   (All arts fields)
New York, NY 10013
212/566-3952

New York City Urban Corps places undergraduate and graduate students within city government agencies. College interns are given the opportunity to experience careers in many areas, including the arts. Students are placed in arts institutions, museums, and with individual artists throughout the New York City area where they work 20 hours each week during the academic year, 35-40 hours per week during the summer. Internships are arranged through college work-study programs, and are paid according to their guidelines.

NEW YORK STATE COUNCIL ON THE ARTS (NYSCA)

915 Broadway, 8th Floor   (Arts councils: various)
New York, NY 10010
212/614-2900

Internship opportunities may be available in a variety of program areas to qualified applicants. No stipend is available, but the learning opportunity is considerable; hours are flexible, as is the internship time period.

NORTH CAROLINA ARTS COUNCIL

North Carolina Department of Cultural Resources   (Community arts
Raleigh, NC 27611   council administration)
919/733-7897

The Community Development Section of the North Carolina Arts Council sponsors a three-month arts administration intern program in which three individuals are chosen to serve an intensive, supervised internship with community arts councils in North Carolina. At each location, the intern is under the supervision of the council executive director or other designated staff member who designs a training program taken from the spectrum of community arts administration: i.e., organizational structure, planning, fund-raising, grantsmanship, financial management, marketing, programming, publicity and promotion, interagency relations, etc. In addition, the interns spend several days over the course of the program with Council staff for information and evaluation sessions. A stipend of $1,000 per month is given to all interns. Applicants must possess a four-year college degree. Evaluation criteria include strong business and administrative abilities, close familiarity with the arts, and ability to accept full-time employment at the end of the program. Individuals chosen will do internship any three consecutive months from September to June. Application deadline is June 1.

OPERA AMERICA, INC.

777 14th Street, NW   (Opera: general management)
Suite 520
Washington, DC 20005
202/347-9262

OPERA America's Fellowship Program offers highly specialized 12-month training programs for entry- and mid-level arts administrators. The areas addressed by the fellowship program include artistic administration, personnel administration, technical production, finanacial management, development, education, marketing, public relations, and volunteer and guild relations. OPERA America pays transportation and a stipend of $1,000 per month. Host companies provide housing.

OPERA America also offers 3- or 6-month internships in its own office for those interested in gaining research and publications experience. OPERA America pays a small daily stipend.

THEATRE COMMUNICATIONS GROUP (TCG)

355 Lexington Avenue   (Performing arts: general management)
New York, NY 10017
212/697-5230

TCG offers internship positions in all areas of their operation, including literary, artists, and management services. Internships are available to college and graduate students for a period of time determined by the intern. There is no stipend, but academic credit may be granted from the student's university.

VISUAL STUDIES WORKSHOP

31 Prince Street   (Museums and galleries)
Rochester, NY 14607
716/442-8676

Internships are offered in gallery- and museum-related operations, including touring exhibitions, media projects, and gallery management.

VOLUNTEER LAWYERS FOR THE ARTS (VLA)

1 East 53rd Street
New York, NY 10022
212/319-2787

General Arts Administration and Development internships are available to college and graduate students during the fall, spring, and summer semesters. Though internships are unpaid, compensation may be available in the form of academic credit.

WALKER ART CENTER

Vineland Place   (Museum and cultural center management)
Minneapolis, MN 55403
612/375-7600

Walker Art Center offers two paid internships. The Curatorial/Education Internship is available to applicants who hold a master's degree in art history or who have commensurate experience with a museum or cultural center. The Design Internship is available to applicants who have completed an MFA in design or who have commensurate experience in an arts or cultural environment.

Internships are 12-month, full-time positions and include a $13,000 stipend, $1000 travel stipend, and a full benefit package. Both programs are grant funded. Applications are due in the spring to begin work in the fall. Applications are available in early March from the Assistant to Curators (612-375-7678) and the Senior Graphic Designer (612-375-7686).

WNET

356 West 58th Street   (Public television)
New York, NY 10019
212/560-2063

The Thirteen College Intern Program is open to college juniors, seniors, and first-year graduate students who live or attend college within the station's viewing area. Interns work during either the fall, spring, or summer semester and receive college credit. Assignments are available in production, marketing, communications, viewer services, and other departments.

YOUNG CONCERT ARTISTS, INC.

250 West 57th Street   (Music and service organizations)
New York, NY 10019
Telephone: 212/307-6655

Internships are open to college students interested in arts administration, and specifically classical music administration. Students may participate in presentation, artist managment, concert operations, auditions, publicity and promotion, or fundraising. There is no salary or stipend, college credit may be arranged.

ARTS AND MEDIA MANAGEMENT SEMINARS, WORKSHOPS, AND INFORMATION CENTERS

ALLIANCE OF RESIDENT THEATRES/NEW YORK (ART/NY)
131 Varick Street, Room 904
New York, NY 10013-1410
212/989-5257

Focus: Off-Broadway and Off-Off-Broadway theatre in New York City.

Publications: ART/NY publications cover a variety of topics on theatre management, including the *Directory of Theatre Membership*, with script submission policies and a *Listing of Performance and Rehearsal Space*, updated regularly.

Information: ART/NY maintains a Job Board and Resource Files on theatre members and a variety of related subjects available to the general public (see Job Referral section of the Career Kit).

AMERICAN ASSOCIATION FOR STATE AND LOCAL HISTORY (AASLH)
172 Second Avenue North, Suite 202
Nashville, TN 37201
615/255-2971

Focus: All aspects of preserving, promoting, and appreciating state, local, and community history in the U.S. and Canada.

Workshops and Seminars: Workshops and clinics conducted at AASLH's annual meeting. Also, numerous three- to five-day workshops and seminars held annually on a variety of topics.

Seminar for Historical Administration: Annual seminar held for historical agency professionals. Seminar covers administration, interpretation, collections, and public awareness of historical organizations. Held each year in Colonial Williamsburg, those interested must apply for acceptance to the program.

Publications: Publishes books on administration, preservation, collections, museums, etc.

AMERICAN ASSOCIATION OF MUSEUMS (AAM)
1225 Eye Street, NW
Suite 200
Washington, DC 20005
202/289-1818

Focus: Museum administration.

Workshops: Cosponsors Legal Problems of Museum Administration—held annually for three days in different locations of the country, conducted by the American Law Institute and the American Bar Association with an emphasis on practical information relating to museum management. Also cosponsor of

Seminar for Historical Administration, conducted by the American Association of State and Local History (see AASLH).

Annual Meeting: Five-day conference held in a different city each year, usually in the spring. More than 100 educational sessions are conducted covering a variety of topics relevant to museums, including administration.

AMERICAN COUNCIL FOR THE ARTS (ACA)
1 East 53rd Street
New York, NY 10022-4201
212/223-ARTS

Focus: Advocacy, arts education, the originating artist, and private-sector support of the arts.

Public Forums: Meetings are held throughout the country to discuss those issues which are the focus of the American Council for the Arts.

Publications: Publishes and distributes books on managing arts organizations including books on finance, law, marketing, fundraising, and general management.

Information Center: Maintains one of the most complete arts libraries outside of the university system, with extensive resources in arts management.

AMERICAN DANCE GUILD, INC (ADG)
31 West 21st Street, Third Floor
New York, NY 10010
212/627-3790

Focus: Dance performance, education, and administration.

Annual Conference: Three-day conference held in a different city each June. Workshops and presentations on all aspects of dance.

Publications: Newsletter, *American Dance*, published six times each year containing news and information for dance professionals and educators.

Seminars and Workshops: Day-long series sponsored throughout the year on many facets of dance. Occassionally acts as presenter for performing arts.

AMERICAN FILM INSTITUTE (AFI)
The John F. Kennedy Center for the Performing Arts
Washington, DC 20566
202/828-4000 (Public Information Office)
1180 Avenue of the Americas, 10th Floor
New York, NY 10036
212/398-6890 (Public Information Office)
2021 North Western Avenue
Los Angeles, CA 90027
213/856-7600 (Public Information Office)

Focus: Film and television.

Seminars, Workshops, and Conferences: Offered in cities around the country, addressing a wide range of current media issues and artistic and professional concerns.

Publications: AFI publishes reference books on many aspects of film and television, including *The American Film Institute Guide to College Courses in Film and Television, Careers in Film and Television,* and *Film and Television: Grants, Scholarships, Special Programs.*

Information Center: The Louis B. Mayer Library provides information and documentation on all aspects of the moving image to Center Fellows, scholars, and researchers by special arrangement.

AMERICAN LAW INSTITUTE—AMERICAN BAR ASSOCIATION
4025 Chestnut Street
Philadelphia, PA 19104
215/243-1630

Focus: Legal problems of museum administration.

Seminar: "Legal Problems of Museum Administration" held annually for three days; covers practical information relating to museum management and legal problems; cosponsored by The Smithsonian Institution, with the cooperation of the American Association of Museums, and held in various locations around the country.

AMERICAN MUSIC CENTER
30 West 26th Street, Suite 1001
New York, NY 10010
212/366-5260

Focus: Promoting recognition and performance of contemporary American music.

Information Center: Primarily for the performing artist, but has some information relevant to management.

AMERICAN SYMPHONY ORCHESTRA LEAGUE (ASOL)
777 Fourteenth Street, NW
Suite 500
Washington, DC 20005
202/628-0099

Focus: Orchestra and general management.

Orchestra Management Seminars: Concentrated week-long seminars addressing various topics related to orchestra management are presented by lecturers from orchestras and consultants in the field; seminars are held in a different location each year.

Volunteer Fundraising Projects Seminars: One-day seminars on how to run volunteer fundraising projects; panel discussions of recruiting and motivating volunteers, promoting fundraising projects, and basic fundraising project planning models; in-depth discussion of specific projects effectively administered by volunteers from across the country.

Orchestra Leadership Workshops: Two-day workshops on topics of interest for orchestras with smaller budgets; offered in regional locations at affordable prices; topics include marketing, finance and administration, volunteer support, building effective boards, increasing the number of individual donors, and increasing the size of gifts.

Staff Training Courses: One- and two-day courses on topics such as marketing, fundraising, concert production, finance, and labor relations; participants include executive directors, department directors, and staff members of professional and volunteer orchestras; courses provide an opportunity to network, discuss specific techniques and procedures, and learn practical ideas that can be put to use immediately.

National Conference: A five-day conference held in a major city in the United States each June; sessions for managers, board members, staff, and conductors; general sessions conducted by leaders in the field; one-day Professional Development Seminars on topics such as time management, supervisory training, long-range planning, and community orchestra management; Employment Opportunities Service available to job seekers and interviewers.

ARTS ACTION RESEARCH (AAR)
(formerly FEDAPT)
205 South Patrick Street
Alexandria, VA 22314
703/739-2722

Focus: Arts management and operations

Programs and Conferences: As a new organization, Arts Action Research replaced FEDAPT in late 1991. AAR plans to consult with arts organizations to help them reconceptualize, restructure, and re-tool; to initiate special research or "laboratory" projects on the structure and operation of arts organizations; to organize and facilitate special workshops and conferences; and to document and disseminate work processes and findings to the field.

Publications: Books published under the FEDAPT imprint: *Market the Arts, Workpapers: A Special Report—The Quiet Crisis, Workpapers 1: Rethinking and Restructuring the Arts Organization,* and *Workpapers 2: Arts Boards: Myths, Perspectives, and New Approaches.* All FEDAPT/Arts Action Research titles are available from the American Council for the Arts (see above).

ARTS AND BUSINESS COUNCIL, INC. (ABC)
25 West 45th Street, Suite 707
New York, NY 10036
212/819-9287

Focus: Arts management and volunteerism.

Corporate Volunteer Training Program: Corporate executives who have volunteered to work with arts organizations through ABC's Business Volunteers for the Arts program (BVA) are offered an intensive arts management orientation covering all aspects of nonprofit arts management.

Seminars: Various seminars and workshops on arts management related issues.

National Programs: There are BVA program affiliates in 30 cities throughout the country. Check with the national office in New York for details about these and other program locations.

ARTS MANAGEMENT
408 West 57th Street
New York, NY 10019
212/245-3850

Focus: Careers, arts management.

Workshops: Several career workshops are presented each year in cooperation with Marymount Manhattan College Arts Management Certificate Program.

Publication: Arts Management, a newsletter.

ARTS MANAGEMENT INSTITUTE
Virginia Tech
Division of Performing Arts
Blacksburg, VA 24601
703/231-5921

Focus: Performing arts management.

Conferences: Two-day conferences are offered a few times each year in Blacksburg, each on a specific topic, such as marketing and board development; Virginia Tech faculty and professionals lead the conferences.

ASSOCIATION OF ARTS ADMINISTRATION EDUCATORS (AAAE)
c/o American Council for the Arts
1 East 53rd Street
New York, NY 10022-4201
212/223-ARTS

Focus: Arts administration and management, higher education programs.

Annual conference: Held each spring at a selected site; members and invited professionals speak on topics of interest; open to college arts administration program heads, as well as associate members and individuals.

Publication: Survey of Arts Administration Training, published biannually by the American Council for the Arts.

ASSOCIATION OF HISPANIC ARTS (AHA)
173 East 116th Street
New York, NY 10029
212/860-5445

Focus: Hispanic arts.

Information Center: Publishes *AHA Hispanic Arts News* 9 times a year. Offers technical assistance to Hispanic groups and individuals.

Training Seminar: Short seminars presented by professionals on topics such as fundraising, marketing, and audience development.

ASSOCIATION OF PERFORMING ARTS PRESENTERS
1112 16th Street, NW
Washington, DC 20036
202/833-ARTS (2787)

Focus: Arts administration, especially presenting organizations.

Summer Workshops: Sessions on arts discipline topics and/or basic skills of presenting.

Leadership Institute in the Arts: The Institute is for experienced arts administrators led by faculty from the Humphrey Institute for Public Affairs, University of Minnesota.

Winter Institute: Workshops are held in New York City prior to the annual conference in December. Topics include artistic direction, arts management, and arts issues.

Annual Conference: The conference is held each December in New York City. Events include small workshop sessions covering a variety of topics, plenary sessions with speakers, display booths staffed by representatives of leading artists, hospitality events, and numerous performances and showings by performing arts groups.

Publications: The Association publishes *Bulletin,* a monthly trade newsletter for presenters and arts administrators. Articles in their quarterly magazine, *Inside Arts,* focus on performing arts issues, trends, and personalities. Other publications on performing arts presentation are listed in their publications catalogue. Complimentary sample copies of the *Bulletin, Inside Arts,* or the catalogue are available upon request.

BANFF CENTRE FOR MANAGEMENT
Arts Management Programs
Post Office Box 1020
Banff, Alberta T0L 0C0
CANADA
403/762-6125

Focus: Arts Management and Museum Management.

Cultural Resources Management: Approximately five seminars are given each year, most at the Banff Centre in Canada; workshops range from intensive three-day sessions to three-week seminars and are designed for entry-level people, middle managers, or executives with practical experience but little formal education in the field; seminars include: "Marketing the Arts," "Management Development for Arts Administrators," "Museum and Art Gallery Management," "Arts Administration Training Program," and "Fundraising for the Arts."

BOX OFFICE MANAGEMENT INTERNATIONAL (BOMI)
333 East 46th Street, #1B
New York, NY 10017
Telephone: 212/949-7350

Focus: Box-office management.

Annual Conference: An annual, four-day conference held in a major world city with a specific theme related to box-office management.

Regional Conferences: Educational, two- to four-day workshops held throughout the world.

Publications: Publications cover such topics as box office and marketing, customer service, and telephone operations. BOMI also publishes a newsletter containing feature articles, results of BOMI surveys, and career opportunities.

CHAMBER MUSIC AMERICA (CMA)
545 Eighth Avenue
New York, NY 10018
212/244-2772

Focus: Chamber music.

Annual Conference: Four-day conference usually held in New York City; workshops on the practical aspects of chamber music presentation, audience development, and career building.

Regional Conferences, Workshops, Training Programs, and Meetings: Several regional events sponsored by CMA on topics such as booking, touring, marketing, fundraising, and organizational development.

Training Seminars: "Art into Business" seminars provide younger musicians with management tools for developing a successful career in chamber music.

Publications: Chamber Music magazine, published quarterly, gives news and commentary on all aspects of the chamber music field, and *CMA Matters*, also published quarterly, offers a technical assistance. Other publications related to management of chamber music ensembles include *Can This Marriage Be Saved?: Interpersonal and Organizational Guidelines for Ensembles, Chamber Music in Our Schools: An Overview and Recommendations, Organizational Manual for Chamber Music Ensembles*, and the National Conference summaries, *Look to the Future* and *Moving Forward*.

CORPORATION FOR PUBLIC BROADCASTING (CPB)
901 E Street, NW
Washington, DC 20004-2006
202/879-9600

System Development Fund: Advanced, mid-level, and entry-level training available for public broadcasting professionals. For CPB funded training opportunities, call (202) 879-9731.

Publication: A Guide to Volunteer and Internship Programs in public broadcasting is published by CPB. To order, call 202/879-9778.

COUNCIL FOR ADVANCEMENT AND SUPPORT
OF EDUCATION (CASE)
11 Dupont Circle, NW
Suite 400
Washington, DC 20036
202/328-5900

Focus: Institutional advancement, fundraising, public relations, publications, and alumni administration.

Conferences, Workshops, and Institutes: Over 100 each year, one to four days in length, on a broad range of topics including fundraising, management, volunteerism, public relations, alumni administration, and publications.

DANCE/USA
777 Fourteenth Street, NW, Suite 540
Washington, DC 20005
202/628-0144

Focus: The American nonprofit dance field, including professional modern dance, ballet, ethnic, jazz and tap dance companies.

Conference and Meetings: A biennial national conference, semi-annual business meetings for member managers, and annual meetings for service organization directors and artists, including artistic directors, independent choreographers, and other artists working in the field. The focus is on artistic, production and management topics of interest.

Publications: Their newsletter *Update*, published 7 times per year, and *Journal*, a quarterly publication, contain job listings (see the Job Referral section of the Career Kit).

DONORS FORUM OF CHICAGO
53 West Jackson, Suite 430
Chicago, IL 60604
312/431-0260

Focus: Grants development.

Workshops and Seminars: The Forum is an association of independent and corporate foundations that provides services to its members; workshop schedules vary.

THE FOUNDATION CENTER
79 Fifth Avenue, 8th Floor
New York, NY 10003
212/620-4230
1001 Connecticut Avenue, NW, Suite 938
Washington, DC 20036
202/331-1400
312 Sutter Street
San Francisco, CA 94108
415/397-0902
1442 Hanna Building
1422 Euclid Avenue
Cleveland, OH 44115
216/861-1934

Focus: Fundraising.

Libraries: The Foundation Center's mission is to collect, organize, and disseminate factual data on foundation and corporate philanthropy. The Center maintains a wide range of reference materials on grantmakers in two national collections in New York and Washington, DC, and two regional collections in Cleveland and San Francisco. The Center also operates a network of more than 180 Cooperating Collections in host nonprofit organizations in all 50 states, Australia, Canada, Mexico, Puerto Rico, the Virgin Islands, Great Britain, and Japan. For a complete list of host organizations, call 1-800-424-9836.

Publications: The Foundation Center publishes numerous books, including directories describing foundations, grants indexes, nonprofit technical assistance, books about the nonprofit sector, and issues for foundations. For a free publications catalog, call 1-800-424-9836 (outside NY state) or 212-620-4230.

THE FUND RAISING SCHOOL
550 West North Street, Suite 301
Indianapolis, IN 46202-3162
317/274-7063 (in Indiana), or 800/962-6692

Focus: Fundraising.

Courses: Taught in various locations across the country and designed to teach the principles and techniques of fundraising; courses are given for beginners, experienced practitioners, and volunteers and trustees; continuing education credits are offered.

THE GRANTSMANSHIP CENTER
1125 West 6th Street, 5th Floor
Los Angeles, CA 90017
213/482-9860

Focus: Grantsmanship and planning.

Mini-courses, Seminars, and Workshops: For training in writing grants, management, planning, and resource development; courses are offered in response to the critical needs of nonprofit organizations.

GREATER PHILADELPHIA CULTURAL ALLIANCE (GPCA)
320 Walnut Street
Philadelphia, PA 19106
215/440-8100

Focus: Not-for-profit service organization for professional cultural organizations and individuals in the Philadelphia area.

Information Center: GPCA offers a JobBank and Resource Library. The JobBank consists of listings available from member organizations as well as placement newsletters. The Resource Library contains directories, research reports, funding guidelines, periodicals, and newsletters, and books on fundraising, audience development, board development and arts management.

Workshops and Roundtables: GPCA offers two series of workshops for members on topics related to managing cultural organizations. Roundtable discussion groups are a source of ongoing dialogue for representatives of member organizations.

Publications: Short Subjects, GPCA's newsletter, is published 11 times a year. It contains information about GPCA programs and services, legislative updates, job listings, and funding and member information (see Job Referral section of the Career Kit). Other publications include *The Space Directory,* listing of cultural facilities for rent in the greater Philadelphia area; *Membership Directory and Resource Guide,* listing basic information about GPCA member organizations and media and legislative contacts; and *For Immediate Release,* a guide to the media.

INTERNATIONAL ASSOCIATION OF AUDITORIUM MANAGERS INC. (IAAM)
4425 West Airport Freeway, Suite 590
Irving, TX 70562
213/255-8020

Public Assembly Facility Management School at Oglebay: A ten-day program on all aspects of managing public assembly facilities. The program is divided into two annual sessions, each lasting five days. Certified Facility Executive points and Continuing Education Units are awarded to all who complete the program.

Conferences: IAAM Annual Conference and Trade Show is held over 4 days during the summer (locations vary).

Publications: IAAM News is a monthly publications that includes job listings (see Job Referral section of the Career Kit.). IAAM also publishes *Facility Manager Magazine,* a quarterly publication.

INTERNATIONAL SOCIETY OF PERFORMING ARTS ADMINISTRATORS (ISPAA)
6065 Pickerel Drive
Rockford, MI 49341
616/874-6200
Focus: Performing arts and presenting organizations.
Annual Conference: Usually held in New York City for four days in December; includes workshops and speeches given by prominent members of the profession.
Annual International Congress: Annual congress of arts administrators from around the world; sessions address issues from an international perspective.
Publication: Performing Arts Forum newsletter contains news and information on ISPAA members and activities; sometimes includes announcements of jobs in performing arts administration.

MEREDITH COLLEGE, OFFICE OF CONTINUING EDUCATION
Cultural Resources Management Program
3800 Hillsborough Street
Raleigh, NC 27607-5298
Focus: Performing and visual arts management for women.
Part-time Program: Provides training for the management of organized cultural activities; the program is intended for women who are college graduates and have an interest in cultural resources; all courses are given on the Raleigh campus; certificate awarded after completing 150 hours of classroom time, which can be extended over a five-year period.

MID-AMERICA ARTS ALLIANCE
912 Baltimore Avenue, Suite 700
Kansas City, MO 64105-1731
816/421-1388
Annual Conference: Offer a number of workshops and panel discussions covering administrative topics such as marketing and development. Contact the organization for further information about location and dates of upcoming conference.

MUSEUM OF TELEVISION AND RADIO
(formerly Museum of Broadcasting)
25 West 52nd Street
New York, NY 10019
212/621-6600
Focus: Broadcasting
Seminars: Over 50 seminars covering a wide variety of topics are offered to the public each year, including some seminars via live satellite broadcast; seminars are conducted by celebrities in the field of broadcasting.

NATIONAL ACADEMY OF RECORDING ARTS AND SCIENCES (NARAS)
303 North Glen Oaks Boulevard
Suite 140
Burbank, CA 91502-1178
213/849-1313
(Chapters in Los Angeles, Chicago, New York City, Atlanta, Nashville, Memphis, and San Francisco)

Focus: Music recording.

Seminars: Seminars conducted on an ad hoc basis by individual NARAS chapters; occasionally address topics of interest to managers.

THE NATIONAL ASSEMBLY OF LOCAL ARTS AGENCIES
927 15th Street, NW
12th Floor
Washington, DC 20005
202/371-2830

Focus: Local arts councils

Information: On local arts councils and conferences; seminars are offered on local and regional levels.

Annual Conference: In a different region of the country each year; workshops and speakers on topics relating to arts councils.

NATIONAL ASSEMBLY OF STATE ARTS AGENCIES (NASAA)
1010 Vermont Avenue, NW
Suite #920
Washington, DC 20005
202/347-6352

Focus: State arts councils.

Annual Meeting: Three-day annual meeting covers topics relating to arts councils; the meeting is held in a different city each year and is open to the public.

Executive Directors Institute: Professional development sessions attended by executive directors of NASAA members. The bi-annual Institute lasts for five days.

Mid-Year Leadership Conference: An annual meeting for chairs, executive directors, and council members to provide them with an opportunity for professional development and for lobbying in Washington. The conference lasts one and one-half days.

NATIONAL ASSOCIATION FOR CAMPUS ACTIVITIES (NACA)
13 Harbison Way
Columbia, SC 29212
803/732-6222
800/845-2338

Focus: Booking live and film entertainment on university campuses.

Annual Conference: Conference held each year includes educational sessions on topics including administration, such as promotion and publicity, facilities management, strategic planning, and others. Conference open to NACA members and representatives of affiliated organizations.

NATIONAL ASSOCIATION OF BROADCASTERS (NAB)
1771 N Street, NW
Washington, DC 20036
202/429-5300

Focus: Television and radio—management and careers.

Annual Conference: Presents workshops and speakers on aspects of broadcast management and technology.

Information: On career development; pamphlets include *Careers in Television* and *Careers in Radio*.

NATIONAL DANCE ASSOCIATION
(An association of The American Alliance for Health, Physical Education, Recreation and Dance [AAHPERD])
1900 Association Drive
Reston, VA 22091
703/476-3400

Focus: All forms of dance.

Conventions: Annual AAHPERD national convention is held in a different city each year. Also, five district conventions are scheduled annually throughout the nation.

Publications: NDA's monthly newspaper, *Update*, contains news, association developments, job listings, and other information for dance professionals (see Job Referral section of the Career Kit). NDA also publishes *Spotlight on Dance*, a quarterly newsletter and *Dance Dynamics*, a bi-annual journal.

NATIONAL GUILD OF COMMUNITY SCHOOLS OF THE ARTS (NGSCA)
P.O. Box 8018
Englewood, NJ 07631-8018
201/871-3337

Focus: Community arts education.

Annual Conference: Held in November; presents speakers and workshops on aspects of community arts education, including fundraising, personnel relations, and career development.

Chapter Workshops: Regional chapters offer one-day workshops on specific topics, such as board relations and management.

Arts Management in Community Institutions (AMICI) Summer Institute: A 12-day annual summer institute held in June or July. A residential program held in a different location each year, it is designed to help develop management skills for administrators at small or emerging community arts education institutions. Topics include organizational structure, fundraising, financial management, image and visibility, in-house and outreach programs, and personal development.

Publication: The Guild's newsletter, *Guildnotes,* is sent to members about every six weeks.

THE NATIONAL VOLUNTEER CENTER
1111 North 19th Street
Arlington, VA 20009
703/276-0542

Focus: Volunteerism.

Annual Conference: National conference on volunteerism with seminars, regional information sharing and skills building workshops.

Information Services: The Center disseminates information about volunteering.

NATIONAL TRUST FOR HISTORIC PRESERVATION
1785 Massachusetts Avenue, NW
Washington, DC 20036
202/673-4000

Focus: Museums and historical associations.

Publications: Preservation News and an annual supplement *Preservation Education.*

Conferences: Annual conference in October for both organizations and individuals.

NEW SCHOOL FOR SOCIAL RESEARCH
66 West 12th Street
New York, NY 10011
212/741-5690

Focus: Media, careers, music, fine arts.

Workshops: From one-day to twelve-week sessions on topics ranging from careers in cable to media spot-buying; non-credit courses are open to the general public; check the bulletin for course offerings and tuition rates. Both credit and non-credit courses are offered.

NEW YORK UNIVERSITY
Robert F. Wagner Graduate School of Public Service
40 West Fourth Street, 738 Tisch Hall
New York, NY 10003
212/998-7400

Focus: Arts and nonprofit management, fundraising.

Courses: Courses on various topics, including administration, financial management, marketing and fundraising for nonprofit and cultural organizations; course offerings vary each semester.

Institutes: The Summer Institute in Management of Nonprofit Organizations is a five-day series of classes held on consecutive Fridays, covering a variety of areas related to managing nonprofit organizations. Occasionally, the school also offers the Institute on Cultural Leadership—call for further details.

OPERA AMERICA
777 14th Street, NW
Suite 520
Washington, DC 20005
202/347-9262

Focus: Opera and musical theatre management.

Annual Conference: provides a yearly forum in which to participate in discussions of important issues for opera company personnel, trustees, and opera enthusiasts. The conference, held in December or January, offers five days of sessions, performances, and special events.

OPERA America Information Service: (formerly Central Opera Service) provides resources on opera and musical theatre from a computerized database as well as paper files.

PROFESSIONAL ARTS MANAGEMENT INSTITUTE (PAMI)
408 West 57th Street
New York, NY 10019
212/245-3850

Focus: Arts management.

Institute: A three-day program offered annually in New York City each November, covers subjects such as audience development, budgeting and finance, fundraising, and general management; features prominent speakers from the profession; small group seminars and workshops are also included.

PUBLIC INTEREST PUBLIC RELATIONS, INC.
225 West 34th Street, Suite 1500
New York, NY 10001
212/736-5050

Focus: Public relations.

Publication: Promoting Issues and Ideas: A Guide to Public Relations for Non-profit Organizations is published by and available at the Foundation Center, New York City (see above).

SANGAMON STATE UNIVERSITY, COMMUNITY ARTS MANAGEMENT PROGRAM
Shepherd Road
Springfield, IL 62794-9243
217/786-6535

Focus: Arts administration.

Sangamon Institute in Arts Administration: A two-week course covering long-range planning, financial management, evaluation techniques, information retrieval, fundraising, career planning, legal aspects of arts management, and other topics; small-group workshop format; offered on campus each summer.

SOUTHERN ARTS FEDERATION
1293 Peachtree Street, NE
Suite 500
Atlanta, GA 30309
404/874-7244

Focus: General management and presenting.

Job-Alike Conferences: This program brings together individuals holding similar jobs in the member arts agencies from the nine-state region; program directors are brought together to discuss common problems.

Southern Arts Exchange: Annual session held in different cities in the Southeast, with related seminars of presenting the arts in the community.

THEATRE COMMUNICATIONS GROUP (TCG)
355 Lexington Avenue
New York, NY 10017
212/697-5230

Focus: Theatre management.

Information: TCG collects and publishes data on the theatre operations in the United States, focusing on nonprofit professional resident theatre companies.

Publications: Theatre Profiles, published biennially, is a survey of noncommercial theatres throughout the U.S.; *Theatre Facts,* available to member theatres, has information on finances and productivity; *Theatre Directory* lists theatres, artistic and managing directors, board chairmen, and related information; *American Theatre* magazine is a monthly forum for the theatre profession, but also reaches a broad-based readership interested in the arts and culture; covers acting, directing, government, trustees, management and other related areas. *ArtSearch* (see TCG under the Job Referral section of the Career Kit).

UNITED STATES INSTITUTE FOR
THEATRE TECHNOLOGY (USITT)
10 West 19th Street, Suite 5A
New York, NY 10011
212/924-9088
Focus: Theatre—design, management, and technical aspects.
Workshops and Seminars: While USITT deals primarily with aspects of technical theatre production and design, some management seminars are offered to member organizations and individuals at their annual conference.

VOLUNTEER LAWYERS FOR THE ARTS
1 East 53rd Street
New York, NY 10022
212/977-9270
Focus: Legal education, representation and advocacy for artists and arts organizations.
Biweekly Seminars: Held throughout the year in New York City to provide information regarding legal matters facing artists such as obtaining not-for-profit corporate and tax-exempt status, contracts, copyright, etc.
Lectures and Seminars: Conducted nationally for arts groups on subjects such as contracts, copyrights, tax and legal problems of non-profits, board liability, and legislation affecting arts groups and individual artists.
Arts Law Line: Legal questions concerning artists and arts organizations are answered daily by calling VLA at (212) 977-9271.
Special Conferences: Held periodically on specific themes of importance to artists nationwide.
Workshops: The essentials of art law for lawyers interested in volunteering their services to assist VLA clients.

WESTAF (WESTERN STATES ARTS FEDERATION)
236 Montezuma Avenue
Santa Fe, NM 87501-2641
505/988-1166
Focus: State arts agencies of the western United States.
Information: WESTAF provides information as it becomes available on seminars, workshops, and conferences presented by and for the constituent state arts organizations.
Publication: The National Arts JobBank (see the Job Referral section of the Career Kit).

REFERRAL SERVICES, MEMBERSHIP ASSOCIATIONS AND PERIODICALS WITH JOB LISTINGS

The following chart lists publications and referral services that announce job openings and/or assist with job placement. In addition, you may want to check with your local and state arts councils, which often receive requests from the arts organizations in their area. Also check with the national associations that represent the councils: the National Assembly of State Arts Agencies (1010 Vermont Avenue, NW, Suite 920, Washington, DC 20005) and the National Assembly of Local Arts Agencies (927 15th Street, NW, 12th Floor, Washington, DC 20005).

It is important to receive information as soon as possible after a job has become available. The chart, therefore, lists the "turnaround time," or the time it takes for the periodical or referral service to get the new job information to you. This is determined by such things as publication deadlines, the frequency of the publication, and the mailing time—based on the type and class of material mailed. The average number of jobs listed was determined by a sampling of recent publications or by direct contact with the organization. The cost listed is often the cost of

Organization Name and Address	Fields Covered	Publication and/or Service
ADVERTISING AGE 220 East 42nd Street Suite 930 New York, NY 10017	Advertising and marketing positions industry-wide	*Advertising Age*
ALLIANCE OF OHIO COMMUNITY ARTS AGENCIES (AOCAA) c/o Fine Arts Council of Trumbull County P.O. Box 48 Warren, OH 44482	All nonprofit arts disciplines in Ohio, with a concentration on community arts council positions	*Community Arts News*
AMERICAN ASSOCIATION FOR STATE AND LOCAL HISTORY 172 Second Ave., N. Suite 202 Nashville, TN 37201	History museums and historical societies	*History News* magazine (bimonthly) *History News Dispatch* (monthly newsletter)

membership, which entitles one to a subscription and use of any available job services unless otherwise noted. Note that in some instances the costs listed may be the student, or lowest, rates.

Some of the publications listed below are much more than job listings. *AVISO,* for example, features articles of interest to the museum professional. *Symphony* magazine, although short on the number of classified listings, has a section called "Musical Chairs" that includes news of who has left what position and who has taken which new job. This type of information can tell you a great deal about the field: which areas of the country seem to be fertile and growing, what the qualifications are for particular jobs, and which companies or organizations have a high rate of personnel turnover. Several local publications have been listed because they consistently list available jobs; there are many other local publications around the nation that you may wish to consult. Publishers and organizations often change their addresses and their rates and formats, so that no list such as the following can be completely up to date. To verify such information, consult the periodical section in a library or check with the library at the American Council for the Arts.

Turnaround Time	*Average Number of Jobs Listed*	*Cost*	*Comment*
7 days	40	$79 for 52 weeks	
10 weeks	4	Free	One of the most consistent newsletters on the state level
6 weeks	25-30	$50 membership	Thorough job descriptions; best source for positions in historical organizations and museums.

Organization Name and Address	Fields Covered	Publication and/or Service
AMERICAN ASSOCIATION OF MUSEUMS (AAM) 1225 Eye Street, NW Suite 200 Washington, DC 20005 202/289-1818	Professional museum jobs of all types, including managerial positions	*AVISO* *Museum News* (bimonthly)
AMERICAN DANCE GUILD, INC. (ADG) 31 West 21st Street 3rd Floor New York, NY 10010 212/627-3790	Education, and administration positions in dance	Job Express Registry Career Counseling
AMERICAN HISTORICAL ASSOCIATION AND REVIEW 400 A Street, SE Washington, DC 20003 202/544-2422	College, university and historical museum administration and other positions	Employment Information Bulletin, a section of the newsletter *Perspectives*
AMERICAN SYMPHONY ORCHESTRA LEAGUE 777 14th St., NW Washington, DC 20005 202/628-0099	Orchestra and some other performing arts positions in areas of management, marketing, fundraising, education and operations	Administrative Service Announcements *Symphony* magazine
ASSOCIATION FOR EDUCATION, COMMUNICATIONS & TECHNOLOGY 1025 Vermont Ave.,NW Washington, DC 20005 202/347-7834	Educational television and the communications media	*ECT Newsletter* and referral service

Turnaround Time	Average Number of Jobs Listed	Cost	Comments
4 to 6 weeks	80	$33 per year; $3 for single issues $38 per year; $7 for single issues	The best source for administrative openings in museums
4 weeks	9-20	Members: $7/month or $18 for three months; Nonmembers: $12/month or $33 for three months Membership fees range from $25 to $600	Individual counseling for dancers, students, and professionals
4 to 6 weeks	250 maximum; depends on time of year	Available to members only. Membership fees range from $25 to $85 per year	Nine issues published each academic year. Most listings are for academic positions
2-3 weeks	10-15	Available to members only. Membership $75 annually.	The best single source for orchestra management positions.
5-8 weeks	3	Members only; Included in $75 membership dues	
2-4 weeks	12-15	$50 regular membership; $20 students; Free to members upon request.	The service is a jobs clearinghouse; positions are listed in the monthly newsletter

Organization Name and Address	Fields Covered	Publication and/or Service
ASSOCIATION OF INDEPENDENT VIDEO AND FILM MAKERS/ FOUNDATION FOR INDEPENDENT VIDEO & FILM (AIVF) 625 Broadway, 9th Floor New York, NY 10012 212/473-3400	Film and video	*The Independent* AIVF *Independent Directory*
ASSOCIATION OF SCIENCE/TECHNOL- OGY CENTERS (ASTC) 1025 Vermont Ave., NW Suite 500 Washington, DC 20005 202/783-7200	Exhibit, education and administrative positions at science museums	*ASTC Newsletter*
BOX OFFICE MANAGEMENT INTERNATIONAL (BOMI) 333 East 46th Street New York, NY 10017	Career opportunities throughout the world, mainly U.S.	Newsletter BOMI/SEARCH— referral service
BROADCASTING MAGAZINE 1705 DeSales Street, NW Washington, DC 20036 202/659-2340 (Office also at: 630 Third Ave. New York, NY 10022 212/599-2830	Positions in all electronic media	*Broadcasting* magazine
CEO JOB OPPORTUNITIES UPDATE 2011 Eye Street, NW Suite 600 Washington, DC 20006 202/331-3828	National listings of openings in trade associations, professional societies and foundations. Some museum and arts council listings.	*CEO Job Opportunities Update* (biweekly newsletter)
THE CHRONICLE OF PHILANTHROPY 1255 23rd Street, NW Suite 775 Washington, DC 20037	National listings of a wide variety of positions in nonprofit management	Biweekly newspaper

Turnaround Time	Average Number of Jobs Listed	Cost	Comment
2 months	6	$25 students; $45 others; includes all services	The Notices section sometimes lists employment opportunities Lists members' skills. Made available to employers.
2 months	8	$30 per year ($40 for overseas subscriptions)	Detailed job descriptions
6-8 weeks Up to 2 weeks (mail); 1 day (fax)	4	$160 membership per year	Issues job bulletins
1 week	75-100	$85 per year for 52 issues	
1-2 weeks	50-60 CEO level; 40-50 senior staff level (salaries above $50,000)	7 issues, $90; 13 issues, $160; 26 issues, $300	
1-2 weeks	70-80 per issue	$57.50 for 24 issues	

Organization Name and Address	Fields Covered	Publication and/or Service
COLLEGE ART ASSOCIATION OF AMERICA 275 Seventh Avenue New York, NY 10001 212/691-1051	College teaching, studio, and administrative visual arts positions; some fine arts museum openings	"Careers" positions listings
CORPORATION FOR PUBLIC BROADCASTING 901 E Street, NW Washington, DC 20004 202/879-9731	All jobs in public radio and television	Public Broadcasting Jobline
COUNCIL ON FOUNDATIONS, INC. 1828 L Street, NW Washington, DC 20036 202/466-6512	Fundraising, arts, and social services , foundations, philanthropy	*Foundation News* (bimonthly)
DAILY VARIETY 5700 Wilshire Blvd., #120 Los Angeles, CA 90036 213/857-6600	Film and the media	*Daily Variety*
DANCE/USA 777 14th Street, NW Washington, DC 20005 202/628-0144	Nonprofit professional dance fields; primarily administrative positions	*Update* *Journal*
THE FOUNDATION CENTER 79 Fifth Avenue, Eighth Floor New York, NY 10003 212/620-4230	A variety of foundations and nonprofit organizations	Listings with a focus on jobs in fundraising and development
GREATER PHILADELPHIA CULTURAL ALLIANCE 320 Walnut Street Philadelphia, PA 19106 215/440-8100	Many arts disciplines at all levels of experience	*Short Subjects* Job Bank Skills Library

Turnaround Time	Average Number of Jobs Listed	Cost	Comment
2 months	1,300 annually	$27 for non-members; free to members	Job openings mailed 6 times per year; placement orientation and interview sessions at annual conference in February
1-7 days (updated weekly)	125 per week	Free	24-hour recorded telephone service. Call: 800/582-8220 or 202/393-1045
Up to 2 months	5	$29.50 per year	Has a classified section listing jobs not often found in other publications; usually high level, executive positions
2 days	25	$129 per year	
4 weeks Quarterly	7 7	$30 per year; free to members	
1 week	50	Free	The library maintains a binder listing a variety of jobs in foundations and nonprofit organizations
5 weeks	40	$15 per year	Mostly greater Philadelphia area listings.
Immediate	Varies	Free to job seekers	Member organization and placement newsletter listings available 5 days a week.
Immediate	Hundreds	Free to job seekers	Resumes and work samples of arts management job seekers.

Organization Name and Address	Fields Covered	Publication and/or Service
INTERNATIONAL ASSOCIATION OF AUDITORIUM MANAGERS 4425 West Airport Freeway, Suite 590 Irving, TX 75062 214/255-8020	Operations and general management positions in arts centers and auditoria	*IAAM News.*
NATIONAL ARTS EDUCATION ASSOCIATION 1916 Association Drive Reston, VA 22091 703/860-8000	Visual arts administrative positions in colleges and museum education programs	*NAEA News* Job Placement Bureau
	All visual arts-related positions	*National Arts Placement* (9 issues per year)
NATIONAL ASSOCIATION OF BROADCASTERS 1771 N Street, NW Washington, DC 20036 202/429-5300	Television, radio, and cable	NAB Employment Clearinghouse
NATIONAL DANCE ASSOCIATION, an associate of the AMERICAN ALLIANCE FOR HEALTH, PHYSI-CAL EDUCATION, RECREATION, AND DANCE 1900 Association Drive Reston, VA 22091 703/476-3436	Most jobs are in education	Referral service *Update*

Turnaround Time	Average Number of Jobs Listed	Cost	Comment
1 month	8-12	$48 for one-year subscrip-tion(12 issues)	Jobs in theaters, auditoriums, convention centers, arenas and stadiums
10 weeks	10	$35 member-ship fee; $12 for students	Very specialized, with an emphasis on teaching and other education positions.
All positions listed are current	50	$50 member-ship fee (but may vary by state); $60 conference registration fee; all fees are somewhat lower for students.	Job listings, resumes, and interviews held at the annual Spring Convention. Job seekers must be NAEA members. Listing organizations do not need to be members.
1-4 weeks	75-100	Members: $20/year; Nonmembers: $40/year	Also lists competi-tions, internships, grant and fellowship opportunities
			An advisory service that assists women and minorities and also provides career counseling
All current positions	Approx. 250	Available to members only; fees range from $25 to $80	There is an employment service and referral program at the annual convention
1-2 month	50 (number of listings is highly variable)	Available to members only	

Organization Name and Address	Fields Covered	Publication and/or Service
NATIONAL GUILD OF COMMUNITY SCHOOLS OF THE ARTS (NGCSA) P.O. Box 8018 Englewood, NJ 07631	Music, dance, and visual arts education administration	Employment listing and referral service
NEW YORK TIMES 229 West 43rd Street New York, NY 10036 212/556-1234	All sectors of the arts and media industry; all positions	*New York Times,* Sunday edition Careers in Education and Employment sections
OPERA AMERICA 777 14th Street, NW Suite 520 Washington, DC 20005 202/347-9262	All nonprofit opera-related issues	*OPERA America Intercompany Announcements*
SOCIETY OF BROADCAST ENGINEERS P.O. Box 20450 Indianapolis, IN 46220 317/253-1640 Jobline: 317/253-0474	Technical and engineering positions in the media industry	SBE Jobline
SOUTHEASTERN THEATRE CONFERENCE 506 Stirling Street UNC-Greensboro Greensboro, NC 27412	Professional, university and community theatre positions in the Southeast, Puerto Rico, and the Virgin Islands	Job Contact Bulletin Job Contact Service
THEATRE COMMUNICATIONS GROUP (TCG) 355 Lexington Avenue New York, NY 10017 212/697-5230	Performing and visual arts; primarily administrative, production, and educational positions	*ArtSearch*

Turnaround Time	Average Number of Jobs Listed	Cost	Comment
4 weeks	4-6	$60 membership	Job descriptions sent to members
5 days	Varies	$1.50 per issue; $1.75 outside New York City tristate area	A majority are entry-level positions; development and academically related positions appear in Education section
5 weeks	5		Not sent to individuals, may by available through OPERA America or your local opera company
Up to 1 week	10	$30 per membership	Members can call in for job listings announced via phone
3 weeks	15-35	$35/year individual membership; $15/year students	Bulletin is mailed to members monthly. Most listings are for academic positions.
	500, Spring 50, Fall	To use the service: membership fee plus $5 Job Contact fee.	Interviews at March and September conventions for a variety of jobs in theatre. Resumes kept on file year-round and forwarded to employers as requested.
2 weeks	200-400	$48 annual subscription fee for 23 issues	Also lists career development opportunities such as internships; one of the most widely read especially on each coast

Organization Name and Address	Fields Covered	Publication and/or Service
VARIETY (Cahners Publishing Company) 475 Park Avenue S. New York, NY 10016 212/779-1100	All arts and media fields	*Variety*
WESTERN STATES ARTS FEDERATION 236 Montezuma Ave. Santa Fe, NM 87501 505/988-1166	All arts disciplines: performing, production, technical, academic and agency positions	*The National Arts JobBank*

Turnaround Time	*Average Number of Jobs Listed*	*Cost*	*Comment*
5 days	10	$129 subscription fee for 52 issues per year	Classified ad section with Employment Opportunities; reaches all level positions.
2 weeks	90-100	$18 for 3 mos. $24 for 6 mos. $36 for 12 mos. (2 issues per month)	The only national employment listing in all disciplines and areas of arts careers; free listing to nonprofit employers; includes comprehensive job descriptions, salary levels, deadlines.

ABOUT THE AMERICAN COUNCIL FOR THE ARTS

Founded in 1960, the American Council for the Arts (ACA) is a national organization whose purpose is to define issues and promote public policies that advance the contributions of the arts and the artist to American life. To accomplish its mission, ACA conducts research, sponsors conferences and public forums, publishes books, reports, and periodicals, advocates for legislation that benefits the arts before Congress, and maintains a 15,000-volume specialized library. ACA is one of the nation's primary sources of legislative news affecting all of the arts and serves as a leading advisor to arts administrators, individual artists, educators, elected officials, arts patrons, and the general public.

BOARD OF DIRECTORS

ABOUT THE AUTHORS

Stephen Langley, author of *Theatre Management in America*, a textbook on the subject used internationally, and of *Producers on Producing*, heads the graduate program in Performing Arts Management at Brooklyn College of the City University of New York, where he is a professor in the Department of Theatre. As Managing Director of the Falmouth Playhouse on Cape Cod for nearly two decades, General Manager of the Brooklyn College Center for the Performing Arts for ten years, and as manager, consultant, and advisor for a variety of other arts projects, he has hired and placed literally hundreds of aspiring arts administrators. After earning degrees from Emerson College in Boston, the Central School of Speech and Drama in London, and the University of Illinois, Dr. Langley published his book on theatre management, which is one of the most important on the comparatively new files of arts management, and one of the first to define the profession. He is a former president of the Association of Arts Administration Educators.

James Abruzzo is Managing Director, National Nonprofit Practice of Kearney Executive Search, a division of A.T. Kearney, one of the top five management consulting firms in the world. In this position, he is responsible for managing executive searches and consulting projects for a wide range of clients, including major cultural and entertainment companies in the United States and abroad.

Mr. Abruzzo's views on the arts appear regularly in the national print and electronic media and he is co-author of the forthcoming ACA Book *Acquired Taste*. He is on the national advisory board of the U.S. Committee for UNICEF and chairman of the board of the Burgdorff Cultural Center. He has also served on the arts management faculties of Baruch College and Columbia University.